Global Humanities
Studies in Histories, Cultures, and Societies

04/2016
Stereotypes and Violence

Global Humanities

04/2016

Stereotypes and Violence

Edited by Frank Jacob

Neofelis Verlag

Global Humanities – Studies in Histories, Cultures, and Societies
04/2016: Stereotypes and Violence
Ed. by Frank Jacob

German National Library Cataloguing in Publication Data
A catalogue record for this book is available from the German National Library:
http://dnb.d-nb.de

Cover Design: Marija Skara
Editing & Typesetting: Neofelis Verlag (mn/ae)
Printed by PRESSEL Digitaler Produktionsdruck, Remshalden
Printed on FSC-certified paper.
ISSN: 2199-3939
ISBN (Print): 978-3-95808-113-0
ISBN (PDF): 978-3-95808-163-5

Contents

Editorial

Our lives are determined by stereotypes, no matter if we want it or not, no matter if we try to resist them or not. The famous American writer Walter Lippmann (1889–1974) understood this dilemma and emphasized it in his famous book *Public Opinion* (1922). He said that "symbolic pictures" would determine the human interrelations especially in times of war or crisis, when people developed a particular fear that was capable of exploiting the otherwise harmless symbols:

> In a more normal public life, symbolic pictures are no less governant of behavior, but each symbol is far less inclusive because there are so many competing ones. Not only is each symbol charged with less feeling because at most it represents only a part of the population, but even within that part there is infinitely less suppression of individual difference. The symbols of public opinion, in times of moderate security, are subject to check and comparison and argument. They come and go, coalesce and are forgotten, never organizing perfectly the emotion of the whole group. There is, after all, just one human activity left in which whole populations accomplish the union sacrée. It occurs in those middle phases of a war when fear, pugnacity, and hatred have secured complete dominion of the spirit, either to crush every other instinct or to enlist it, and before weariness is felt.[1]

These "symbolic pictures", however, were not only extremely dangerous in a period that was mainly characterized by fear or anger. They also helped to understand a world "out of reach" for the understanding of the individual, why they had consequently to be described as steady determinants of the course of human history. Lippmann explained, that

> [t]he world that we have to deal with politically is out of reach, out of sight, out of mind. It has to be explored, reported, and imagined. Man is no Aristotelian god contemplating all existence at one glance. He is the creature of an evolution who can just about span a sufficient portion of reality to manage his survival, and snatch what on the scale of time are but a few moments of insight and happiness. Yet this same creature has invented ways of seeing what no naked eye could see, of hearing what no ear could hear, of weighing immense masses and infinitesimal ones, of counting and separating more items than he can individually remember. He is learning to see with his mind vast portions of the world that he could never see, touch, smell, hear, or remember. Gradually he makes for himself a trustworthy picture inside his head of the world beyond his reach.

While human beings consider themselves to be independent, not controlled by external influences but internal reasoning, stereotypes are important for the daily life interactions of every human being. The ways we chose friends or more

1 Walter Lippmann: Public Opinion. University of Virginia American Studies Program 2002–2003. http://xroads.virginia.edu/~Hyper2/CDFinal/Lippman/ch01.html (accessed 19.10.2016).

general, people we link to, is highly influenced by such stereotypes, even if we, especially as a consequence of political correctness, claim that they don't. Robert Cantwell argued for the inevitability of stereotypes as an essential part of human interactions, because the

> [s]tereotype belongs to the world of appearances, and like other illusions wrought out of appearances [...] it places the subject at the center of the social cosmos, secure in the capacity of his or her own mind to know and hence to master the world. Indeed it is difficult to imagine any representation of the human character without recourse to stereotype, in which the process of recognition seems to begin.[2]

Stereotypes often serve as a tool that helps people to explain particular group related phenomena by dividing the groups themselves into so called in- and out-groups.[3] This differentiation is needed to homogenize the out-group and use them as an 'abstract' other to strengthen the identity of the members of the imagined in-group by contrasting themselves towards the other group.[4] The behavior of in-group members is therefore very often impacted by existent stereotypes that had been formulated within this group.[5] To study so-called ethnic attitudes and political, racial, or social prejudices stereotypes were often analyzed in the past to explain the existent interrelationships between the different factors.[6] The sociologist James W. Rinehart defined the difference between prejudice, stereotype, and discrimination very early, but regardless of his definition emphasized the relation between these important sociological parameters: "Prejudice is customarily defined as a feeling of hostility toward the members of racial, nationality, and ethnic groups; stereotypes, as the beliefs people have about such

2 Robert Cantwell: On Stereotype. In: *New England Review* 13,2 (1990), pp. 53–78, here p. 74.

3 For a discussion of such explanatory models, see Craig McCarthy / Vincent Y. Yzerbyt / Russel Spears (eds): *Stereotypes as Explanations. The Formation of Meaningful Beliefs about Social Groups*. Cambridge: Cambridge UP 2002. See also Gordon W. Allport: *The Nature of Prejudice*. New York: Basic1979.

4 On out-group homogeneity, see Charles M. Judd / Bernadette Park: Out-Group Homogeneity. Judgements of Variability at the Individual and Group Levels. In: *Journal of Personality and Social Psychology* 54,5 (1988), pp. 778–788. For a survey on possible in- and out-group dynamics, see Michael A. Hogg / Dominic Abrams (eds): *Intergroup Relations. Essential Readings*. Philadelphia: Psychology 2001, pp. 129–266.

5 For the so-called common sense explanation that is related to the establishment of a stereotype in such a described scenario, see Miles Hewstone: Attribution Theory and Common Sense Explanations. An Introductory Overview. In: Miles Hewstone (ed.): *Attribution Theory. Social and Functional Extensions*. Oxford: Blackwell 1983, pp. 1–26.

6 With regard to such studies different approaches toward the stereotype and its manifestations have been chosen. See Margot Heinemann: *Sprachliche und soziale Stereotype*. Frankfurt am Main: Lang 1998; Thomas Petersen: *Visuelle Stereotype*. Köln: von Halem 2009; Martina Thiele: *Medien und Stereotype. Konturen eines Forschungsfeldes*. Bielefeld: Transcript 2015.

members; and discrimination".[7] For Rinehart, "[s]tereotypes are sets of beliefs, usually stated as categorical generalizations, that people hold about members of other groups. These beliefs are ordinarily oversimplified"[8] and are very often based on historical traditions. A stereotype is therefore very often the expression of an intergroup relationship which is expressed through "a mental image which lumps together members of a group and associates them with particular traits."[9] The U. S. law professor Jody Armour therefore also correctly defined stereotypes as "well-learned internal associations about social groups that are governed by automatic cognitive processes."[10]

While in some national environments these internal associations are based on race, which for example "continues to be an American obsession"[11], in others ethnicity, economic standing, gender, sex, language, political values etc. might play a more important role. However, what Earl Smith named "social typing" and what "can best be understood as a manifestation of ethnocentric behavior, by members of the dominant group"[12] (i. e. in-group) is usually expressed to secure its dominant social and economic position within an existing society. Historically seen, as the U. S. historian Eugen Weber emphasized, the explanation for its existence seems to also be very simple.

> The word is modern, the reality it describes is ageless. Equally so the tendency to attribute particular characteristics to places, or to animal groups, including groups of humans. Greeks had stereotyped views about Persians and Egyptians, Romans about Greeks and Gauls. But the national stereotypes we live with began to take shape in the Middle Ages. It is in the eleventh and especially in the twelfth century that we find them formulated, as members of different ethnic groups rub against each other on pilgrimages, on crusades and in the new schools then springing up in cities such as Paris.[13]

In the middle ages the first stereotypes were formulated in written forms and exchanged by the students at the educational centers of the medieval world,

7 James W. Rinehart: The Meaning of Stereotypes. In: *Theory into Practice* 2,3 (1963): Intergroup-Relations Education, pp. 136–143, here pp. 136–137.

8 Ibid., p. 137.

9 Earl Smith: An Analysis of the Social Stereotype with Special Reference to African-Americans. In: *Humboldt Journal of Social Relations* 8,1 (1980/81), pp. 61–82, here p. 61.

10 Jody Armour: Stereotypes and Prejudice: Helping Legal Decisionmakers Break the Prejudice Habit. In: *California Law Review* 83,3 (1995), pp. 733–772, here p. 733.

11 Ibid., p. 772.

12 Smith: An Analysis, p. 61.

13 Eugen Weber: Of Stereotypes and of the French. In: *Journal of Contemporary History* 25,2/3 (1990), pp. 169–203, here p. 169.

from where they would spread to eventually become part of the national culture in later centuries.[14]

The negative stereotypes, history has created and our time still conserves, generally show certain characteristics:

1. The minority group portrayed is not inferior in any absolute sense, but only relative to the standards of the dominant group.
2. The stereotype gives a highly exaggerated picture of importance to a few characteristics – usually negative.
3. Some supposed traits are invented and made to seem reasonable by associating them with other tendencies that may have a kernel of truth.
4. Favorable tendencies are either omitted entirely or insufficiently stressed.
5. The stereotype fails to show how the dominant or other groups share the same tendencies or have unfavorable characteristics of their own.
6. There is little room for change.
7. The assigned traits are thought of as intrinsic or even self-willed.
8. There is no room for individual variation.[15]

These negative images, however, are not universal but rather an expression that is related to a specific space at a specific time. In addition, while not all stereotypes are inherently malicious, negative stereotypes (e.g. about violence) may act as self-fulfilling prophecies and trigger the very behavior they dictate.[16]

The establishment of a stereotype is also stimulated by the idea of injury or loss as it had been tentatively created by another out-group within the society, e.g. immigrants or refugees.[17] We can consequently argue, that the more someone feels to be negatively impacted by another out-group, the higher are the chances for the establishment of a negative stereotype, which is related to this particular

14 Weber: Of Stereotypes and of the French, p. 169.

15 George Simpson / Milton Yinger: *Racial and Cultural Minorities*. New York: Harper & Row 1965, p. 119, cit. in Smith: An Analysis, p. 62.

16 Jeffrey Levine / Edward G. Carmines / Paul M. Sniderman: The Empirical Dimensionality of Racial Stereotypes. In: *The Public Opinion Quarterly* 63,3 (1999), pp. 371–384, here p. 381.

17 These stereotypes very often lead to a political exploitation of fear from immigrants or refugees as has been obvious during the U.S. presidential election campaign of the Republican Party or the reaction of the German AfD party during the 'refugee crisis' of the last two years. For these positions, see Ann Coulter: ¡Adios, America! The Left's Plan to Turn Our Country into a Third World Hellhole. Washington, DC: Regnery 2015; Alexander Gauland: Alternative für Deutschland fordert vorübergehenden Aufnahmestopp für Flüchtlinge, 29.09.2015. https://www.alternativefuer.de/alternative-fuer-deutschland-fordert-voruebergehenden-aufnahmestopp-fuer-fluechtlinge-gauland-auch-um-der-fluechtlinge-willen-muss-deutschland-jetzt-die-notbremse-ziehen/ (accessed 19.10.2016).

group. Similar stereotypes had been created with regard to Asian immigration during the 19th century, when Chinese or Japanese workers were depicted as a competition for work and jobs within the borders of the United States.[18] Anti-Chinese stereotypes were made popular by missionaries or politicians.[19] Such stereotypes were later transported by Hollywood movies and television series alike, which seem to have the ability to conserve such popular assumptions and hand them over from generation to generation of audiences.[20]

This conservation of stereotypes is responsible for the still existing impact of such beliefs in many societies of our modern world. While some groups develop stronger stereotype based antagonisms towards out-groups than others,[21] the existence of stereotypes per se is a problem that is endangering a peaceful together in modern societies. Obviously, "racial negativity remains a primary determinant of white Americans' attitudes toward a range of race-related policies, including affirmative action, welfare providing the foundation for political preferences for some spending, and capital punishment"[22], and the stimulation of fear in the United States and Europe alike is still a useful tool to secure political influence for right wing oriented politicians that claim to save jobs or Western culture from foreign competition and infiltration. Racial or ethnic presettings of the homogenous in-group are consequently reacting against an imagined and solely imagined threat from outside of the group, almost naturally leading to a conflict between the two groups, expressed, to name just one

18 On Chinese immigration in the US, see Gunter Barth: *Bitter Strenght. A History of the Chinese in the United States, 1850–1870*. Cambridge, MA: Harvard UP 1964; Ronald Takaki: *Strangers from a Different Shore. A History of Asian Americans*. Boston: Little, Brown 1989.

19 For missionary perspectives, cf. Justus Doolittle: *Social Life of the Chinese*, vol. 2. New York: Harper 1895. On politicians and anti-Chinese stereotypes, see Thomas F. Gossett: *Race. The History of an Idea in America*. Dallas: Southern Methodist UP 1963, pp. 289–291. Anti-Asian feelings became globally popular and were subsumed by the term "yellow peril". On the idea of a "yellow peril", see Heinz Gollwitzer: *Die gelbe Gefahr. Geschichte eines Schlagworts, Studien zum imperialistischen Denken*. Göttingen: Vandenhoeck & Ruprecht 1962.

20 Albert H. Yee: Asians as Stereotypes and Students. Misperceptions That Persist. In: *Educational Psychology Review* 4,1 (1992), pp. 95–132, here p. 98. Lynn S. Neal: "They're Freaks!" The Cult Stereotype in Fictional Television Shows, 1958–2008. In: *Nova Religio: The Journal of Alternative and Emergent Religions* 14,3 (2011), pp. 81–107, analyzed the stereotype of cult within 50 years of television series and was able to emphasizes the power of conservation which television had on popular stereotypes of the 1950s that were still present in television shows of the 2000s.

21 Shayla C. Nunnally: Racial Homogenization and Stereotypes. Black American College Students' Stereotypes about Racial Groups. In: *Journal of Black Studies* 40,2 (2009), pp. 252–265, here p. 252.

22 Ibid., p. 263.

example, by a resistance to blend neighborhoods with people who are not part of the in-group.[23] Regardless of the fact that some of the out-groups will be able to integrate and become part of the society, racial or ethnic stereotypes might not fully disappear and remain strong in determining the perception of this particular group.[24]

What is particularly worrying with regard to such stereotypes is the obviously decreasing resistance to use violence towards members of the out-groups, may it be racial violence or hate crimes in the United States or violence against refugees in Europe.[25] The latter increase of violence is also related to the change of the image of a refugee. While refugees were seen as heroes, who for political reasons had to escape from home during the Cold War,[26] they are now solely considered as economically motivated refugees, who, as stated in many right wing commentaries, like 'parasites' or 'natural catastrophes' 'invade' Europe to gain from the exploitation of the hard working European. The trauma of war, suffering, and loss that many of the refugees experienced seems to play a minor role for those who want to stop the European support. Very often, this depiction as a burden for the society is predominant. However, in reality, refugees should be considered as an economic chance for the nation state that acts as a host.[27] To prevent

23 Reynolds Farley / Charlotte Steeh / Maria Krysan / Tara Jackson / Keith Reeves: Stereotypes and Segregation. Neighborhoods in the Detroit Area. In: *American Journal of Sociology* 100,3 (1994), pp. 750–780, here p. 750; Jon Hurwitz / Mark Peffley: Public Perceptions of Race and Crime. The Role of Racial Stereotypes. In: *American Journal of Political Science* 41,2 (1997), pp. 375–401, here p. 376. One example could be the resistance by German communities to accept refugee camps in their villages or cities. Frank Drieschner: Flüchtlingsunterkünfte. Wer protestiert warum? In: *Die Zeit*, 14.04.2016. http://www.zeit.de/2016/17/fluechtlingsunterkuenfte-hamburg-proteste-blankenese-oberschicht (accessed 19.10.2016).

24 Yee: Asians as Stereotypes, pp. 95–96. Especially adolescents seem to react stronger to stereotypes and if they internalize them, will also react, following them, in their adulthood. See Owen Gill: Urban Stereotypes and Delinquent Incidents. In: *The British Journal of Criminology* 16,4 (1976), pp. 321–336; Ronald O. Pitner / Ron Avi Astor / Rami Benbenishty / Muhammad M. Haj-Yahia / Anat Zeira: The Effects of Group Stereotypes on Adolescents' Reasoning about Peer Retribution. In: *Child Development* 74,2 (2003), pp. 413–425.

25 Paul Blickle et al.: Gewalt gegen Flüchtlinge. Es brennt in Deutschland. In: *Zeit Online*, 03.12.2015. http://www.zeit.de/politik/deutschland/2015-11/rechtsextremismus-fluechtlings unterkuenfte-gewalt-gegen-fluechtlinge-justiz-taeter-urteile (accessed 19.10.2016); Heinrich Schmitz: Rechte Hassbürger und Meinungsfreiheit. Eine Kapitulationserklärung. In: *Tagesspiegel*, 10.08.2015. http://www.tagesspiegel.de/politik/rechte-hassbuerger-und-meinungsfreiheit-eine-kapitulationserklaerung/12167486.html (accessed 19.10.2016).

26 Vanessa Pupavac: Refugees in the 'Sick Role'. Stereotyping Refugees and Eroding Refugee Rights. In: *New Issues in Refugee Research*, Research Paper No. 128. UN Refugee Agency, August 2006, p. 1.

27 Alexander Betts / Louise Bloom / Josiah Kaplan / Naohiko Omata: *Refugee Economics. Rethinking Popular Assumptions*. Oxford: Humanitarian Innovation Project 2014, pp. 16–20.

violence against the members of an out-group, it is important to understand and explain how stereotypes work and in how far they stimulate the increase of violence.

The present issue of *Global Humanities* will therefore analyze this special relationship from different angles. Oliver Betts starts with an analysis of the history of "wandering workers" in the Anglophone world to show how stereotypes were created by a fear for competition against foreign workers and a preassumed loss that would have been related to it. Barbara Manthe continues by discussing the interrelationship of racist stereotypes and violence in Germany since 1980 to further identify the reasons for stereotypes and their violent impact on society. That many of these stereotypes are also religion-related is emphasized by Benjamin Nickl, whose contribution deals with German anxieties and their creation by clichéd fears of Muslim otherness.

The second section analyzes gender related stereotypes. Sylvia Sadzinski is dissecting the relationship between stereotypes and rape myths in relation to the race of the stigmatized "men of color", who are regularly depicted as perpetrators of sexual violence against women. Bojan Perovic continues the section when he explores the gender based violence in Serbia and discusses the role of stereotypes and entertainment for such crimes. Andrew Fuyarchuk eventually highlights a gendered epistemology and harrassment in a recent case of science scandal, due to which Dr. Nancy Olivieri was harrassed for the doubts she expressed towards a new experimental drug and for which she was confronted with the political violence of the pharma industry.

The final section deals with one particular group of victims of stereotypes and violence: the Roma. Victoria Shmidt highlights the contemporary situation of Roma in the Czech Republic, while Biba Hadziavdic and Hilde Hoffmann discuss the persistence of Roma related stereotypes and their impact on the current European film.

The broad perspective of the volume shows that the danger of stereotypes and its interrelationship to a continuingly growing potential for a violent eruption is evident. The only way to decrease the danger is to embrace the unknown, to mediate between in- and out-groups, to cross imagined distances and to remember that those in supposed out-groups are also human. Only then, society can be equalized, violence diminished and internal as well as external peace be secured.

Frank Jacob

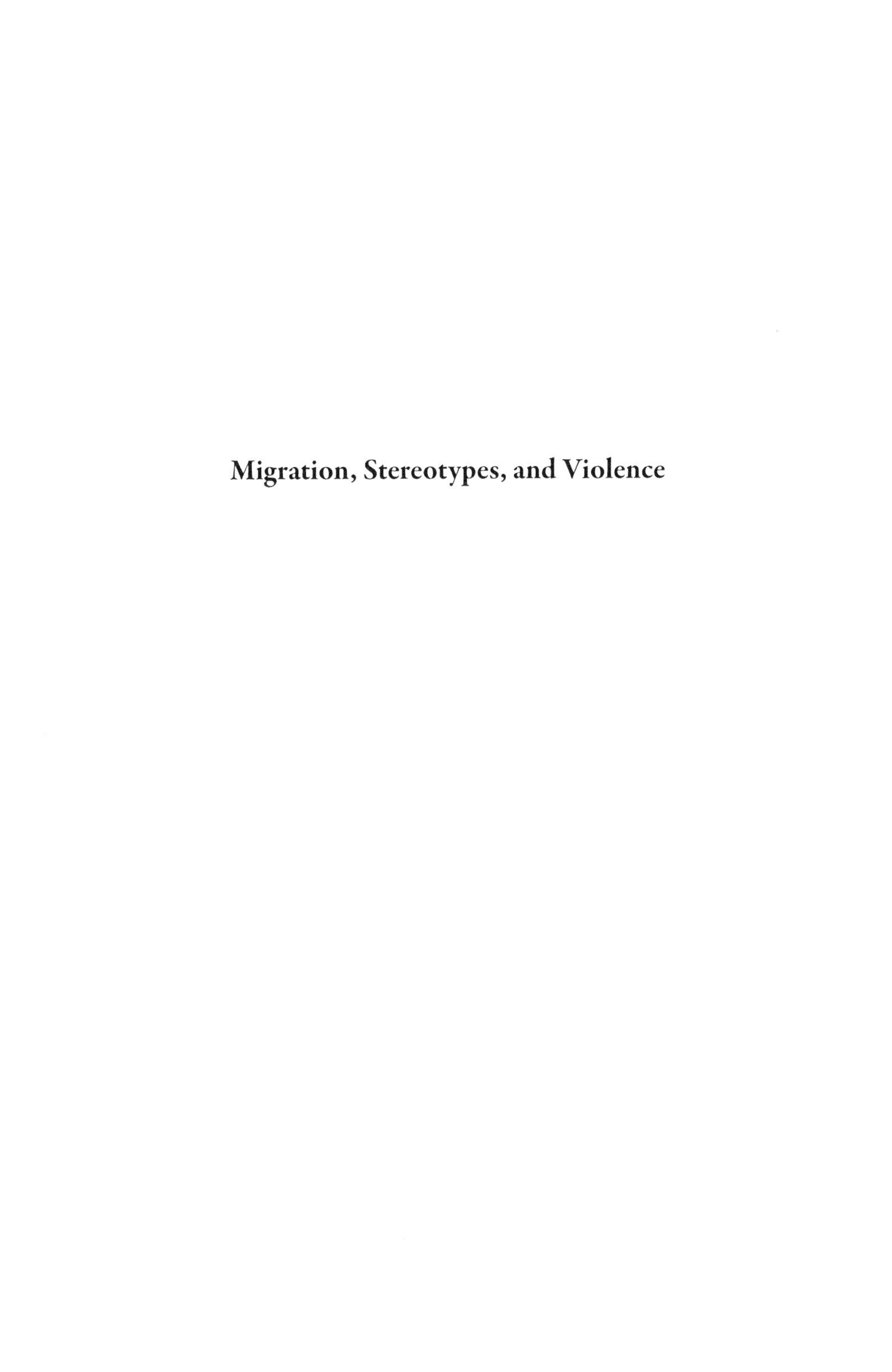

Migration, Stereotypes, and Violence

The Wandering Worker

Violence and Casual Labor in the Modern Anglophone World

Oliver Betts

At some point in the 1850s the Reverend Edward Monro, incumbent of Harrow Weald on the edge of London, saw a man who had been cut in half by an express train. Monro visited the camp that had formed along the half-finished railway siding, where the body lay in hospital, and felt chastised. "The whitened lip and rigid finger of the dead navvy seemed to cry out to every railway parish," Monro recalled, "Oh God, make haste to help us!"[1] This vignette formed a suitably violent beginning to Monro's passionate plea for his fellow clergymen to minister to the wandering laborers, referred to as navvies, who worked the railways of Britain. A product of an industrial age that required vast manpower to fuel the manual-labor needs of infrastructure construction, casual laborers like navvies were a constant feature of the landscape of the changing Anglophone world. Yet they were also, given their mobile and transient nature, a shifting feature of industrial society. Existing on the edges of society, with few of the social contacts needed to anchor them in support networks or local communities, casual laborers in the nineteenth and early twentieth centuries left little in the way of source material behind for the historian.[2] Depicted instead through the eyes of other authorities, who saw the wandering lives of these workers as an inherently alien patina of chaos and confusion, casual laborers were routinely portrayed through a series of stereotypes as living violent lives and, as Monro's text demonstrates, frequently experiencing violent deaths.

The work of railway navvies, their name derived from 'navigators' due to their original employment digging navigation canals, offers two significant insights into the stereotyping of casual laborers as violent in the modern world. Firstly, as the railways spread across the nineteenth-century world, they carved a path across the landscape that escaped very few commentators. In 1862 navvies engaged in constructing the Midland Railway in London tore through the

1 Edward A. Monro: The "Navvies" and How to Meet Them. A Letter to a Friend. In: *The Church and the Million* II (1857), p. 5.

2 Raphael Samuel: Comers and Goers. In H.J. Dyos / Michael Wolff (eds): *The Victorian City. Images and Realities*, vol. 1. London: Routledge / Kegan Paul 1973, pp. 123–160, here p. 123

churchyard at St. Pancras. The Vicar complained to his MP, outraged at how the workmen were "hacking the coffins to pieces and throwing the bones about"[3]. According to some reports they played football with the skulls. The architect supposed to be supervising, a young Thomas Hardy, recalled the event twenty years later in verse, evoking the "jumbled patch of wrenched memorial stones" that the navvies had left behind.[4] This violent intrusion into the landscape, from blasting tunnels to digging cuttings, allows an insight into more recent wide-scope studies of violence and the public obsession with it. As Richard Bessel has recently argued, the modern world has seen the definitions of violence shift from the perspective of the committer of violence to a victim-centric perspective, the latter encompassing not just physical acts of aggression but also "that which is violence in the eye, or ear, of the beholder".[5] Tearing up the landscape and laying in the infrastructure of a new, mechanical, age the reliance of navvy workers on sheer physical strength, often working with few tools and in harsh conditions, navvies were not just seen as the perpetrators of violence but, as Monro's text demonstrates, also the sufferers of violent circumstance and situation as well.

Secondly, stereotypes surrounding the violent nature of navvy life and work shed historical light on the contemporary issues facing casual labors around the globe today. Whilst Raphael Samuel, in his influential study of urban "Comers and Goers" such as navvies, is too hasty in his conclusion that these ways of life were dying off by the end of the nineteenth century, such labor conditions, and the stereotypes attached, certainly existed within a defined timeframe.[6] It would be inappropriate to label the current workers busily engaged in the Cross-rail project beneath London as navvies; with their twenty-first century technical skill-sets, health and safety culture, and more settled lifestyles, modern railway construction workers are not seen as being immured in the cultures of violence of their forebears. Yet the frantic period of railway construction that transformed the world between 1840 and 1940, the heyday of the pre-mechanical construction culture that fostered the 'violent' navvy, has striking parallels with today. Shifting cultures of casual labor continue to exist in the developed Western world but, even more pertinently, the cultures of transient labor beyond the West, such as

3 House of Commons: Hansard, 25.02.1867. http://hansard.millbanksystems.com/ (accessed 16.09.2016).

4 Thomas Hardy: The Levelled Churchyard. In: Id.: *Selected Poems*, ed. by Bob Blaisedell. New York: Dover 1995, here p. 29–30.

5 Richard Bessel: *Violence: A Modern Obsession*. London: Simon & Schuster 2015, p. 8–10.

6 Samuel: Comers and Goers, pp. 123–127.

China's *liudong renkou* (floating population) continue to be marked by a hostility from governmental and local sources that draws heavily on discussions of violence.[7] Spanning the Anglophone world between 1840 and 1940 this article will demonstrate how casual migrant labor provoked such cultural stereotyping from a range of social, cultural, and political spheres but also how, through the open-ended nature of these stereotypes, such processes continue to shape the perception of mobile casual labor around the world to this day.

Stereotyping the Violent Navvy

Navvies were always defined by their work. Elizabeth Garnett, the founder of the *Navvy Mission*, attempted to describe to the un-initiated what was so significant about the navvy and his lifestyle. Even a boy as young as twelve, she argued, could be a navvy. "Our boy" she claimed, imagining a fictive navvy lad for the narrative, "is very independent. Let his ganger or his father ill-treat him, and he will go off without permission to some other work".[8] Most navvies she admitted, were not born to the system though, and were instead brought into "the ranks", but the result of "whether a navvy is born one, or whether he adopts the profession" was the same.[9] The wandering work consumed him. In her attempts to raise funds for her missionary work amongst the navvies Garnett had a vested interest in presenting them as hard-working and deserving figures, but she was by no means alone in this view. Navvies were inextricable from the work that shaped them. In 1887 the Duke of Argyll, in a debate over the character of Irish workmen, argued that placed "in favorable circumstances" the Irishman could be transformed. As a navvy he was a productive figure.[10] By the 1870s their connection to manual labor was so carefully defined that mechanical excavators became known, in a British context, as steam navvies.[11] A navvy was his work.

The manual nature of this work, repeatedly emphasized as intensely physical, was the root of the violent stereotypes that defined the image of the navvy. Their very bodies betrayed the physicality of their work. Dr Francis Cade, brought in to conduct a post-mortem in 1909, testified in court that the dead man "was a

7 Linda Wong: China's Urban Migrants – The Public Policy Challenge. In: *Pacific Affairs* 67,3 (1994), pp. 335–355, here p. 335.

8 Elizabeth Garnett: *Our Navvies: A Dozen Years Ago and Today*. London: Hodder & Stoughton 1885, pp. 2–3.

9 Ibid., pp. 3–4.

10 House of Commons: Hansard, 22.04.1887. http://hansard.millbanksystems.com/ (accessed 14.09.2016).

11 Oxford English Dictionary Online: Navvy. http://www.oed.com/ (accessed 22.04.2016).

very muscular and powerful man of the navvy type; there was very little fat and the muscles were extremely thick".[12] Ford Maddox Brown arranged a group of them, digging away, in the center of his 1865 *Work* emphasizing, as George Dart has argued, "the absolute centrality of manual labor" in the period.[13] The language used to describe navvies was infused with that of strength and muscular force. They were "hulking" according to *Punch* in 1865[14] whilst an 1846 Select Committee found them "hard worked [... and] exposed to great risk of life and limb".[15] This depiction of navvies as hard men built by their rough employment filtered through into the press. In *The Young Boss*, an 1895 short story for youths, Walter Gibb, the titular young boss, is sent to manage a construction project in the Canadian West. He has to earn, through hard work and the display of masculine temper in standing up for his authority, the respect of his workforce comprised of "rough navvies, wholly uneducated, much given to horse-play and brawling".[16] Violence was seen, in many cases in the press, as the natural offshoot of their occupation.

The stereotype was particularly sharp when it came to the particular facets of the navvy life that troubled the wider British public. As Julie Marie-Strange has noted with regards to homeless men and women in Victorian Britain, towards the end of the nineteenth century mobile populations that stood in contrast to the increasingly settled norms of society were the increasing subject of a range of reactions, from sympathy to suspicion, that at once both "problematized [...] and proposed solutions".[17] The mobility of navvies, whom even a sympathetic Garnett depicted as "a great nomadic tribe" roaming the land, increasingly formed an unsettling tenet of their supposed character in the press.[18] Descending on new construction projects by order of their masters, the sheer number and mobility of navvies was presented as threatening. Trying to assess the

12 Old Bailey Proceedings Online: March 1909, Trial of Castleton, Hannah (29, laundress). http://www.oldbaileyonline.org, version 7.2 (accessed 22.04.2016).

13 Brown, Ford Maddox. 1852–1863. *Work*. Painting. Manchester Art Gallery. George Dart: The Reworking of "Work". In: *Victorian Literature and Culture* 27,1 (1999), pp. 69–96, here p. 72.

14 Anon: The Banishment of the Beggars. A New Tramp Chorus. In: *Punch*, 27.05.1865, p. 209.

15 Report from the Select Committee on Railway Laborers, 1846. In: *Reports from Committee*, vol. XIII, 22.01.–28.08.1846. London: Her Majesty's Stationary Office 1846, pp. 1–535, here p. 427.

16 William Edward Thomson: The Young Boss. In: Id.: *Walter Gibbs the Young Boss and Other Stories*. Toronto: Briggs 1896, pp. 1–134, here p. 97.

17 Julie-Marie Strange: Tramp: Sentiment and the Homeless Man in the Late Victorian and Edwardian City. In: *Journal of Victorian Culture* 16,2 (2011), pp. 242–258, here p. 257.

18 Garnett: *Our Navvies*, p. 6.

number of navvies in Britain at any given point in the nineteenth century is complicated as the men themselves shifted in and out of casual labor. Before a Parliamentary Committee in 1846 one of the major labor contractors, Samuel Peto, could only attest to employing "about 9000" on his projects.[19] One local official in Dumfriesshire reported to the same Parliamentary Committee that some 7,000 men had descended on the local area to construct the railway line in the space of a few months.[20] Crowded into shanty-town settlements along the lines they were building, the press frequently portrayed navvies as inhabiting a space where the veneers of civilization were at their thinnest.

Drink, which urban reformers waged a considerable battle to counter in the accessible spaces of the city, was portrayed as the fuel that fires the violence of the navvy in the hinterlands of reforming influence. There were, the Dumfriesshire official reported, "constant scenes of drunkenness, riot, and all sorts of disturbance"[21]. Nor was his rural part of Scotland an exception; the 1846 Committee heard evidence of navvy violence in areas as diverse as the Edinburgh region, Croydon, Kendal, and Liverpool.[22] As J. Carter Wood has observed, violence was one of the most talked about areas of social concern in the nineteenth century and, without a doubt, this observation should be extended into the twentieth.[23] Navvies proved a reliable short-hand for casual violence in newspapers. In 1847, irate and drunken, navvies smashed up the Bull Inn in Preston the night before the local Conservative Party was due to meet there.[24] The following year a contractor, paying his men in a public house, was set upon and beaten by disgruntled navvies who had been drinking away the pay he had already given them.[25] Incidents like these, which were reported in small segments in newspapers often under "Court Circular" or "Police News" headings that summarized a series of crimes for the interested reader in sensational fashion, kept the stereotype of the navvy whose violence was fueled by his heavy drinking alive. A blend of fictional and real violence, in stories and in crime reporting, was supplemented by a wider stereotype of the excessive navvy given to drink because of his high wages and all-or-nothing attitude. "Them Dratted

19 Report from the Select Committee on Railway Laborers, 1846, p. 506.

20 Ibid.

21 Ibid., pp. 506–507.

22 Ibid., pp. 31–33, 160, 166, 195.

23 J. Carter Wood: Criminal Violence in Modern Britain. In: *History Compass* 4,1 (2006), pp. 77–90, here p. 83.

24 Preston Races. In: *Bell's Life and Sporting Chronicle*, 01.08.1847, p. 5.

25 Riot and Robbery by Railway Laborers. In: *Bell's Life and Sporting Chronicle*, 09.07.1848, p. 3.

Girls" lamented one spoof parenting article in the satirical magazine *Fun* in 1888 "each of my seventeen daughters eats as much per day as three ordinary navvies".[26] So commonplace was the stereotype that, during a Commons debate in 1877, one MP declared he could easily spare his fellow members detailed description of the many "cases of drunken navvies dashing out the brains of their paramours and murdering their children" that littered the press.[27] It was a stereotype of violent over-indulgence, fed by a selective process of reporting and interpreting news about casual laborers in the press, which proved deeply convincing to the Victorian public.

Subjects of Violence

Emphasizing the process by which the casual laborer, in the public eye, became a violent and rough stereotype remains only one facet of their position in Victorian culture. The changing definitions of violence in the modern world, as Bessel has noted, repositioned discussions of violence to shift from perpetrator to victim as the focal point. He sees this as an on-going process that found particular purchase in the later twentieth-century, but examining the reputations of railway navvies in the wider Anglophone world reveals that the turn of the century saw navvies repositioned as victims of violence in some cases.

Concerns about casual labor beyond the British Isles, where the ethnic composition of casual labor forces was more diverse, indicates a more complex process of stereotyping where navvies could be as much the victims of violence as the perpetrators. Labor migration within the southern part of Africa relied, at the turn of the twentieth century, on a "tramping system" of mobile labor. In an effort to avoid the large scale columns and wagon-trains that could elicit hostile reaction from rural tribes, particularly the Zulus, railways, sugar plantations, and mines all encouraged migrants to make their own pathways to employment. The result, as Patrick Harries has highlighted, was often the arrival of exhausted and emaciated African laborers at the work camps, especially those high on the cold Kimberly Plateau. It was a process of exploitation that elicited alarmed comments from many observers. Whilst migrating black laborers were figures of anxiety for some in colonial Africa they were, for others, a subject of sympathy; as much victims of violence as potential perpetrators.[28]

26 Them Dratted Gals. In: *Fun*, 11.04.1888, p. 156.

27 House of Commons: Hansard, 13.07.1872. http://hansard.millbanksystems.com/ (accessed 16.09.2016).

28 Patrick Harries: *Work, Culture and Identity: Migrant Laborers in Mozambique and South Africa c. 1860–1910.* Portsmouth, NH: Heinemann 1994, pp. 28–34.

The nuanced, even in places contradictory, stereotype of the casual laborer as one who could conceivably both commit and suffer violence was brought into stark relief when the ethnic compositions of workforces came under scrutiny. The importation of Chinese coolie labor into South Africa in the 1900s elicited a series of impassioned responses that portrayed the laborers in question in broad-brush stereotypes.[29] From the perspective of the Transvaal community into which they were arriving the coolies were violent disruptors of the precarious balance between white and black labor already in place. Anxieties about the supposedly shifty and unreliable character of the Chinese laborers, seen in some cases as an almost willful desire to disrupt and disturb rather than a purely physical process of violence, was for detractors of the scheme seemingly embodied by the riots and disturbances at labor camps and the necessity of extra policing to prevent against theft and desertion.[30] Even the pro-coolie labor scheme position, as embodied by figures such as High Commissioner Lord Selborne, relied on such stereotypes. As *The Spectator* reported in 1905 Selborne's case rested on the process of "improved management" and that the violence of the Chinese coolie, like the "more disorderly, riotous, and criminal" black laborer, would eventually be brought under control.[31] For those who opposed coolie labor, however, these men were the victim of violent exploitation. In a letter to *The Times*, referenced in news periodicals afterwards, M. P. John Seely raised the specter that the restrictive employment contracts would be illegal under English Common Law and implored a newspaper that was known for its "consistent and courageous support of liberty to take up the cause of these victims of legal violence."[32] Both competing sides of the debate over coolies relied upon stereotypes of violence where either the coolies or the contractors were the perpetrators.

Whilst questions of ethnicity doubtless shaped the discussion of casual labor in South Africa, this confusion over the navvy as both violent and victimized was replicated in Britain itself. Examining the reactions to Chinese railway labor in the American West, where they were employed in building the California arm of the Trans-Continental Railway, alongside discussions of navvies in Britain itself reveals a similar uncertainty over how violence was related to the processes and

29 Rachel Bright: *Chinese Labor in South Africa 1902: Race, Violence, and Global Spectacle.* London: Palgrave Macmillan 2013, pp. 95–139.

30 Persia Crawford Campbell: *Chinese Coolie Emigration to Countries within the British Empire.* London: Cass 1971, pp. 172–173, 194–199.

31 The Blue Book Published Last Week. In: *The Spectator*, 16.12.1905, p. 2.

32 John Seely: The Proposed Importation of Chinese Labor into the Traansvaal. In: *The Times*, 12.01.1904, p. 11.

people of casual railway labor. Although much of the language surrounding the Chinese in the Western USA had distinctly racial over-tones, with a sympathetic 1888 article explaining their passivity as the result of "slavish instincts [...] accustomed to oppression", the tension between the dueling stereotypes of violent laborers on the one hand and exploited workers on the other manifested itself in similar fashion in both countries. The same 1888 American article complained that Chinese railway laborers, unable to speak English, were brutally used by white overseers who had even killed some workers through over-discipline.[33] Samuel Peto meanwhile, a contractor who employed some 9,000 navvies in Britain, testified before a Parliamentary Committee that he was almost powerless to prevent the "truck system" by which corrupt masters and merchants sold laborers overpriced supplies and split the profits.[34] Whilst newspaper accounts of navvy and coolie violence, ranging from riot to theft, sustained public conviction that these men were violent and disruptive, there was certainly evidence of exploitation and the violent control system in both cases for those who believed the navvy or coolie to be a victim.

Furthermore, whilst it is tempting to read these conflicting stereotypes of casual labor and violence through an ethnic lens, closer examination of these accounts reveals that the open-ended nature of 'the navvy' as he appeared in the late nineteenth-century press often superseded cultural stereotypes rooted in discussions of race. Whilst in an American context the belief that a Chinese coolie's aptitude for physical work might stem from a different cultural background to that of his white co-worker for many his manual labor still demanded a begrudging respect. In a similar vein so was the Irish worker in Britain able to be subsumed by the broader cultural stereotypes surrounding navvy work. Irish migrants made up, well into the twentieth century, a significant proportion of the floating casual labor force in mainland Britain, particularly pulled to the temporary world of railway construction. Whilst a comprehensive historical literature has identified the often complex stereotype of the violent 'Paddy', a stalwart of the sensational Victorian press, this image is complicated when the cultural baggage surrounding the navvy is brought into the frame of discussion.[35] "Do not tell me that the Irish Laborer is incapable of labor" the Duke of Argyll

33 *The Youth's Companion*, 12.01.1888, p. 1.

34 Report from the Select Committee on Railway Laborers, 1846, pp. 497–503.

35 See, for instance, Lynn Hollen Lees: *Exiles of Erin: Irish Migrants in Victorian London*. Manchester: Manchester UP 1979; Frances Finnegan: *Poverty and Prejudice: A Study of Irish Poverty in York 1840–1875*. Cork: Cork UP 1982; Michael de Nie: *The Eternal Paddy: Irish Identity and the British Press 1798–1882*. Madison: University of Wisconsin Press 2004.

argued in the House of Lords in 1887, "I never saw any navvies work better".[36] Mr Peto, in 1849 speaking in the Commons itself, argued that "some of the best 'navvies' employed in this country were Irishmen; and they were remarkable for their industry, temperance, and constant application to work"[37]. The violent reaction to ethnic groups of casual migrants, from the Chinese in California to the Irish in England and lowland Scotland, should not be underestimated, but the extent to which these ethnic stereotypes of violence, passivity, or feckless-ness were able to filter into the more embracing image of the navvy is significant indeed. The Irishman's "passion", the Coolie's "subservience", or the floating population of rural migrants in India which, as Ian Kerr notes, British officials came to consider a "natural" element of how they understood the caste society of the time, cast alternately as both strengths and faults could be easily folded into the wider umbrella concept of the railway navvy.[38]

The Uses of the Violent Navvy

One of the reasons why this confused stereotype, wherein the violence of the railway navvy could either be a boon to physical construction or a curse of disruptive anarchy, remained so prevalent in late nineteenth and early twentieth-century society was because such a dichotomy was reinforced by the demands of the modern state. Nowhere was this more obvious than in warfare in the Anglophone world, particularly Britain's overseas conflicts. From the Crimean War, through the entanglement of Empire, and into the new century British military ventures relied upon railways and, consequently, the use of navvy labor. The "Balaklava Railway Corps", as the men were called, shipped out to the Crimea in the winter of 1854 to begin construction on a railway to enable the distribution of supplies to the British Army in the peninsula.[39] "No-one can yet decide on the exact value of this auxiliary" *The Times* mused as the first ships left Britain for the war, but if a track had already been built, the newspaper felt sure, a great deal of "toil, suffering, and death" on the part of the soldiers would have been prevented.[40] The article itself reflected the positive view of the navvy and his work, listing the rough work ahead of the men, their heavy-duty clothing

36 House of Lords: Hansard, 22.04.1887. http://hansard.millbanksystems.com/ (accessed 06.09.2016).

37 House of Commons: Hansard, 09.07.1849. http://hansard.millbanksystems.com/ (accessed 15.09.2016).

38 Ian J. Kerr: *Building the Railways of the Raj 1850–1900*. Oxford: Oxford UP 1997, pp. 100–103.

39 Dick Sullivan: *Navvyman*. London: Coracle 1983, pp. 143–147.

40 The Balaklava Railway Corps. In: *The Times*, 28.12.1854, p. 9.

and pre-prepared equipment (a stark contrast to an Army unprepared for siege warfare in the Crimea at the time), and the organizational and disciplinary efforts of masters like Peto who ran the scheme. Their presence, and their rapid construction of the railway in challenging conditions, set the tone for how the navvy was seen through the lens of military and imperial patriotism. By the time of the Mahdist War in the Sudan in 1885 the potential for navvy violence in a conflict zone was being presented as a positive; whilst Lord Cecil, in the House of Lords, raised queries about how men "not [...] of the strictest sobriety" would cope in the "tropical sun",[41] the satirical *Moonshine* punned that if attacked "the enemy will find them on their metal".[42] Emblematic of the jingoism of the late Victorian period perhaps, but also of how the physical challenge of war, with the stark face of modern violence it presented, affected how the "violent" navvy was portrayed when drawn into its spiral.

This dichotomy between positive and negative stereotypes of the violent navvy, and his uses or abuses, is perhaps most starkly rendered in the wartime account of John Ward. Ward, was at various points in his life a canal-navvy, a railway-navvy, a union-organizer, and a Member of Parliament. Having founded a Navvy's Union in 1889, at the outbreak of the First World War he used his connections in and experience with labor organizations to raise five work battalions for the front.[43] By 1919, however, he and elements of these units of the Middlesex Regiment had been shipped to Siberia to aid in the Allied intervention in the Russian Civil War. As Brad Beaven has recently summarized in his work on patriotism and popular culture in modern Britain, collective attitudes to the nationalistic and imperialistic calls to arms have long been the subject of intense historiographical debate.[44] Whilst Bessel has asserted, quite rightly, that the First World War has become "the benchmark for understanding what modern war came to signify" which he essentially sees as "mass violence and senseless sacrifice",[45] Beaven has emphasized the importance of the decade and a half between the Boer War conflict and the outbreak of the Great War, particularly when it came to the reception of calls to arms amongst working-class

41 House of Commons: Hansard, 09.03.1885. http://hansard.millbanksystems.com/ (accessed 16.09.2016).

42 Railing by Contract. In: *Moonshine*, 07.03.1885, p. 117.

43 Marc Brodie: Ward, John (1866–1934). In: Lawrence Goldman (ed.): *Oxford Dictionary of National Biography*. Oxford: Oxford UP 2004. http://www.oxforddnb.com/view/article/36733 (accessed 22.04.2016).

44 Brad Beaven: *Visions of Empire: Patriotism, Popular Culture, and the City 1870–1939*. Manchester: Manchester UP 2012, pp. 90–94.

45 Bessel: *Violence*, pp. 138–139.

communities like navies.[46] Ward not only embodied those contradictions himself, having been one of those navvies in the Sudan whose potential for violent patriotism was presented in *Moonshine*, but also experienced the contrasting stereotypes of the violent navvies, either valorous and valorized or rebellious and despised, first hand in the campaign in Russia itself.[47]

The railways of Russia, particularly the Trans-Siberian where Ward and his men were posted, were caught up in the chaos of revolution and civil war. Nominally under the control of the White movement and their Allied supporters, station towns and lines were frequently interdicted by Bolshevik insurgents. Violence was everywhere.[48] Yet Ward was convinced that it was the product of a minority. The average Russian navvy, who he was struck to discover included a fair number of women, was a figure for Ward who embodied the same rough qualities as his British counterpart – doughty, tough, and determined to defend his own rights. "They presented many characteristics of the average British workmen" he wrote after one meeting. Indeed so immured was Ward in his positive, British-based, stereotype of the positive navvy that throughout his text he insisted that the violence came from elsewhere.[49] At a meeting in Irkutsk he spotted in the crowd "half a dozen" radicals, not railwaymen but instead hardened revolutionaries "composed of the very worst elements in the towns" determined on "the spoliation and assassination of every decent man".[50] In truth Bolshevik partisans were in constant operation and drew considerable strength from disaffected groups of railwaymen in nominally "White" controlled areas, indeed accounts of conflict with partisan groups in Ward's own account reflect this, but for the MP and ex-navvy the seductive vision of the stalwart casual laborer, who needed rescuing from the clutches of the professional revolutionaries and their insane predilection for political violence, was simply too appealing.[51] "It was quite clear to me that the Russian workmen were tired of the Revolution" he concluded after meeting with another group of Russian navvies "they were promised an Eldorado and realized Hell instead".[52] They were, in essence, victims of political violence rather than perpetrators.

46 Beaven: *Visions of Empire*, p. 94.

47 Brodie: Ward, John (1866–1934).

48 Orlando Figes: *A People's Tragedy. The Russian Revolution 1891–1924*. London: Pimlico 1997, pp. 651–653.

49 John Ward: *With the Die-Hards in Siberia*. London: Cassel 1920, ch. XVII, unpaginated.

50 Ibid., unpaginated.

51 See, for instance, Jamie Bisher: *White Terror: Cossack Warlords of the Trans-Siberian*. London: Routledge 2005, pp. 157–191.

52 Ward: *With the Die-Hards*, p. 85.

Casual Labor Violence since the Navvies: China's *Liudong Renkou*

After 1870, Samuel has argued, the casual laborers of the late Victorian period were in decline. School Boards sought out their children for fixed-term education, speculative builders seized their traditional campsites, and local government scrutinized the sources of informal employment, credit, and accommodation that supported their nomadic lifestyles.[53] Whilst recent studies have emphasized the continuance of such casual migratory labor lifestyles in Britain, particularly amongst self-defined traveler groups, they also point to the economic instabilities urbanization and the regulation of employment has wrought on more mobile casual labor economies.[54] As early as the 1890s, when the last mainline railway in Britain began construction, questions were being raised about just how defined the image of the navvy was; in 1893 *The Spectator* criticized those who felt that "every unemployed weaver or watchmaker is a ready-made navvy" and that the unemployed could be put to casual labor work regardless of their social backgrounds or employment histories.[55] Yet by the 1920s the figure of the navvy was increasingly diffused by work-schemes that put the unemployed to the construction and excavation tasks that navvies had traditionally dominated.[56] Although casual railway labor continued into the mid-century, the navvy, violent or otherwise, was an increasingly anachronistic stereotype in twentieth-century Britain.

It is important to note that these stereotypes of casual labor, originally associated with the figure of the navvy, continue to resonate in areas where the frenetic pace of modern construction continues. Contrasting the navvies with another group of casual workers, caught up within a similar context of construction work, social isolation, and cultural stigma, demonstrates just how pervasive the stereotypes of violence that surround the casual worker can be. The case of China's "floating population", the so-called *liudong renkou*, illustrates well these important continuities.

China's expansion, at the dawn of the twenty-first century, is vast even for the student of the railway and construction mania that gripped Victorian Britain

53 Samuel: Comers and Goers, p. 153.

54 Margaret Greenfields / Andrew Ryder / David Smith: Gypsies and Travelers: Economic Practices, Social Capital, and Embeddedness. In: Joanna Richardson / Andrew Ryder (eds): *Gypsies and Travelers: Empowerment and Inclusion in British Society*. Bristol: Policy 2005, pp. 101–116, here pp. 101–103, 109, 113–114.

55 The Legal Poor. In: *The Spectator*, 30.12.1893, p. 9.

56 See, for instance, the debate about navvies and unemployed men on a County Durham drainage scheme, House of Commons: Hansard, 09.03.1925. http://hansard.millbanksystems.com/ (accessed 16.09.2016).

and helped to spawn the array of images that surrounded the navvy. Motorways have grown from 180 miles to over 30,000 since the 1980s, the number of cities from 200 in the 1970s to almost 700 now, and in 2003 alone China constructed some 28 billion square feet of housing.[57] The rapid pace of growth has been fueled by the *liudong renkou*. A substantial part of China's modernization, numbering some 16% of the total population in 2010, "floaters" are, it is important to note, not completely the same as the navvies of turn-of-the-century Britain. The earlier figure of the Chinese Coolie was often, as discussed above, conflated with the navvies in the nineteenth and twentieth centuries. The term coolie, like navvy, denoted a lower social status that the historian Ross Forman has argued linked it to other British Imperial adoptions for subordinates such as the use of the Indian term "ayah".[58] By 1920 two British officers and students of Asian languages serving as part of the Chinese Labor Corps in France during the First World War felt able to conflate navvy and coolie in print. Introducing a translated compendium of Coolie Work Songs in the *Bulletin of the School of Oriental and African Studies* they claimed that the "mental caliber" of coolies "can be compared with that of the international navvy".[59] Despite these parallels the state system the *liudong renkou* inhabit sets them apart from both navvies and coolies. Defined by the Household Registration Regulations of 1958 (the *hukou*), or rather their movement from their registration district, floating casual laborers in China exist on the fringes of a state-regulated system that has no parallel in the late Victorian age.[60] Yet, like the navvies, their presence in the social landscape of the developing nation state has seen a number of stereotyped views of their lifestyles and place in society emerge, shedding further light on the stereotyping of the casual laborer as both victim and perpetrator of violence in the modern world.

Recent social upheavals in China, particularly in the developing fringe of Xinjang in the north-west of the country, have provoked reaction in both China itself and in the Western media. An area of population influx, particularly of ethnic Han Chinese, tensions between these migrant newcomers and

57 Thomas J Campanella: *The Concrete Dragon: China's Urban Revolution and What It Means for the World*. New York: Princeton Architectural Press 2008, pp. 14–16.

58 Ross G. Forman: *China and the Victorian Imagination: Empires Entwined*. Cambridge: Cambridge UP 2007, p. 38.

59 A. Neville / J. Whymant: Chinese Coolie Songs. In: *Bulletin of the School of Oriental and African Studies* 1,4 (1920), pp. 145–166, here p. 146.

60 C. Cindy Fan: Settlement Intention and Split Households: Findings from a Survey of Migrants in Beijing's Urban Villages. In: *China Review* 11,2 (2011), pp. 11–41, here p. 12; Wong: China's Urban Migrants, pp. 335–336.

the Muslim Uyghur population bubbled over into riots and demonstrations in 2009.[61] Triggered by an earlier incident in Shaogun, Guangdong Province, far to the south, where a bout of anti-Uyghur violence was provoked amongst locals after reports circulated of Uyghur migrant workers having raped a Han woman, protests in Xinjang turned to violence as the police and military were brought in to disperse the crowds.[62] Whilst these conflicts are to some degree products of ethnic tension they are also, when placed within a wider context of *liudong renkou* migration in China, typical of the profound anxieties provoked by the movement of casual labor. "Vagrants without jobs [...] are said to be responsible for between one-third and 70 percent of all criminal activities in Chinese cities", summarizes Linda Wong, arguing that as which so much relating to the floating population "whether this is true or exaggerated is hard to tell".[63] Suspicion fuels the treatment of migrants even though, as sociologist Børge Bakken has pointed out, even un-official methodologies that attempt to circumvent misleading official statistics on crime, such as household interviews, fail to tap into the realities of crime as experienced by the *liudong renkou* themselves.[64] "The image of the floater as a potential criminal breeds fear among city dwellers" Wong concludes.[65]

For others, however, the floating casual laborers of twenty-first century China are victims not criminals. In December 2012 a CNN editorial online asked whether this system of internal migration in China was akin to "Apartheid".[66] The vast majority of *liudong renkou* are peasants, indeed many are referred to specifically as peasants (*nongmin-gong*) and, driven by poor standards of living in rural areas in contrast to the potential wages rumored to exist in cities and on major construction sites, they arrive in cities across China daily in search of work.[67] Whilst news events have, in some cases, raised the specter of the violent

61 James A. Millward. *Eurasian Crossroads: A History of Xinjiang.* New York: Columbia UP 2007, pp. 285–286.

62 Xinhau News Agency: Guandong Toy Factory Brawl Leaves 2 Dead, 118 Injured, 27.06.2009. http://www.china.org.cn/china/news/2009-06/27/content_18023576.htm (accessed 22.04.2016); Hu Yinan / Lei Xiaoxun: Urumqi Riot Handled 'Decisively, Properly'. In: *China Daily*, 18.07.2009. http://www.chinadaily.com.cn/china/2009-07/18/content_8444365.htm (accessed 22.04.2016); Jane Macartney: China in Deadly Crackdown after Uighurs Go on Rampage. In: *The Times*, 05.07.2009.

63 Wong: China's Urban Migrants, pp. 340–341.

64 Børge Bakken: Comparative Perspectives on Crime in China. In: Id. (ed.): *Crime, Punishment, and Policing in China.* Lanham: Rowman & Littlefield 2007, pp. 64–100, here p. 71.

65 Wong: China's Urban Migrants, p. 341.

66 Madison Park / Cy Xu: Is Migrant System China's Apartheid?. In: CNN, 25.12.2012. http://edition.cnn.com/2012/12/25/world/asia/china-migrant-family/ (accessed 22.04.2016).

67 Hsiao-Hung Pai: *Scattered Sand: The Story of China's Rural Migrants.* London: Verso 2012, p. 2.

casual laboring figure reminiscent of critical stereotypes of the navvies, other accounts have instead focused on these workers as victims. Hsia-Hung Pai, a journalist who travelled China interviewing and documenting the lives of casual laborers, reflects repeatedly in her account on the harshness of the modern industrial life thrust upon these often young, poorly educated, and unskilled migrants. Harsh working conditions, exploitation by unscrupulous employers, and repeated scandals of child labor, all serve to create in her account a powerful and moving vision of the Chinese casual laborer as a victim of the violence of modern industry.[68] Nor is she alone; the CNN editorial opens with a description of the squalid conditions migrant casual labor faces in Chinese cities – "The chipped walls of Guo Jigang's tiny home are bandaged together with clear packing tape".[69] The space itself is a violent intrusion into the lives of the migrants. Pai presents her subjects as ground down by it. One migrant brings her back to a shared flat to see his poetry; "there must have been at least a dozen people living there besides him" she noted but added that Ren Jianguo "didn't seem to care about the mess or lack of space".[70] The *liudong renkou*, she concludes, despite being labelled a "security risk" by the state and the Chinese media, face profound maltreatment from institutions and settled urban society themselves in their quest to "earn quickly and send money home".[71]

Like the Victorian navvies they exist as stereotypes, rather than individuals, in the public eye, alternately feared as potential sources of violence and pitied as those at most risk in a society modernizing at break-neck speed. Historian Elizabeth Weber has observed, in her studies of Qing era texts dealing with Chinese coolie labor, that the violence visited upon the coolies served two literary purposes in Chinese society. The sufferings of the coolies in novels represented "both foreign cruelty" and the Chinese state's "impotence in preventing that cruelty"; an analysis similar to the anxieties about the cruelty of the railway age in Garnett's text and the concerns about life in modern China uncovered by Pai.[72] Navvies, coolies, and the *luidong renkou* have all been reduced to figurative elements in these texts, victims of violence that represent the rough-edges of the modern world.

68 Ibid., pp. 32–33, 36, 50–53.

69 Park / Xu: Is Migrant System China's Apartheid?

70 Pai: *Scattered Sand*, p. 21.

71 Ibid., p. 292.

72 Elizabeth E. Weber: Reimaging Coolie Trajectories: The Triumphant Return as Political Statement in Late Qing 'Coolie Fiction'. In: *Literature Compass* 13,5 (2016), pp. 300–310, here p. 307.

Conclusion

In 1867 the *English Women's Domestic Magazine* published an article exploring the place of women in America, especially in the Western states that at the time were being shaped by mass migration and the coming of the railways. In Utah territory, it observed, could be found "a listless, indolent crowd of Pawnees, smoking and drinking on the Pacific road, while their squaws were laboring on the railway line as navvies [...] she has a thousand toils to endure".[73] It was a small comment in a wider column about the spread of Mormonism and the place the faith held for women in America that neatly encapsulated the contrasting stereotypes surrounding navvies. There are, of course, important cultural readings to this piece as well, considering the prevailing stereotypes that surrounded Native American tribes like the Pawnee, but the contrast to other accounts of navvies across the Anglophone world is striking. Casual labor on the railways is displayed, in one vignette, as both a latent threat of disruptive violence and as victimized by harsh conditions and working environments. The navvy stands out as both victim and perpetrator.

In attempting to assess the cultural stereotypes that surrounded casual labor in the period this paper has relied chiefly upon outside sources, ranging from newspapers through to political debate, that reflect an avowedly middle-class and up perspective. It has purposefully not delved into the realities of violence for casual workers in the period. Interpersonal violence served a myriad of purposes between 1840 and 1940, but these were not always fully understood, or even particularly considered, in the wider cultural stereotypes that were built up around figures such as the navvy. "The life is a strange one" observed Garnett, who spent more time with navvies than many commentators, "isolated, and free, differing from that of his fellow countrymen and unknown to them".[74] Stereotyped views of the navvy were built up through peripheral contacts, fleeting and chance, for many outside observers and were maintained, as with so many cultural stereotypes, by assumption and confirmed belief based on a few selectively interpreted facts. Mobile, rootless, and operating on the fringes of increasingly settled and urban societies, both navvy labor at the end of the nineteenth century and the *liudong renkou* at the end of the twentieth embodied social unease and changing attitudes to violence.

As both creators and captives of the vast industrial changes of the modern world it was not a contradiction for them to be both victim and offender. They exist

73 Women in America. In: *English Women's Domestic Magazine*, 01.08.1867, p. 418.
74 Garnett: *Our Navvies*, p. 5.

within brutal landscapes of industrial change. From the iron and steel hub of Middlesbrough in 1907, with its "pillars of cloud by day [... and] pillars of fire by night" as one contemporary put it, through to Chengdu in 2012, so changed by development as to prove almost unrecognizable to Pai after only a decade, the spaces and places of the industrializing modern world provoke a cacophony of noises, sights, smells, and tactile environments.[75] It produces, as this study has endeavored to show, a tautology of interlocked stereotypes; migrant casual labor is prone to violence, filling the cityscape or construction site with its riotous behavior, but is also the product of the slower and more insidious violence of the world it inhabits, caught in the throes of modernizing change. Bessel may be right that, as with the ending of the navvy-age in the mid twentieth century in the West, rising living standards both reduced the social space and economic instabilities that encouraged violence amongst many workers, but shifting the focus beyond the boundaries of the post-war West reveals arenas where such stereotypes of violence continue to find purchase.[76] Casual migrant workers, of course, come from a range of backgrounds, cultures, and desires, and remain vastly more complex than any stereotype can allow. But in the sweeping currents of prevailing popular culture this does not matter. Here they embodied, and continue to embody, the conflicted attitude modern society has to industrial change and its attendant social upheavals.

75 Lady Florence Bell: *At the Works: A Study of a Manufacturing Town*. London: Virago 1985, p. 12; Pai: *Scattered Sand*, pp. 41–48.
76 Bessel: *Violence*, pp. 273–274.

Racism and Violence in Germany since 1980

Barbara Manthe

Introduction and Definitions

In the past thirty-five years, racist violence and the far-right in the Federal Republic of Germany (FRG) have been entwined. Foreigners are not only the most at-risk victims of right-wing perpetrators, but activists from the far-right are the most common culprits of racist violence.[1] However, the post-war far-right in Germany has not always significantly engaged in racially-motivated violence. Such deeds began to appear in the 1980s, corresponding with societal developments and changes inside the right-wing scene.

This article provides a historical insight into the violence that emerged from racist stereotypes and ideology in West Germany since 1980, and also considers East Germany (former German Democratic Republic or GDR) after 1990. The text draws attention to outrages committed by right-wing groups or individuals, since this group comprises most assailants of race-based violence. Following a brief discussion of definitions, the article demonstrates that extreme-right violence against non-German citizens has a decade-long history. While right-wing offenders were mainly driven by anti-communist, antisemitic and nationalist motives until the 1970s, the number of racist assaults distinctly increased after 1980. After the reunion with the GDR in 1990, racist violence escalated; different types of attacks occurred, such as premeditated murders, street violence by individuals or smaller groups, mass riots and arson attacks. Since the former GDR was the setting of the highest rate of right-wing motivated crimes after 1990, it is important to specify the preconditions there and examine the contemporary circumstances in the western parts of Germany. This paper also explains why racist violence rose after 1980; some determinants of the violence were economic and societal changes, discourses on migration and the emergence of the skinhead movement. In a further section, I draw attention to the neo-Nazi milieu that emerged in the early 1990s, which constituted the political home of the "National Socialist Underground" (*Nationalsozialistischer Untergrund*, or the NSU). Furthermore, the article examines the crucial impact of racist writing that circulated among the extreme right, such as the *Turner Diaries* (a popular

1 Todesopfer rechter Gewalt seit 1990. http://www.zeit.de/gesellschaft/zeitgeschehen/todesopfer-rechter-gewalt (accessed 27.03.2016).

novel propagandizing a "race war"), and how the NSU possibly drew inspiration from racist manuals and novels. In conclusion, the article highlights how German society continues to struggle with identifying underlying racist motives when it comes to violence.

When speaking of racist violence by right-wing actors, it is necessary to take a look at ethnically-driven nationalism. Unlike in other countries, civic identity and nationhood in Germany was linked to the *Volk* – belonging to the German *Volk* was determined by descent and blood, not by choice or by immigration. This concept emerged as a counterpart of the French idea of 'nation' in the early 19th century; legitimized by a biologistic concept of 'race', belonging or non-belonging to the German *Volk* and the notion of ethnic homogeneity became a crucial question in National Socialism. After 1945, society dissociated from National Socialist ideology, but the idea remained that all Germans had a common ethnic background. The citizenship law of the FRG based on the principles of *ius sanguinis* defined German nationality by bloodline and ethnic background. Debates on immigration thus always involved a debate on who belonged to Germany and who did not; ethnic nationalism already formed the basis for violent racism in Germany after 1980, and the boom in racism in the 1990s can be explained by the rise in nationalism during the German reunification that was linked to feelings of superiority over presumed "foreigners".[2]

I synonymously use the terms 'far-right' and 'right-wing' to define the attitudes, activities and behaviors of those that assume the racial or ethnic inequality of men and deduce from that belief an unequal treatment of men; seek ethnic homogeneity; assess community over individual liberties and oppose pluralism and democratization.[3] Although the ideology of the far-right is not consistent and features a variety of conceptions and goals, its visions for society are, generally speaking, anti-democratic, nationalistic, racist and antisemitic.[4] Violent activities by the far-right should not be interpreted as deeds isolated from society, but must be analyzed in their societal and historical context. It is also important to draw attention to how society and third parties – bystanders, for instance – respond to these behaviors.

2 Cynthia Miller-Idriss: *Blood and Culture. Youth, Right-wing Extremism, and National Belonging in Contemporary Germany*. Durham / London: Duke UP 2009, pp. 46–47, 52.

3 Fabian Virchow: *Nicht nur der NSU. Eine kleine Geschichte des Rechtsterrorismus in Deutschland*. Erfurt: Landeszentrale für politische Bildung Thüringen 2016, p. 7.

4 Richard Stöss: *Rechtsextremismus:* Begriff – Struktur – Analyse. In: Kurt Bodewig / Rainer Hesels / Dieter Mahlberg (eds): *Die schleichende Gefahr. Rechtsextremismus heute*. Essen: Klartext 1990, pp. 61–64.

Racism as a Primary Issue among the Far-Right

Although racism had always been an integral part of right-wing ideology, the far-right developed surprisingly few specific racist activities before 1980. The actions during 1950 and 1980 were mainly driven by antisemitism, anti-communism and attempts to stop the critical reappraisal of the National Socialist past. Furthermore, a more general objective was the restoration of the (National Socialist) *'Reich'*. Several arson attacks against asylum seekers (as well as other outrages) committed by the German Action Groups (*Deutsche Aktionsgruppen*, or DA) throughout the year 1980 indicated the outset of racist violence in Germany, which still has yet to cease. The DA was a small group with at least five members, founded and led by the former lawyer Manfred Roeder. He politically targeted many things since beginning his political career in the 1970s, such as sex shops and sex movies.[5] In 1980, he gathered a group of sympathizers who carried out attacks throughout the country. During an arson attack against a refugee hostel in Hamburg in August 1980, two Vietnamese refugees were killed. Police detained the group after two members were caught writing the phrase "Foreigners out" (*Ausländer raus*) on a motorway sign.[6] As far as we know today, the activities of the DA were part of the first racist attacks against immigrants in the FRG; therefore, the group's racist acts inspired others among the far-right in West Germany.

Migration and the agitation against "super-alienation" (*Überfremdung*) have become main topics among the far right. It is important to note that migration to Germany had already been happening often since the 1950s when the first recruitment agreements between Germany and Italy, Turkey, Spain and other South-European and North-African countries were made to overcome labor shortages in the FRG.[7] Immigration was thus not 'new' to German society, but it is fair to state that in German society, the idea that immigrants should stay in their 'host country' for good was a new one.

The 1980s were characterized by societal developments, economic and political changes, as well as debates concerning migration and multiculturalism. Discussions on integration and the question of remigration were recurring themes throughout the 1980s.[8] The conditions under which 'guest workers' lived in the

5 Andrea Röpke / Andreas Speit: *Blut und Ehre. Geschichte und Gegenwart rechter Gewalt in Deutschland*. Berlin: Links 2013, p. 47.

6 Stefan Aust / Dirk Laabs: *Heimatschutz. Der Staat und die Mordserie des NSU*. München: Pantheon 2014, pp. 87–88.

7 Jochen Oltmer: *Migration im 19. und 20. Jahrhundert*. München: Oldenbourg 2010, pp. 52–54.

8 Klaus Hecking: Kohl wollte offenbar jeden zweiten Türken loswerden. In: *Der Spiegel*, 01.08.2013. http://www.spiegel.de/politik/deutschland/kohl-wollte-jeden-zweiten-tuerken-in-deutschland-loswerden-a-914318.html (accessed 15.02.2016); Mit der Nadel einen Brunnen graben. In: *Der Spiegel* 43,9 (1989), pp. 70–90.

FRG had changed; a shrinking job market and increasing unemployment rate had seemingly jeopardized the support for – or at least indifference toward – immigrant workers that could be observed previously among the German population. Insufficient integration policy, a lack of appropriate education for 'guest worker' children and the uncertainty of their eventual place in society led to segregation and impeded upward social mobility.[9] Although 'guest workers' were discriminated against in terms of housing, wage and education, many Germans perceived migrants as a social or cultural threat. Opinion surveys depicted in 1980 that up to forty-four percent of the West German population were hostile toward immigrant workers; the attitudes largely depended on the socio-economic status, education level and political position of the respondents.[10]

At the same time, migration to Germany transformed. The politics of inner-European labor recruitment came to an end while a growing number of refugees fled civil wars and poverty; they sought asylum in West Germany, where political asylum was guaranteed.[11] This development gave occasion to an asylum debate that was sustained by the new Conservative-Liberal government under Chancellor Helmut Kohl – the debate was revived in the early 1990s, a topic to which this paper will return later. At the same time, issues concerning multiculturalism arose and raised questions about how people in Germany wanted to live together and if the state was seen as an immigration country.[12] The disadvantages of migration were primarily debated, which fueled racist and right-wing groups. It is therefore not surprising that members of the neo-Nazi party National Democratic Party of Germany (*Nationaldemokratische Partei Deutschlands,* or NPD) launched a 1980 racist campaign under the slogan "Citizens' Initiative for Halting Foreigners" (*Bürgerinitiative Ausländerstop*) that promoted segregation and remigration.[13]

Before that time, though, the German far-right had primarily concentrated on nationalist issues concerning the divided Germany, the allied occupation and

9 Marilyn Hoskin: Public Opinion and the Foreign Worker. Traditional and Nontraditional Bases in Germany. In: *Comparative Politics* 17,2 (1985), pp. 193–210, here pp. 195–196, 208.

10 Ibid., pp. 200–206.

11 Ulrich Herbert: *Geschichte der Ausländerpolitik in Deutschland. Saisonarbeiter, Zwangsarbeiter, Gastarbeiter, Flüchtlinge.* München: Beck 2001, p. 242.

12 Stefan Neubert / Hans-Joachim Roth / Erol Yildiz: Multikulturalismus – ein umstrittenes Konzept. In: Iid. (eds): *Multikulturalität in der Diskussion. Neuere Beiträge zu einem umstrittenen Konzept,* Opladen: Leske + Budrich 2002, pp. 9–29, here pp. 9–10.

13 Rita Chin: *The Guest Worker Question in Postwar Germany.* New York / Cambridge: Cambridge UP 2007, p. 153.

the attempts to restore the *Reich*. These objectives faded into the background in favor of ethnocentric racism and nationalism.

In the same year the DA operated, another explicitly racist group emerged in West Germany: the Ku Klux Klan (KKK). Originally located in the United States, the KKK attempted to establish branches at several Air Force bases in the FRG. The members of these groups were US soldiers, but they also sympathized with German neo-Nazis, as the West German magazine *Stern* investigated in 1981. American and German racists held regular meetings and went 'on patrol' together. Although the Klan members from the US provided informational material and racist magazines for the Germans, it is notable that the domestic neo-Nazis expressed their own specific brand of racist thoughts. *Stern* journalist Gerhard Kromschröder quoted a young German: "Our enemies are not only the Niggers. Together with our American comrades we fight as German patriots against every foreign race. Against Russians, Turks and all those wogs that overflow our country".[14]

The ideological reorientation of the far right in the FRG went along with a radicalization of the neo-Nazi scene that started in the 1970s and culminated in 1980; eighteen people were killed during right-wing terrorist attacks, thirteen of them during the Munich *Oktoberfest* bombing in September 1980.[15] New generations of neo-Nazis were willing to commit severe outrages, even murder. Right-wing terrorist networks emerged, building secret armories and robbing banks to prepare for lethal attacks.[16]

Lone actors were also part of this developing scene. Despite acting alone, they were seldom completely detached from the right-wing scene. Helmut Oxner is a prime example – on June 24, 1982, he shot visitors at a discotheque in Nuremberg, injuring several guests and killing two African-Americans. Afterwards, he fired at seemingly foreign pedestrians on the street, murdering an Egyptian man. Before committing suicide, Oxner said to the policemen at the scene: "I only fire at Turks." Oxner was already known to the police as a neo-Nazi and for the illegal possession of firearms. The magazine *Der Spiegel* stated that the offender was a sympathizer of the NPD, whose Nuremberg branch had held anti-immigrant rallies in the last two years.[17]

14 Gerhard Kromschröder: Die weißen Rächer aus der Eifel. In: *STERN* 34,23 (1981), p. 163.

15 Röpke / Speit: *Blut und Ehre*, pp. 50–51.

16 Virchow: *Nicht nur der NSU*, pp. 13–21.

17 Lebende Zeitbomben. In: *Der Spiegel* 36,27 (1982), pp. 32–35.

The Emergence of the Skinhead Movement and the Escalation of Racist Violence

Since the mid 1980s, more and more cases of street violence against first- and second-generation immigrants have been reported.[18] While legal actions and trials involving militant neo-Nazi groups occurred earlier,[19] a new subcultural phenomenon vigorously developed. Imported from England, the skinhead culture proved extremely popular in Germany, not only among a politically neutral music scene but also among mainly young people with a right-wing and racist outlook on the world. Different from right-wing parties and groups, this subcultural movement was diffuse in nature; it was not an official organization with memberships and a defined ideology, but a subcultural milieu that was also linked to the Punk scene in the early 1980s and was constantly evolving. Nevertheless, bands and individuals who were part of the scene were known for racist utterances. The West German music group *Böhse Onkelz*, for instance, which had its roots in the Punk scene, published the racist song *Türken raus* (Turks out) in 1982 and thereby marked the orientation of this new movement toward a racist and nationalist approach. The subculture radicalized; consequently, more and more young people became skinheads for political reasons and joined neo-Nazi groups at the same time. The neo-Nazi scene and the skinhead culture in West Germany inspired each other, and to some extent merged into one milieu.[20]

The most significant burst of racial violence came after 1990. In 1990, 309 acts of race-driven violence were counted, but it should be pointed out that these acts only concerned West Germany. Throughout the course of German reunification, the number of right-wing outrages in reunified Germany increased from 1,492 per year in 1991 to its peak of 2,639 in 1992, followed by 2,232 violent acts per annum in 1993. In 1994, violence went down to 1,489 violent crimes per year, and the decrease has continued until the late 1990s.[21] It is important to highlight that these numbers only cover officially reported crimes; there is an estimated number of unrecorded cases marked as not politically motivated. The

18 Sabine Stamer: Manche lernen Karate. In: *Die Zeit*, 16.01.1987. http://www.zeit.de/1987/04/manche-lernen-karate/komplettansicht (accessed 22.02.2016).

19 Bernhard Rabert: *Links- und Rechtsterrorismus in der Bundesrepublik Deutschland von 1970 bis heute*. Bonn: Bernard & Graefe 1995, p. 238.

20 Christian Dornbusch / Jan Raabe: 20 Jahre Rechtsrock. Vom Skinhead-Rock zur Alltagskultur. In: Iid. (eds): *RechtsRock. Bestandaufnahme und Gegenstrategien*. Münster: Unrast 2003, pp. 19–50, here pp. 26–31.

21 Michael Minkenberg: *Die neue radikale Rechte im Vergleich. USA, Frankreich, Deutschland*. Opladen / Wiesbaden: Westdeutscher Verlag 1998, p. 306.

largest number of these right-wing attacks was driven by racism, however, and most of these crimes occurred in the new eastern states of Germany.[22] This is a significant fact that the paper will elaborate on later.
Different types of attacks can be identified, such as street violence by individuals or smaller groups, mass riots, arson attacks and planned murders. The article will return to the latter when it comes to homicides committed by the National Socialist Underground (NSU). Street violence certainly represented the largest amount of racist assaults in the early 1990s; attacks against not only immigrants, but also against left-wing youths, homeless people, homosexuals, Jews, Sinti, Roma and disabled people occurred daily in Germany. Groups of neo-Nazis performed unequivocal manhunts, where the victims were often severely injured or even killed.[23] Beating up foreigners – regardless of whether the "foreigner" had a German passport or not – became a brutal pastime among right-wing youths and young adults, encouraged by the idea of building "Nationally Liberated Zones", a euphemism for a no-go area for immigrants and other "enemies" of the far-right.[24] Although the term has to be handled carefully because of its propagandistic nature, it indicates the far-right activists' attempts to establish cultural hegemony in their social environment. The concept also suggests that neo-Nazis should become economically independent from the "system" by starting their own businesses, for instance.[25]

Racist Riots and Arson Attacks

Mass riots were another form of racist violence that particularly stirred the attention of the national and international media. It is remarkable that not only neo-Nazis participated in these riots, but also 'ordinary citizens'. Well-known cases were the riots in Hoyerswerda (Saxony, September 17–23, 1991) and

22 Richard Stöß: *Rechtsextremismus im Wandel.* Berlin: Friedrich-Ebert-Stiftung 2007, p. 159.

23 Such as the Angolan Amadeu Antonio Kiowa, who was killed on November 25, 1990, in Eberswalde (East Germany) by a gang of 60 neo-Nazis, or the Kurd Nihad Yusufoglu, who was stabbed to death by a skinhead on December 28, 1990, in Hachenburg (West Germany). Frank Jansen / Johannes Radke / Heike Kleffner / Toralf Staud: 149 Todesopfer rechter Gewalt. In: *Der Tagesspiegel*, 31.05.2012. http://www.tagesspiegel.de/politik/rechtsextremismus/toedlicher-hass-149-todesopfer-rechter-gewalt/1934424.html (accessed 23.02.2016).

24 Burkhard Schröder: *Im Griff der rechten Szene. Ostdeutsche Städte in Angst.* Reinbek: Rowohlt 1997, pp. 155–159.

25 Gideon Botsch: Die extreme Rechte als „nationales Lager" – „Versäulung" im lebensweltlichen Milieu oder Marsch in die Mitte der Gesellschaft? In: Christoph Kopke (ed.): *Die Grenzen der Toleranz. Rechtsextremes Milieu und demokratische Gesellschaft in Brandenburg. Bilanz und Perspektiven.* Potsdam: Universitätsverlag 2011, pp. 57–81, here pp. 78–79.

Rostock (Mecklenburg-Vorpommern, August 22–26, 1992), both cities in eastern Germany, where rioters attacked asylum hostels for days. In Rostock, up to 3,000 people gathered in a housing complex in the district of Lichtenhagen and cheered the mob when it first attacked a shelter for Roma who had fled Romania. The police evacuated the refugees three days later amid general applause of the crowd. The following night, the rioters attacked a neighboring house where 150 Vietnamese workers lived – the attackers threw stones and Molotov cocktails and prevented the fire service from extinguishing the flames. The residents managed to escape from the roof and through a neighbor's house.[26] In this case, good fortune alone prevented fatalities.

Almost immediately after the event, journalists and other observers levelled blistering criticism at how reluctantly police and authorities had handled the crisis in Rostock. The number of police deployed during the riots was far too small to seize control of the situation or to detain the offenders, but even later on, official investigations would never completely hold anyone responsible.[27] The political context, however, was deep – the events of Rostock could be seen as a symptom and manifestation of the political climate during that time, since immigration and asylum law were in the spotlight of contemporary political discussion. Much like in the 1980s, the growing number of asylum seekers who came to Germany – the numbers of which exceeded 440,000 in 1992[28] – gave occasion to heated debates with noticeably racist undertones. The media and politicians did not often explicitly condemn violence against immigrants, but rather they expressed sympathy toward the offenders. For instance, the conservative Minister of the Interior of Mecklenburg-Vorpommern, Lothar Kupfer, revealed a "certain understanding" for the rioters and the applauding bystanders in Rostock.[29]

At the beginning of the 1990s, political parties argued over asylum law reform in the German constitution, which had thus far guaranteed an absolute right to political asylum. The conservative parties sought to restrict that guarantee while amending Article 16 of the constitution to the effect that asylum seekers entering from a secure country (so-called safe third states) may not invoke the right

26 Röpke / Speit: *Blut und Ehre*, pp. 94–102.

27 Thomas Prenzel: Rostock-Lichtenhagen im Kontext der Debatte um die Einschränkung des Grundrechts auf Asyl. In: Id. (ed.): *Rostock-Lichtenhagen. Kontext, Dimensionen und Folgen der rassistischen Gewalt*. Rostock: Universität Rostock 2012, pp. 9–29, here pp. 20–24.

28 Indeed, the recognition rate only amounted to 4.3 % in 1992. Ibid., p. 11.

29 John Eisenhammer: Mistakes Admitted in Effort to End Rostock Riots. In: *The Independent*, 28.08.1992. http://www.independent.co.uk/news/world/europe/mistakes-admitted-in-effort-to-end-rostock-riots-john-eisenhammer-in-bonn-describes-the-dilemma-that-1542896.html (accessed 25.02.2016).

of asylum. During the riots of Rostock on August 21 and 22, 1992, the Social Democratic Party of Germany (SPD) recalled its vote against the amendment, a decision that paved the way for the revision of Article 16 by the German parliament in May 1993.[30]

Two different yet parallel interpretations claim to explain the authorities' reluctance to immediately terminate the riots in Rostock. One opinion assumes that politics themselves had failed; authorities were overwhelmed and the police commander misjudged the situation.[31] Another interpretation ventured that politicians deliberately let the violence escalate to precipitate a decision on asylum law reform. The journalist Jochen Schmidt – who was part of a camera crew that was trapped with the Vietnamese workers in the burning house during the riots – even argued that the violence was staged as a 'controlled escalation' to light a beacon in the asylum debate.[32] In retrospect, elements of both explanations are likely to be true; the authorities undoubtedly reacted reluctantly, but politicians also took advantage of the situation. Whether the violence was willingly expedited or left to escalate is an unresolved matter.

Besides the cases of direct violence, arson attacks against the houses of immigrants became more and more frequent. As previously mentioned, this kind of crime had already occurred in the 1980s, but the sheer volume of assaults in the 1990s dismayed politicians and the public alike. The most notable attacks took place in Mölln (Schleswig-Holstein, November 23, 1992) and Solingen (North Rhine-Westphalia, May 29, 1993) where neo-Nazis set family homes on fire at night. Eight women of Turkish origin died during the assaults. Although other arson attacks with more fatalities were carried out in the following years, the outrage of Mölln and Solingen lingered in the public's memory for several reasons. Firstly, both attacks were executed in western Germany, which confounded the common view that right-wing and racist violence was only a problem in the eastern states. Secondly, the targets were not refugee hostels in a remote district, but family homes in a German neighborhood. Thirdly, police quickly arrested the perpetrators in both cases, who instantly confessed. They undoubtedly belonged to the right-wing scene and their crimes were racially motivated; since the backgrounds of arson attacks were seldom elucidated at that time, this case was an exception. Finally, the aggression and sheer tragedy that overcame the Genç and

30 Prenzel: Rostock-Lichtenhagen im Kontext, pp. 25–26.

31 Ibid., p. 23.

32 Jochen Schmidt: Politische Brandstiftung. Warum 1992 in Rostock das Ausländerwohnheim in Flammen aufging. Berlin: Edition Ost 2002; Anklang an Weimar. In: *Der Spiegel* 46,41 (1992), pp. 18–29.

Arslan families was beyond question; the youngest victim was only four years old. The fact that all victims were female – in contrast to common fatalities of neo-Nazi street violence in which mostly men were killed – certainly intensified public outcry. The public response to the arson attacks, especially to Mölln and Solingen, differed from ambiguous reactions to riots, while some had an indifferent view on street violence. In the winter of 1992, several hundred thousand people took part in demonstrations against racial violence, which were mainly organized by journalists and local initiatives.[33]

Causes of Racist Violence

The reasons for the outburst of racist violence in Germany in the early 1990s have been widely discussed. It is unquestionable that right-wing parties like The Republicans (*Die Republikaner*, or REP) or the German People's Union (*Deutsche Volksunion*, or DVU), which had achieved success in West German elections for several years, exacerbated the political atmosphere with their racist slogans.[34] In any respect, the political climate was tense and a pervasive racist attitude among the German population found expression in acclaiming right-wing activities against immigrants. In a 1992 survey, 38 % of all Germans approved of "right-wing tendencies because of the immigrant problem".[35]
Although the situation in the former German Democratic Republic can be characterized by an extremely active neo-Nazi scene, escalating street violence and a relatively higher homicide rate than in the west, it would be a mistake to simply displace the problem to eastern Germany. Certainly, the new eastern states had seen rapid changes within the last few years – the GDR's former institutions underwent a loss of authority, which created a political vacuum that could not be entirely absorbed by the West German authorities. East German police and justice were neither consent nor able to consequently proceed against the far-right. As a result, right-wing extremists felt reinvigorated and created spaces of hegemony to which violence was inextricably linked. Furthermore, professional youth work and many social and cultural offerings to young people had broken off after the reunification. Angela Merkel, the then Federal Minister for Women and Youth, implemented an action program against aggression and violence in 1992 in order to handle the situation, but this attempt only led to a stabilization

33 Norbert Kostede: Erleuchtung für die Politik. In: *Die Zeit*, 29.01.1993. http://www.zeit.de/1993/05/erleuchtung-fuer-die-politik/komplettansicht (accessed 07.03.2016).
34 Röpke / Speit: *Blut und Ehre*, p. 99.
35 Anklang an Weimar, p. 19.

of right-wing structures. Many newly hired youth workers were overwhelmed by the numerous and confident neo-Nazis who soon seized the chance to take over youth clubs and other youth facilities. Albeit many West German neo-Nazis saw the opportunity to agitate the east and took part in violent acts, the crucial role of East German neo-Nazis must not be underestimated. In particular, those who re-emigrated after having left the GDR as so-called 'deserters from the republic' played an important part in constituting a right-wing scene in the east that had covertly existed before 1989.[36] Ingo Hasselbach, for example, a former right-wing leader who left the scene shortly after 1992, participated in the rioting in Rostock. He wrote in his autobiography: "People like me have motivated others through racist slogans to throw stones and Molotov cocktails on outnumbered defenseless persons, not only in Rostock-Lichtenhagen."[37] However, he claimed that the Rostock incident had not been planned from the outside, which consolidates the assumption that the violence was not only a move by the organized right-wing scene but a form of violent dynamics that brought together neo-Nazis, sympathizers and 'ordinary neighbors' alike.

Given the special situation in the east, racist violence in all its forms also occurred in the western parts of Germany, but in smaller numbers. It would be misleading to explain this imbalance as a result of a 'different mentality' without regarding other socio-economic factors that could shed light on the situation. Eastern Germany had relatively more rural and sparsely populated regions with fewer immigrants than the west, and large regions in the new states were deprived and affected by unemployment, which led to an interior migration – particularly by better-qualified people. These aspects, especially in the context of socio-economic deprivation and disintegration among a certain part of the population, do not necessarily elicit racist and right-wing attitudes but are likely to strengthen them.[38] Although it is important to distinguish between attitudes and behaviors, a person with a racist attitude can change under certain conditions into an activist, for example, if the political climate encourages racist actions or if a strong right-wing scene creates group dynamics. This process can be observed in eastern Germany during the early 1990s.

36 Liane Richter / Klaus Niebuhr: Unaufgearbeitetes Schlüsseljahrzehnt. In: *der rechte rand* 23,137 (2012), p. 21.

37 Ingo Hasselbach / Winfried Bonengel: *Die Abrechnung. Ein Neonazi steigt aus.* Berlin / Weimar: Aufbau 1993, p. 146.

38 Oliver Decker / Elmar Brähler: *Vom Rand zur Mitte. Rechtsextreme Einstellung und ihre Einflussfaktoren in Deutschland.* Berlin: FES 2006, pp. 17–18.

The Genesis and Crimes of the National-Socialist Underground (NSU)

Racist violence, as well as the actions of the militant far-right, declined until the end of the 1990s due to the banning of several important neo-Nazi organizations and the restructuring of the right-wing scene. The resentful political climate also settled after the 'asylum compromise' in 1993, yet racist street violence continued, albeit on a lower level, and it should be pointed out that the public interest in violent activities of the far right was still very low. In 1998, the year the NSU terrorists Uwe Mundlos, Uwe Böhnhardt and Beate Zschäpe went underground, right-wing and racist violence was almost a non-issue in German society. In retrospect, however, disregarding the militant scene of the late 1990s was a severe error. The decrease of racist assaults did not necessarily indicate that a vigorous and militant scene had not grown, especially in the east. The young neo-Nazis in the late 1990s had grown up witnessing violent crimes against immigrants as not only hesitantly persecuted by the authorities and supposedly necessary to some parts of the population, but also a sign of significant political potency. Hence, many smaller neo-Nazi milieus flourished in the new states that exerted regional domination by resorting to violence; a right-wing lifestyle thus became socially acceptable in many places.[39]

The cultural and political perception of the riots of Rostock and similar happenings resulted in not only German neo-Nazis commemorating these events, but also the rise of international sympathizers. Music featured prominently in this process, as well; for instance, the British neo-Nazi rock band No Remorse released a 1996 album bearing the cynical title *Barbecue in Rostock*, referring to the Rostock riots.[40] The title song blatantly glorifies racist violence and murder, even though the Turks had not been the targets in Rostock:

> Didn't want their town filled with scum,
> so they got together and made petrol bombs.
> Then one cold, starry night,
> they set them filthy Turks alight!
> There's a barbecue in Rostock, you better come!
> How do you like your Turks? Do you like 'em well done? [...]
> It's time these Turks got to know,
> that Deutschland's youth are on patrol. [...]
> But things got hot in Solingen,
> 'co's Deutschland's youth did it again![41]

39 David Begrich: Die Quellen des Hasses. In: *Blätter für deutsche und internationale Politik* 57,1 (2012), pp. 43–46, here p. 44.

40 Ryan Shaffer: British, European and White: Cultural Constructions of Identity in Post-War British Fascist Music. In: Nigel Copsey / John E. Richardson (eds): *Cultures of Post-War British Fascism*. Oxon / New York: Routledge 2015, pp. 142–160, here p. 151.

41 No Remorse: Barbecue in Rostock. (*Barbecue in Rostock*, 1996).

In order to understand the NSU's deeds, it is crucial to point out that its members Mundlos, Böhnhardt and Zschäpe came from these milieus. They were not only part of the militant neo-Nazi group Thuringian Homeland Security (*Thüringer Heimatschutz*, THS), but they and many of their supporters were also connected to German branches of the international neo-Nazi network Blood & Honour that promoted White Power music, organized concerts and distributed right-wing and racist ideas among the scene.[42]

Between January 1998 and November 2011, when the NSU was uncovered, the group committed at least ten murders, two bomb attacks and several bank robberies. The activities of Mundlos, Böhnhardt and Zschäpe, who were backed by a yet unknown number of supporters, aroused one of the largest political scandals in the history of the republic. A federal inquiry committee that was constituted in 2012 by the *Bundestag* – the national German parliament – investigated that the prosecution and secret services not only failed to track down the neo-Nazis in hiding, but also incorrectly assessed the acts of violence as offenses committed by cross-border organized crime groups, which they concluded from the immigration backgrounds of most of the victims. Police suspected that the relatives of the homicide victims concealed information on alleged criminal activities of their murdered husbands, fathers and sons and investigated the victims' backgrounds.[43] The media indifferently donned the series of murders with the degrading title of the "Kebab Murders" (*Dönermorde*).[44]

The true motives for the crimes remained unbeknownst to authorities and the general public until the day of uncovering in 2011. The inquiry committee paid particular attention to the role of the domestic intelligence service (*Verfassungsschutz*) and their informants, but how close the informants came to the terrorist cells and whether the *Verfassungsschutz* knew about the existence of the NSU or not are still unresolved matters.[45] Until today, numerous details of the thirteen-year long underground activities of the NSU have not been clarified, but it is beyond any doubt that the motives of the terrorists were driven by racism. The

42 Wolf Schmidt: Blut- und Ehre-Mörder aus Jena. In: *die tageszeitung*, 15.02.2012. http://www.taz.de/!5093882/ (accessed 11.03.2016).

43 Deutscher Bundestag, 17. Wahlperiode: *Beschlussempfehlung und Bericht des 2. Untersuchungsausschusses nach Artikel 44 des Grundgesetzes.* Drucksache 17/14600, 22.08.2013, pp. 497–499, 731–735.

44 Fabian Virchow / Tanja Thomas / Elke Grittmann: *„Das Unwort erklärt die Untat". Die Berichterstattung über die NSU-Morde – eine Medienkritik.* Frankfurt am Main: Otto Brenner Stiftung 2015, pp. 21–25.

45 See for more detailed information, Deutscher Bundestag: *Beschlussempfehlung und Bericht des 2. Untersuchungsausschusses nach Artikel 44 des Grundgesetzes*; Aust / Laabs: *Heimatschutz*.

two bombing attacks in Cologne in 2001 and 2004 were directed against Iranian, Turkish and Kurdish immigrants; almost all murder victims were of Turkish and Kurdish origin, and one Greek man was presumably killed because the perpetrators thought he was a Turk. It may be assumed from the existing evidence that the NSU selected their murder victims, since they were male, immigrants and young enough to father children.[46]

Racist Writing as Terrorist Inspiration

Although much of the NSU's inner workings remained undetected hitherto, there are many indications that the terrorists did not act without inspiration from outside sources. The idea of leaderless resistance – small cells or lone wolves who independently executed violent actions and terrorist attacks – was widely discussed in the neo-Nazi scene in the 1990s. Combat 18 (with "18" standing for AH – Adolf Hitler), founded in the UK as an armed wing of Blood & Honour in the early 1990s, specifically propagated right-wing terrorism based on the principles of leaderless resistance. In Germany, Combat 18 was not a formal organization but rather a label and guide for terrorists on the far-right. Several manuals circulated among the extreme right, such as the paper *The Way Forward* composed by a Norwegian neo-Nazi in 2000. He wrote:

> There are many ways of spreading fear and terror amoung [*sic*] the enemy. [...] We must simply work on, seizing every opportunity to under mind [*sic*], sabotage and destroy the anti-White forces, while recruiting, organizing and training our comrades of all ages and White nations for the coming conflicts.[47]

The author later published a pamphlet called *The Field Manual*, where the reader could find practical instructions for terrorist activities.[48] The novel *The Turner Diaries*, written in 1978 by the American racist William Luther Pierce, garnered particular appeal. The book depicts a fictional scenario in which a racist organization undergoes guerrilla warfare against the US government. The book is perforated by racist and anti-Semitic violent fantasies that end in the mass extermination of Jews and blacks. The protagonist, Earl Turner, is a member of the organization who implements terrorist attacks and murders. In *The Hunter*, the

46 Andreas Speit: Zu alt, um umgebracht zu werden. In: *die tageszeitung*, 16.10.2013. http://www.taz.de/!5057111/ (accessed 14.03.2016).

47 Max Hammer: *The Way Forward*. Selfpublishing, 2000, pp. 13, 15.

48 Eike Sanders / Kevin Stützel / Klara Tymanova: Taten und Worte – Neonazistische „Blaupausen" des NSU. https://www.nsu-watch.info/2014/10/taten-und-worte-neonazistische-blaupausen-des-nsu/ (accessed 19.03.2016).

sequel to *The Turner Diaries*, a man becomes a serial killer and, among other acts, assassinates 'interracial couples'.[49] The books point to a supposed necessity for a race war sparked by terrorist attacks and therefore, they are intended to trigger overreactions by the government or the black or Jewish community. As per the books, the white population is expected to join the race war on the side of the racists and bring the conflict to an end. Political involvement is implied to be non-essential and sometimes even unproductive.

The impact of this literature must not be underestimated as an ideological weapon. *The Turner Diaries* not only inspired terrorist groups like The Order in the United States, but also lone wolf activists like David Copeland, who conducted three bombing attacks in London in 1999, hurting several hundred people and killing three.[50] The deeds of these groups and individuals in turn inspired new publications that called for the beginning of a race war. The German version of *The Stormer,* a Combat 18 magazine, even provided instructions on how to imitate Copeland's crimes in 2003. Under the title "How to build a Dave Copeland Special", the booklet printed a manual for the construction of a nail bomb the way Copeland had done.[51] Earlier literature, particularly National Socialist publications, figured into this milieu as well, but more in a nostalgic way as this literature did not adjust to modern neo-Nazism. Parties and militant organizations alike published journals and booklets in West Germany, but spreading them among a non-organized milieu was challenging. In the 1990s, concerts and big demonstrations opened up new means of distribution. Fanzines, novels and terrorist manuals attracted the neo-Nazi scene with its subcultural context and its overt glorification of violence more than the propaganda of right-wing parties.

In the late 1990s, racist writing had fed a militant milieu that had become eager to attack. It is certainly no coincidence that the NSU emerged from the Blood and Honor milieu that discussed leaderless resistance and armed struggle. The modus operandi of killing citizens and planting bombs without leaving any indication that this was a politically motivated crime strikingly resembles the discussed conceptions of starting a race war. Indeed, however, *The Turner Diaries*

49 Eike Sanders: Was ein ehrbarer Mann tun muss. Der Roman „Hunter" von William Pierce als Vorlage für den Lone Wolf Terrorist. https://www.nsu-watch.info/2015/05/was-ein-ehrbarer-mann-tun-muss/ (accessed 19.03.2016).

50 Sanders / Stützel / Tymanova: Taten und Worte – Neonazistische „Blaupausen" des NSU.

51 Deutscher Bundestag: *Beschlussempfehlung und Bericht des 2. Untersuchungsausschusses nach Artikel 44 des Grundgesetzes*, p. 165.

were confiscated from two defendants in the NSU case,[52] and in August 2014, the novel was introduced as evidence at trial.[53]

The investigative authorities and the *Verfassungsschutz* did not attribute the homicides and the bombings to the three neo-Nazis in hiding until the discovery of the NSU in 2011, and they essentially ignored any signs that pointed to the right-wing scene. However, the domestic intelligence service of the Federal Republic of Germany (*Bundesamt für Verfassungsschutz*, BfV) reflected on the possibility of right-wing terrorism. In June 2000, three months before the first NSU murder, BfV principal Heinz Fromm spoke about "certain rudiments of the emergence of terrorist structures", and that "We know from neo-Nazis who prepare for the armed struggle."[54] Furthermore, he pointed out that police had found weapons and explosives in the right-wing scene. A few years later, in July 2004, the BfV approached the North Rhine-Westphalian domestic intelligence state office pointing toward an eventual correlation between the bomb attack in Cologne that had just taken place in June 2004 and the Copeland bombings in 1999. The BfV highlighted that a nail bomb was used in both cases and that the crime scene in Cologne was a district mainly inhabited by immigrants. Furthermore, the BfV referred to the aforementioned bomb building instructions in the *Stormer*.[55] This suggestion was eventually discarded, and police instead concentrated on investigations concerning organized crime and drug dealing.

Until today, the exact impact that racist publications had on the NSU cell was undetermined, or if it imitated its modus operandi from books like the *Turner Diaries* or *The Hunter*. However, it seems fair to state that in the 1990s and 2000s, the violent German neo-Nazi scene not only extensively adopted, translated and spread the booklets, manuals and novels, but also regarded them as welcome inspiration for their strategies.

Contemporary Racist Violence

Although the crimes committed by the NSU were at their peak in the 2000s, the first decade of the 2000s was not free of race-related atrocities – they simply occurred less frequently than in the early 1990s. The debates concerning

52 Robert Andreasch: Gelder für die Widerstandsbewegung. In: *der rechte rand* 26,156 (2015), p. 11.

53 Vorwürfe gegen Verfassungsschutz. In: *die tageszeitung*, 06.08.2014. http://www.taz.de/!5036048/ (accessed 20.03.2016).

54 Deutschland droht Terror von rechts. In: *Welt am Sonntag*, 13.06.2000.

55 Deutscher Bundestag: *Beschlussempfehlung und Bericht des 2. Untersuchungsausschusses nach Artikel 44 des Grundgesetzes*, p. 707.

multiculturalism that mainly addressed 'guest workers' and refugees in the 1980s began to focus on Islam in the following decades, and religion as a main instrument of differentiation extended the notion of the "foreign" workers. Controversies over Muslim women wearing headscarves can be observed in the late 1980s and reached their first climax in the 1990s, and this controversy was paired with a brand of racism that alleged not biological, but cultural differences among people. Muslims and Islam in general were ascribed mainly negative attributes, and by that logic, the headscarf represented a backwards and misogynistic culture. But the debate went beyond the headscarves; the notion of a "parallel society", where migrants live by their own rules and customs, merged with an integration debate that merely passed on the responsibility for integration to the immigrants disregarded previous failed integration policies.[56] After the September 11 attacks in 2001, the debate on Islam and international terror soon fused with a general discussion on the integration of Muslims in Germany, which led to a rise of anti-Muslim violence. This anti-Islam sentiment was brought to action through arson attacks against mosques and the race-motivated murder of Marwa el-Sherbini in 2009.[57]

Since 2013, an increasing number of people from Eastern Europe and the Arab countries fleeing to Germany has led to a rise of racist violence against these refugees – this violence, sadly, has likely not yet reached its peak. Numerous 'Anti-Asylum initiatives' – which were occasionally founded and headed by organized neo-Nazis, but frequently consisted of a mixture of 'ordinary citizens' and right-wingers – protested against refugee hostels throughout the whole country.[58] In a process lasting for several years, the amount of racist attacks, especially against accommodating refugees, has exploded since 2015. In that year, the number of criminal acts against refugee hostels was more than four times as high as the previous year. The amount of violent crimes has increased fivefold[59], and authorities

56 Claudia Nikodem: Kopfzerbrechen um das Kopftuch: oder die Frage, wie mit Differenz umgegangen wird. In: Markus Otterbach / Erol Yildiz (eds): *Migration in der metropolitanen Gesellschaft. Zwischen Ethnisierung und globaler Neuorientierung*. Münster: Lit 2004, pp. 141–152, here pp. 144–146.

57 Andrea Dernbach: Stiche ins Herz. In: *Die Zeit*, 27.10.2009. http://www.zeit.de/gesellschaft/zeitgeschehen/2009-10/prozess-marwa-dresden (accessed 20.03.2016).

58 Andrea Röpke: Protest gegen Flüchtlinge: Rechter Aufruhr in Schneeberg. In: *Der Spiegel*, 04.11.2013. http://www.spiegel.de/panorama/gesellschaft/schneeberg-in-sachsen-rechter-protest-gegen-fluechtlinge-a-931711.html (accessed 20.03.2016).

59 Julian Heißler: Deutlich mehr Anschläge auf Asylbewerberheime, 13.01.2016, https://www.tagesschau.de/inland/anschlaege-asylunterkuenfte-bka-101.html (accessed 20.03.2016).

have warned of new emerging right-wing terrorism.[60] Despite the fact that in 2015, unlike in the early 1990s, the media reported favorably about refugees and the strong civil society that has come to oppose racism and violence, latent racist attitudes are apparently firmly anchored in wide parts of the population.[61]
German society still struggles with identifying racist motives when it comes to violence, and this becomes particularly apparent in the discussion about the exact number of right-wing murders since 1990, many of which are race-driven. While the German government counted 75 right-wing motivated homicides between 1990 and 2015, journalists, NGO's and victim counselling centers estimated at least 152 fatalities.[62] On the one hand, this discrepancy results from the official standards that police authorities impose on the cases, and also from a reluctance with which the courts recognize racist or right-wing motivations, particularly since racist and violent criminals often do not unveil their dispositions after the deed. On the other hand, the mismatch reveals a more fundamental social problem: apart from short periods of increased interest, society's awareness of racist violence has always been low. Victims of racist assaults often belong to marginalized groups and, for a long time, did not have lobby groups. Germany lacks hate crime legislation, which means that ambiguous cases may not be investigated as race-related crimes.
This article showed that racist violence has continued since the 1980s and has provoked all forms of violence: homicide, arson attacks, mass riots and terrorism. In the case of the NSU cell, it became clear that racist activities, racist music and racist writings have created a milieu that inspired and radicalized more terrorists. The early 1990s and the years after 2013 are two periods when racist violence gathered momentum and evolved into a group dynamic in which offenders felt vindicated. A major challenge that society now has to face is the "culture of wide impunity" toward racist outrages that has facilitated the emergence of right-wing terrorist structures in the 1990s[63]. Even today, however, the

60 Furcht vor neu organisiertem Rechtsterrorismus. In: *Die Zeit*, 28.08.2015. http://www.zeit.de/politik/deutschland/2015-08/bka-fluechtlingsunterkuenfte-straftaten-rechtsextremismus-dokumentation-bundesinnenministerium (accessed 20.03.2016).

61 See Oliver Decker / Johannes Kiess / Elmar Brähler: *Die stabilisierte Mitte. Rechtsextreme Einstellung in Deutschland 2014*. Leipzig: Kompetenzzentrum für Rechtsextremismus- und Demokratieforschung 2014.

62 Bundesregierung korrigiert Opferzahl rechter Gewalt nach oben. In: *Die Zeit*, 27.07.2015. http://www.zeit.de/gesellschaft/zeitgeschehen/2015-07/rechte-gewalt-zahl-der-toetungsdelikte-bundesregierung (accessed 20.03.2016).

63 Virchow: *Nicht nur der NSU*, p. 94.

rate of solved crimes relating to racial motivations is meagre.[64] A direct comparison between the racist assaults of the 1990s and the violence in the 2000s proves difficult, since societal conditions vary widely. But it became clear that whenever the public sphere debated immigration, integration or multiculturalism and displayed a heated countenance, they ultimately spurred racist outrage.

64 Julian Heißler: Deutlich mehr Anschläge auf Asylbewerberheime. In: *Tagesschau*, 13.01.2016. https://www.tagesschau.de/inland/anschlaege-asylunterkuenfte-bka-101.html (accessed 20.03.2016).

Modern German Anxieties

Generalized Muslimness as New Nationalist Politics in the West

Benjamin Nickl

From International to National Politics

Much of Western politics and state governance have focused on the fight against religious radicalism since the Islamist terror attacks of 9/11 in the United States. That the mainstream media and politicians of Western countries have referred to this focus in public discourse as a war on terror was, according to John Sides and Kimberly Gross, a predictable phenomenon. The two political scientists insist that the simplification of Muslimness as a potential menace to society was effective on the public imagination of Christian majority populations in countries like America. Sides and Gross point out that the social and political complexity of 9/11 circulated in Western societies as an issue of violent Muslimness. The generalization worked because it justified the Western hemisphere's attacks on Iraq and Afghanistan as the epicenters of an Islamist threat.[1] The identities of millions of Afghans and Iraqis were amalgamated into a general ethnocentrism, a matter which seminal works of researchers such as Andrew Shryock and Marc Helbling have shown to be part of a historical Orientalism, as described in the important contribution of Edward Said.[2] Shryock calls it "the grand

1 John Sides / Kimberly Gross: Stereotypes of Muslims and Support for the War on Terror. In: *The Journal of Politics* 75,3 (2013), pp. 583–598, here p. 583.

2 Edward Said: *Orientalism* [1979]. New York: Vintage 1994, pp. 3–9. Said's *Orientalism* greatly influenced the discussion of idealized Muslimness in the public imagination of Western societies. Said's postcolonial theorem fostered critical discussion among scholars about the discursive construction of ideological binaries between West and East. It is useful to place the term "Islamophobia", which first appeared as an "unfounded hostility towards Muslims and therefore fear or dislike of all or most Muslims" in a 1991 Runnymede Trust Report, in that discussion about Western xenophobic histories and Europe's colonial rhetoric, too. I discuss here the contemporary stereotype of Western selves and Muslim others with access to critical scholars such as Daniel Martin Varisco, who provides judicious criticism of Said's forceful polemic in *Reading Orientalism: Said and the Unsaid*. Seattle: University of Washington Press 2012, pp. 11–13. Varisco details crucial aspects of gender-blindness in Said's argument as echoed in feminist readings of *Orientalism* in Christine Anne Holmlund: Displacing Limits of Difference: Gender, Race, and Colonialism in Edward Said and Homi Bhabha's Theoretical Models and Marguerite Duras's Experimental Films. In: *Quarterly Review of Film & Video* 13,1–3 (1991), pp. 1–22, here p. 8, and in Frances White: Africa on My Mind: Gender, Counter Discourse and African-American Nationalism. In:

collapse of geography, culture, and history conveyed in terms like 'the Muslim world'"[3], while Helbling talks of Islamophobia and Neo-Orientalization in the twenty-first century.[4] Western Muslimness in the new millennium is a selective construct of a good Muslim versus bad Muslim binary, as both Shryock and Helbling argue. And indeed, the generalization of Muslim identities is also an effective political strategy. The fear of Muslim terrorists has helped the leaders of nations such as the United States and Great Britain to gain voters' support for military interventions in Muslim majority countries and stricter refugee laws, according to Todd Green.[5]

Yet the widespread fear of Muslimness in Western societies is no longer a foreign policy issue. Underlying assumptions about Islam's inherent violence have increasingly become a domestic concern for nations like the United States, Denmark and Sweden, who had previously claimed social diversity as a constituent of their national identities.[6] Alexandra Herfroy-Mischler, for instance, offers a historical study of Switzerland's major press agencies. She writes that the print news media helped construct the country's political neutrality during and immediately after World War II as "the dominant and central national narrative"[7]. But the Alpine republic showed that anti-Muslim sentiments had penetrated deeply into Switzerland's national culture with the 2009 referendum on banning minaret towers.[8] Corinne Torrekens and Dirk Jacobs present conclusive evidence that there is also a correlation between the religiosity of certain European migrant groups and their perceived distance to majority societies.[9] Based on the 2010 EURISLAM data set, their findings indicate that similar mechanisms of

Journal of Women's History 2,1 (1990), pp. 73–97, here pp. 74–78. The aspect of gender, however, has resurfaced as an important part of the broader discussion on Muslim violence and the stereotyping of Muslim men in the new century, especially following the events of New Year's Eve 2015/2016 in Cologne, Germany.

3 Andrew Shryock (ed.): *Islamophobia/Islamophilia. Beyond the Politics of Enemy and Friend.* Bloomington: Indiana UP 2010, p. 1.

4 Marc Helbling: *Islamophobia in Western Europe and North America.* New York: Routledge 2013, pp. 4–6.

5 Todd Green: *The Fear of Islam. An Introduction to Islamophobia in the West.* Minneapolis: Fortress 2015, p. 235.

6 Ibid., pp. 12–14.

7 Alexandra Herfroy-Mischler: When the Past Seeps into the Present. The Role of Press Agencies in Circulating New Historical Narratives and Restructuring Collective Memory During and After the Holocaust Transitional Justice. In: *Journalism* 16,1 (2015), pp. 1–22, here p. 2.

8 Ibid., pp. 18–19.

9 Corinne Torrekens / Dirk Jacobs: Muslims' Religiosity and Views on Religion in Six Western European Countries: Does National Context Matter? In: *Journal of Ethnic and Migration Studies* 42,2 (2015), pp. 1–16, here p. 2.

anti-Muslim sentiment are at work in all six countries studied, namely Belgium, France, Germany, the Netherlands, Switzerland, and the United Kingdom.

The accommodation of religious views in Western Europe has gradually moved from international to national concern in relation to Muslim migrants and Islamic terror attacks in France and Belgium. According to Gabriella Lazaridis, however, the recurring headscarf debates in the Netherlands and the more recent Burka and Burkini ban movements in France demonstrate a troublesome escalation of earlier versions of Western acculturation attitudes in almost all countries of Western Europe and Scandinavia.[10] Whether referred to as Kopftuch, foulard, voile, başörtüsü, turban, hoofddoek, or hijab, Beverly Weber writes that the immigrant Muslima, the woman with the veil, first began to emerge in Western Europe as a symbol of Islamist oppression.[11] Both she and her head covering were divorced from vastly different countries of origin and stood in as a Muslim migrant for religiously motivated violence against women. These women constantly lived in fear of abusive husbands who terrorized them in the name of Islam. As soon as the Muslima became upwardly mobile, however, the gendered stereotype of hijab martyrdom turned against secularist critics and intersectional feminists, who demanded that Muslim women discard the headscarf and reject the violent men of Islam. The rekindling of the headscarf debate suggests how volatile the meanings of Islam still are in Europe. Their religious dress reinforces a reductive or simplified story about Muslim women and the many histories of their clothing items, which have become yet again a site for the inclusion and exclusion of Muslims from national communities.

In Germany, the reductive stereotyping of Islamic majority societies and a functional gender bias has been hiding negative sentiments against Muslim minorities in the country. Large segments of the population today indiscriminately display negative emotions and attitudes towards Muslim groups living in and migrating to Germany. The fire was fueled when rape accusations surfaced against hundreds of Muslim men with migration backgrounds who allegedly sexually assaulted and raped women on New Year's Eve in the city of Cologne in 2015/2016. Some of these men are now serving prison sentences or were given suspended sentences. Events like the sexual assault attacks in Cologne have marked the issue of Muslimness as a national security threat on the forefront of German politics. Malte Thran and Lukas Boehnke describe the German

10 Gabriella Lazaridis: *Migrant Women: Maids, Nannies and Nurses, and the Ban on the Headscarf*. London: Palgrave Macmillan 2015, pp. 40–43.

11 Beverly Weber: Hijab Martyrdom, Headscarf Debates: Rethinking Violence, Secularism, and Islam in Germany. In: *Comparative Studies of South Asia, Africa and the Middle East* 32,1 (2012), pp. 102–115, here pp. 102–103.

PEGIDA[12] movement, which began in 2014, as an example of the rapid rise of German Islamophobia in which small right-wing parties and scattered Neo-Nazi collectives could unite.[13] According to Thran and Boehnke, representatives of PEGIDA have construed Germany's approximately four million Muslims, nearly half of whom have German citizenship or permanent residence, as supporters of global Muslim conflicts and the violent "Islamization" of the German nation state.[14] That PEGIDA attracted in mid-January of 2015 "as many as 25,000 Germans from all walks of life at their demonstration marches"[15] illustrates how the bias against Muslimness in Germany could mobilize a deep-seated fear of losing national identity.

Muslim Discrimination and Integration in Germany

Muslimness has become a contested space for Western societies in the new century. The phenomenon of Muslim stigmatization, however, is not entirely new to Germans. Daniel Faas details how the country's complex relationship with domestic Islam mainly began in the 1960s with the large-scale integration of Turkish labor migrants.[16] Faas writes: "[Germany] is home today to around 2.6 million Turkish economic migrants, mostly Sunnis, from an avowedly secular country which has experience with democratic norms and has been in European Union membership negotiations since 2005"[17]. Most of the members of this community descend from Muslims who came to Germany to work and prosper. But the native population in Germany relegated them, their children and their children's children to the periphery of society and to the legal and social margins of the German nation state, according to Hakan Ovuno Ongur.[18] The first generation of Turkish German Muslims was the one to bear the brunt

12 PEGIDA stands for the German phrase "Patriotische Europäer gegen die Islamisierung des Abendlandes", or "Patriotic Europeans against the Islamization of the West". PEGIDA is a far-right movement which originated as a grassroots rally in Dresden in October 2014 to promote anti-Islamic political positions. The movement has since gained in numbers through social media campaigns and online networks.

13 Malte Thran / Lukas Boehnke: The Value-Based Nationalism of Pegida. In: *Journal for Deradicalization* 3 (2015), pp. 178–209, here p. 179.

14 Ibid.

15 Ibid.

16 Daniel Faas: Muslims in Germany. From Guest Workers to Citizens? In: Anna Triandafyllidou (ed.): *Muslims in 21st Century Europe. Structural and Cultural Perspectives*. London / New York: Routledge 2010, pp. 59–77, here p. 59.

17 Ibid., p. 59.

18 Hakan Ovunc Ongur: *Minorities of Europeanization. The New Others of European Social Identity*. New York / London: Lexington 2015, p. 58.

of xenophobic ostracism. Muslim men in particular were regularly Islamized in the public imagination through films and literature, despite their lack of religious fervor in actual fact, nor any display of fanatic radicalism, according to Leslie Adelson.[19] The quintessential image of Turkish German masculinity was that of the poor and uneducated "Ali" in the 1960s and 1970s. In the 1980s came the iconographic cliché of the abusive husband and aggressive father who beats his wife and daughter into obedience according to the rules of Islam and repressive Muslim traditions, explains Heather Benbow.[20]

Christoph Lamm argues that the discourse of Turkish German "otherness" proves the German majority population's reluctance to undergo social change.[21] Turkish German Muslims have lived in Germany for more than half a century, and they have integrated during that time across the social strata just like Muslims who came to Germany from India, Iran, Iraq, Syria, and Afghanistan. They are popular singers, play for the German national football team and have also been elected for office to Germany's state and national parliaments. Turkish immigrants were also successful in establishing lucrative tourist exchanges between Turkey and Germany, and they have made a name for themselves as restauranteurs and tradespeople in several of Germany's larger cities.[22] However, as Lamm points out, politicians of all different camps have reduced individuals with Muslim identities or immigration background in Germany since 9/11 to aggressive collectives. The stereotype is that Muslims live in Islamist ghettos in social exclusion from and out of the reach of the German mainstream and its cultural authority. Consequently, Lamm writes that "the public 'Islamization' of Muslim immigrants is pushed [...] in an effort to conceptualize democratic and secular German identity against a vision of Islam untouched by the Enlightenment and liberal emancipation"[23].

That the stereotyping of Muslimness in German society is a recurring pattern with repetitive images troubles Germany's political establishment. Raymond Taras writes that the ethnic essentialism in Western European countries such as Germany has a long history of bundling "religious, ethnic and cultural prejudices

19 Leslie Adelson: *The Turkish Turn in Contemporary German Literature. Toward a New Critical Grammar of Migration*. New York: Palgrave Macmillan 2005, p. 12.

20 Heather Benbow: *Marriage in Turkish German Popular Culture: States of Matrimony in the New Millennium*. London: Lexington 2015, p. 1.

21 Christoph Lamm: The Muslim Makers: How Germany 'Islamizes' Turkish Immigrants. In: *Interventions* 12,2 (2010), pp. 183–197, here p. 183.

22 Ibid.

23 Ibid.

together"[24]. The anti-Jewish propaganda campaign in which Jewish Germans were portrayed to the German public in the Third Reich to justify genocide and mass murder illustrates this.[25] Parallels with the Holocaust upset particularly the Christian Democrats, who insisted during the decade following 9/11 that Germany was Europe's liberal leader with regards to Muslim integration. Former German President of State Christian Wulff declared unequivocally that Islam is an integral part of German society at the Berlin International Film Festival's opening night in 2010, when the Turkish-German comedy film *Almanya – Welcome to Germany*[26] premiered:[27] "Islam is part of Germany. [...] We must not allow false truths about it, fossilization of prejudice and discrimination"[28]. It was German chancellor Angela Merkel, though, who said in a public speech only one week after Wulff's statement that Germany's utopian multiculturalism of the 1980s had utterly failed to accomplish a sustained integration of Muslims into the wider public.[29] The official results of Anhalt-Saxony's state parliament votes in March 2016 suggest that Merkel pre-empted a continued division between the German majority and Muslim minority population. The right-wing party AfD, which was founded only in September 2013 in Berlin and whose abbreviation stands for Alternative for Germany, received 21.9 percent of all votes and fifteen of the Eastern German state's forty-three direct mandates for parliament. A "rejection of political and religious extremism" as well as a "no" to Muslim asylum seekers and forced migrants from Syria were the main points of the AfD's political program. The self-proclaimed protest movement beat out the Social Democrats as well as the Liberal Left and the Greens, as it urged voters to protect the "traditional values" of Germanness.[30]

24 Raymond Taras: 'Islamophobia Never Stands Still'. Race, Religion, and Culture. In: *Ethnic and Racial Studies* 36,3 (2013): Racialization and Religion. Race, Culture and Difference in the Study of Antisemitism and Islamophobia, pp. 417–433, here p. 417.

25 Ibid., p. 419.

26 *Almanya – Willkommen in Deutschland* (*Almanya – Welcome to Germany*, D 2010, D: Yasemin Samderelli).

27 "Der Islam gehört zu Deutschland". In: *Focus*, 03.10.2010. http://www.focus.de/politik/deutschland/20-jahre-wende/christian-wulff-der-islam-gehoert-zu-deutschland_aid_558481.html (accessed 15.03.2016).

28 "Der Islam gehört inzwischen zu Deutschland. [...] Legendenbildungen, Zementierung von Vorurteilen und Ausgrenzungen dürfen wir nicht zulassen". In: *Handelsblatt*, 03.10.2010. http://app.handelsblatt.com/politik/deutschland/wulff-rede-im-wortlaut-der-islam-gehoert-zu-deutschland/3553232.html (accessed 15.03.2016).

29 Kanzlerin erklärt Multikulti für gescheitert. In: *Die Welt*, 16.10.2010. http://www.welt.de/politik/deutschland/article10337575/Kanzlerin-Merkel-erklaert-Multikulti-fuer-gescheitert.html (accessed 14.03.2016).

30 Stefan Locke: AfD in Sachsen-Anhalt. Wie radikal sind die Köpfe der AfD? In: *Frankfurter*

Muslim Stereotyping and Societal Anxieties in Germany

Germany's self-identification as a democratic society with open borders has suffered since the exponential growth of the influx of Muslim refugees since 2013. There have been a growing number of attacks on asylum shelters and violence against refugee families despite the initial images of joyful Germans who welcomed thousands of predominantly Syrian refugees at train stations in Berlin, Hamburg and Munich and other cities.[31] Some scholars suggest that it is a back-and-forth dance performed by Germans in the context of their ethnocentric immigration and domestic integration policies. Selen Ercan argues that Western European host societies have held heated debates in recent years over the ability to integrate Islam into their majority populations. Ercan insists that Germans have put Muslimness and acts of violence in Muslim families and among Muslim groups on the agenda in their national discussion of civil security.[32] Honor killing in Germany's Muslim community, for example, "acquired a particular and relatively well-entrenched meaning when it first came to fore in 2005 after the murder of Hatun Sürücü; it has since been understood as a culturally specific form of violence illustrating the irreconcilable differences between [Germany's] minority and majority cultures"[33]. As such, as Ercan writes, Muslimness as a social construct and a cultural identity has been "associated with the 'failed multiculturalism' diagnosis"[34], suggesting that Muslim migrants are unable to live as good Muslims among good Germans.

Indeed, the macro politics of ethnic diversity in Germany seem to falter under the weight of Muslim stereotyping. Paul Spickard points out that every act of Islamist terrorism in Western Europe, such as the London bus bombings in 2005 or the street riots in Paris' North African banlieues, reveals only a token inclusion for residents of color and Muslim background.[35] For example, Hamburg-born Turkish-German Aygül Özkan, a politician and member of the Christian

Allgemeine Zeitung, 14.03.2016. http://www.faz.net/aktuell/politik/wahl-in-sachsen-anhalt/afd-in-sachsen-anhalt-wie-radikal-sind-die-koepfe-der-afd-14123900.html (accessed 16.03.2016).

31 Julia Khrebtan-Hörhager: De-Constructing Monoculturalism on the German Screen. A Critical Cultural Reading of On the Other Side. In: *Crossings. Journal of Migration and Culture* 6,2 (2015), pp. 193–209, here pp. 193–195.

32 Erkan Selen: Creating and Sustaining Evidence for 'Failed Multiculturalism'. The Case of 'Honor Killing' in Germany. In: *American Behavioral Scientist* 59,6 (2015), pp. 658–678, here p. 658.

33 Ibid.

34 Ibid., p. 658.

35 Paul Spickard: *Multiple Identities. Migrants, Ethnicity, and Membership*. Bloomington: Indiana UP 2013, p. 11.

Democrats, provoked howls and cheers of protest from "the Right-leaning press"[36] when her colleagues nominated her for a ministerial post in Lower Saxony's state government in 2008. The myth of German mono-ethnicity has made it difficult for ethnic others to overcome the stereotype of the white, Christian German with blue eyes and blonde hair.[37] A small yet influential elite in German society has repeatedly relied on such essentialist thinking to politicize Muslimness in Germany and peg it as the nation's looming downfall. Thilo Sarrazin was a leading member of the Social Democrats and executive board member of the German Federal Bank until he published a book in 2010 entitled *Deutschland schafft sich ab* ("Germany does away with itself").[38] Sarrazin was let go from his duties as board member and caused controversy in his party due to both a distinctly racist and an Islamophobic attitude. In his book, he warns the German reader that the majority of Muslim migrants are unfit to contribute to the future of German society due to their cultural and social volatility.[39]

There exists a peculiar perceived connection between violence and Muslim identities in Germany. It is part of a mutually exclusive discourse on integration, which links an indistinct form of Muslimness to bad ethnic diversity and simultaneously praises individual success stories of integration as examples of good Muslimness and successful ethnic diversity. Joyce Mushaben argues that the Germans have set these dualist terms for Islam without the empirical presence of radicalistic threats.[40] Germany's paradoxical approach to modern multiculturalism stems in part from considerable setbacks in the country's narrative of national progression. Mushaben points out that Germans have celebrated their multicultural diversity since the fall of the Berlin wall in 1989 as a hallmark of modern liberalism. The idea of multiethnic diversity had allowed them to overcome the image of Nazi Germany as well as that of an oppressive regime in the GDR.[41] Specifically, West Germans believed that social capitalism and a strong alliance with American multiculturalism would be the backbone of a cosmopolitan Germanness without historical guilt. Germany's internal stability

36 Spickard: *Multiple Identities*, p. 10.

37 Ibid.

38 Thilo Sarrazin: *Deutschland schafft sich ab. Wie wir unser Land aufs Spiel setzen*. München: DVA 2010.

39 Ibid., pp. 23–25.

40 Joyce Mushaben: *The Changing Faces of Citizenship. Integration and Mobilization Among Ethnic Minorities in Germany*. New York: Berghahn 2008, p. 23.

41 Ibid., p. 25.

would in turn serve as a transnational catalyst for its Europeanisation process.[42] But 9/11 was evidence to the majority of German society that the new Germany could not inspire non-native newcomers to convert their clichéd, backwards and violent Turkish or Arab Muslimness to integrated German Muslimness. Several of the terrorists who directed two passenger planes into the World Trade Centre towers were Muslim immigrants who had lived in Germany for years without causing any problems in their Hamburg and Berlin neighborhoods. The fact that multicultural Germanness had failed to appease the religious radicals assured the wider German public that there was reason for concern if Islam were to remain unregulated in Germany.

As Ruth Mandel argues, one must take into account – for the study of current Muslim stereotypes in Germany – a connection between sociality, history and communal anxieties.[43] Mandel argues that the presumed link between violence and Muslimness is at the core of Germans' fear of too much of or the "wrong kind of ethnic, social, linguistic, and cultural diversity"[44]. She describes how Germany's Muslim others quickly turned into a reductive object of societal instability and hence a threat to the status quo.[45] Deniz Göktürk's various discussions of Turkish German cinema support Mandel's claim. Göktürk posits that the majority population's anxieties and fears of cultural alienation are the focus of a large body of films in Germany. These films warn viewers about the consequences of Muslim behavior that deviates too much from the German norm.[46] For example, the majority of Turkish-German feature films in the 1970s and 1980s showed audiences that violent Muslims had the choice to either become good German citizens, leave the country, or be removed from society via incarceration or death. According to Göktürk, the cautionary tales were largely self-serving. They existed primarily to quell the natives' fears of violent Muslim men who would not shy away from abusing veiled Muslim women or even German women.[47]

That Western European countries like Germany pit Muslimness against their own ideals and cultural values perpetuates the myth of a culture clash, warns

42 Ibid., pp. 38–40.

43 Ruth Mandel: *Cosmopolitan Anxieties*. Durham: Duke UP 2008, p. 5.

44 Ibid., p. 4.

45 Ibid., pp. 3–4.

46 Deniz Göktürk: Turkish Delight – German Fright. Unsettling Oppositions in Transnational Cinema. In: Karen Ross / Deniz Derman (eds): *Mapping the Margins: Identity, Politics and the Media*. New Jersey: Hampton 2003, pp. 177–192, here pp. 179–180.

47 Ibid., p. 183.

Mandel. She also argues that it is an unrealistic myth, as Germans project international problems with Islamist terror onto domestic Muslim residents and even forced migrants. Germans seek to quell their fears of global religious radicalism by signaling to local Muslims that they need to surrender their non-Western identities.[48] Managing Islam locally can thus subdue the threatening stereotype of violent Islamist groups like ISIS, which the West cannot control. German politician and member of the European parliament Bernd Lucke demonstrates the currency of this strategy; the leader of the AfD declared at a party rally in Kamen, North Rhine-Westphalia in March 2015 that Islam is foreign to most Germans.[49] Lucke demanded a ban of burkas and minarets in Germany. A survey of contemporary German cinema suggests that managing the Germans' anxieties and fear of multicultural overload through fiction is still productive. A wave of German films and novels has appeared in the second decade of the new century and focuses on the inherent dangers of violent Islam. Feo Aladag's Turkish-German film drama *When We Leave*[50] focuses on the honor killing of a Turkish-German woman who runs away from her abusive husband. The film received seven awards at the 2010 German National Film Festival, and the German Film Board's selection committee chose it as Germany's official entry in the competition for the Academy Award for Best Foreign Language Film in 2011.

Good Muslim or Islamist Other

Germany's population today comprises a diverse collection of ethnic backgrounds, languages and cultures. The variety of communities in German culture is an empirical fact and historical truth, according to Zeyno Bata.[51] That a growing number of natives want to reject these facts with reductive labels, such as "Islamist radical" or "Muslim terrorist", undermines, in Baran's opinion, the Western ideal under whose banner the conservative nationalists stand, namely tolerance.[52] Baran writes, "This encourages 'us versus them' mentalities, and exacerbates extremism and intolerance among Muslims and non-Muslims

48 Mandel: *Cosmopolitan Anxieties*, pp. 8–11.

49 AfD-Chef Bernd Lucke: „Der Islam ist fast allen Deutschen fremd". In: *Der Spiegel*, 01.03.2015. http://www.spiegel.de/politik/deutschland/afd-chef-bernd-lucke-der-islam-ist-meisten-deutschen-fremd-a-1021187.html (accessed 20.03.2016).

50 *Die Fremde* (*When We Leave*, D 2010, D: Feo Aladag).

51 Zeyno Baran (ed.): *The Other Muslim. Moderate and Secular*. New York: Palgrave Macmillan 2010, p. 2.

52 Ibid.

alike"[53]. Bakare Najimdeen concludes that the majority of Germans hold "a view of Islam as inherently violent"[54] because they refuse to recognize it as modern and have insufficient knowledge about its internal diversity. Fictional works about Islam's antimodernist dangers reinforce the stereotype of Muslims as violent others, as does the actual violence of the Muslims who committed the Charlie Hebdo massacre and the 2015 Islamic State or ISIS attacks in France.[55] Esra Özyürek argues, however, that a simplistic nexus of failed integration, Islamist radicalism and home-grown extremism ignores social realities.[56] She illustrates with a study of three thousand Turkish-Muslims who converted to a Turkish-speaking Protestant movement in Turkey that attitudes against the Christianization of Turkey are "first and foremost nationalist and etatist, not religious"[57]. According to Özyürek, the Western right-wingers' discourse of the Islamist other also fails to explain why only a tiny minority of Muslims in Western countries like Germany participates in Islamist violence, or why four hundred thousand German converts to Islam are conveniently excluded from its representations in the media.[58]

The perceived danger of Muslimness has created a false platform for populist groups such as AfD and PEGIDA. They claim that ISIS' global rise was only possible because nation states relied too much on democratic pluralism instead of fortifying their borders and cultural traditions. However, that the populists' interpretation of modern Islam appropriates Muslimness as radical extremism plays according to Haci-Halil Uslucan into the hands of actual radical movements such as the Hizb ut-Tahrir in Germany.[59] Usclucan points out that the German news and entertainment media play a particularly prominent role in the creation of Muslim stereotypes. He argues that they have a habit of drowning out the beauty and peacefulness of Islam because German audiences expect images of violent Muslims. Furthermore, there is little mention of Islam's existing compatibility with universal human rights in Western Europe – specifically

53 Ibid.

54 Bakre Najimdeen: Muslims and the Charlie Hebdo Saga. In: *Policy Perspectives: The Journal of the Institute of Policy Studies* 12,2 (2015), pp. 81–104, here p. 102.

55 Ibid.

56 Esra Özyürek: Christian and Turkish. Secularist Fears of a Converted Nation. In: *Comparative Studies of South Asia, Africa, and the Middle East* 29,3 (2009), pp. 398–412, here p. 399.

57 Ibid, p. 398.

58 Esra Özyürek: *Being German, Becoming Muslim. Race, Religion, and Conversion in the New Europe*. Princeton: Princeton UP 2014, p. 4.

59 Haci-Halil Uslucan: *Stereotype, Viktimisierung und Selbstviktimisierung von Muslimen: Wie akkurat sind unsere Bilder über muslimische Migranten*. Wiesbaden: Springer 2014, pp. 2–4.

German society, which boasts millions of secular people with a Turkish or Arab background.[60] The leaders of more than two thousand mosques in urban and rural settings have acted in unison to invite local populations to intercultural dialogue forums and to discuss Islamic aspects of Sharia law. In 2014, the Central Council of Muslims in Germany announced that members of all four main branches of Islam should reject violence in the name of religion.[61]

One may argue that scholars who examine Muslim stereotyping and violence have their work cut out for them. Özyürek stipulates that researchers should refocus their discussions on the premise of localness in Islam. The multifaceted histories of religious symbolism and rituals present also a tangible starting point for inquiry into past exchange and similarities between Islam and other faith communities. More studies should focus on the geographical, social and historical grounding of Muslim identities in different forms of the body politic.[62] Özyürek' argument analyses the nation, and its self-proclaimed defenders, as a source of nationalist essentialism. Such an approach favors a comparative framework, which is convincing because transnational connections between Muslim minority populations and Muslim majority countries have shifted to the forefront of recent migration and integration debates. In my view, more work must be done to interrogate the social and civic dimensions of Muslim life, in particular those of Muslim youth, and the multicultural narratives in which state organizations and the media embed them. The field could benefit greatly from generational studies regarding Muslim representation and self-perception. Analyzing the experiences of converts to Islam and the history of people born into the religion would also be productive in understanding some of the emerging political trends in Western Europe and North America. These areas have, however, remained largely underexplored in the scholarship of Muslimness and its discursive history in predominantly Christian societies such as Germany.

60 Uslucan: *Stereotype, Viktimisierung und Selbstviktimisierung von Muslimen*, pp. 2–4.

61 Bethan John: German Muslims Invite All Faiths to Day of Prayer Against Islamic State. In: *Reuters Nachrichtenpresse Mobile*, http://www.reuters.com/article/us-iraq-syria-germany-muslims-idUSKBN0HB24G20140916 (accessed 19.11.2016).

62 Özyürek: *Being German, Becoming Muslim*, pp. 203–207.

"All Men [of Color] are Rapists"[1] or the Grammar of Violence

Stereotypes, Rape Myths and Doing Gender and Race

Sylvia Sadzinski

"Postcolognialism"

Within the first weeks of the year 2016, a few hundred women reported sexual assault, muggings and thefts by large groups of men occurring on New Year's Eve (NYE) 2015, particularly in Cologne, Germany, as well as in Hamburg and Stuttgart. Normally, press and police codes say that references to the origin of the supposed offender should only be made when considered relevant in relation to the crime.[2] Things were handled differently in this case: in eyewitness and police reports, the men were described as "Arabic" or "North African-looking" – specifications that were spread by the media fairly quickly and even before one alleged assailant was arrested.[3] The subsequent broad public discussions were often emotional and led to debates about migrants and refugees in Germany, as well as sexual violence in general. Stereotypes of 'the Arab' and 'the North African man' became ubiquitous and simultaneously correlated with alleged images and stereotypes of women. The discussions reached one of their climaxes on 5 January, 2016, when at a press conference discussing the incidents, Cologne's mayor Henriette Reker stated that for women, "there's always the possibility of keeping a certain distance of more than an arm's length"[4] from strangers in order to avoid and prevent sexual assaults.[5] Additionally, Reker recommended that women stay close to their friends during forthcoming carnival festivities and

1 Marilyn French: *The Women's Room*. New York: Simon & Schuster 1977, p. 433.

2 See, for example, Deutscher Presserat (ed.): *Publizistische Grundsätze (Pressekodex). Richtlinien für die publizistische Arbeit nach der Empfehlung des Deutschen Presserats. Beschwerdeordnung*. Berlin: Deutscher Presserat 2015, p. 10. http://www.presserat.de/fileadmin/user_upload/Downloads_Dateien/Pressekodex_bo_web_2015.pdf (accessed 10.04.2016).

3 Ana Maria Michel / Valerie Schönian / Frida Thurm / Tilman Steffen: Was geschah in Köln? In: *Zeit Online*, 05.01.2016. http://www.zeit.de/gesellschaft/zeitgeschehen/2016-01/koeln-silvester-sexuelle-uebergriffe-raub-faq (accessed 11.04.2016).

4 Kate Connolly: Cologne Attacks. Mayor Lambasted for Telling Women to Keep Men at Arm's Length. In: *The Guardian*, 06.01.2016. http://www.theguardian.com/world/2016/jan/06/cologne-attacks-mayor-women-keep-men-arms-length-germany (accessed 10.04.2016).

5 For a video of the press conference, see https://www.youtube.com/watch?v=KRzfSx-I-3o (accessed 10.04.2016).

other such events.[6] One week after the conference and two weeks after the event itself, journalist Margarete Stokowski coined the term "Postcolognialism" in her online column.[7] By referring to the city where the most assaults were reported and linking it to the theoretical concept of postcolonialism[8], Stokowski gave this period of sexist and racist debates a name.

Sexual violence has been analyzed extensively, especially in law. In the 1970s, the Western feminist movement declared rape as one of its most important issues. Since then, scholars from different scientific fields of arts and humanities have also reflected upon the correlations of sexual violence and gender, and – although far less discussed – the links between rape, gender and race.[9]

In her essay "Fighting Bodies. Fighting Words: A Theory and Politics of Rape Prevention", Sharon Marcus suggests a new reading of sexual violence and rape.[10] From a poststructuralist position, Marcus describes rape as a script and linguistic fact and discourse. Ever since Michel Foucault's *L'Ordre du Discours*, discourses are understood as practices, constantly and simultaneously constructing and reflecting meaning, not only describing realities but producing them.[11]

In this article I will show how gender stereotypes and racial stereotypes are related to ideas and discussions about sexual violence in general and rape in particular. As "an overarching term used to describe any violence, physical or psychological, carried out through sexual means or by targeting sexuality"[12], the term sexual(ized) violence is closely related to (structural) power relations and connected to structural and cultural forms of violence. It is believed that

6 Connolly: Cologne Attacks.

7 Margarete Stokowski: Wie man mit der Mistgabel argumentiert. In: *Spiegel Online*, 14.01.2016. http://www.spiegel.de/kultur/gesellschaft/fluechtlinge-wie-man-mit-der-mistgabel-argumentiert-kolumne-a-1071937.html (accessed 26.02.2016).

8 See, for instance, Edward Said: *Orientalism*. New York: Pantheon 1978; Homi K. Bhabha: *The Location of Culture*. London / New York: Routledge 1994.

9 See, for example, Susan Brownmiller: *Against Our Will. Men, Women and Rape*. New York: Simon & Schuster 1975; Emilie Buchwald / Pamela R. Fletcher / Martha Roth (eds): *Transforming a Rape Culture*, rev. ed. Minneapolis: Milkweed 2005; Angela Davis: *Women, Race and Class*. New York: Random House 1981; Kate Harding: *Asking for It. The Alarming Rise of Rape Culture – and What We Can Do about It*. Boston: Da Capo 2015; Robin Warshaw: *I Never Called It Rape. The Ms. Report on Recognizing, Fighting, and Surviving Date and Acquaintance Rape*. Rev. ed. New York: Harper Perennial 1994.

10 Sharon Marcus: Fighting Bodies, Fighting Words. A Theory and Politics of Rape Prevention. In: Judith Butler / Joan Scott (eds): *Feminists Theorize the Political*. New York: Routledge 1992, pp. 385–403.

11 Michel Foucault: *L'Ordre du Discours. Leçon Inaugurale au Collège de France Prononcée le 2 Décembre 1970*. Paris: Gallimard 1971.

12 Victoria Sexual Assault Centre: What Is Sexualized Violence? http://vsac.ca/sexualized-violence (accessed 26.02.2016).

gender and racial stereotypes, gender norms, myths about sexuality, different social hierarchies and power relations ensure the exercise of sexual violence.[13] Consequently, rape cannot be seen as a purely sexual act, but as a specific form of sexualized power and sexist violence, which "manifests gender differences in the most radical and brutal manner".[14] It will be outlined that the discourse of rape features narrative structures and a "gendered grammar of violence"[15], both ideas of which will be examined in regard to the construction of gendered and racialized images and stereotypes. In addition, stereotypical ideas about rape (in other words, rape myths) lead to victimization and responsibilization, playing an essential part within these processes.

First, a short introduction of constructions of gender and race is given. Next, these theoretical ideas will be enhanced and specified by reflections about stereotypes such as hierarchical orders within these categories of identity. This is followed by an overview of rape myths. The following part confronts rape myths and the discourse of rape. Here, the grammar of violence will help demonstrate how a hierarchical, dichotomous and stereotyped understanding of gender and race is established and simultaneously manifested. This will be underlined by two specific examples of the NYE-debate: the mayor's advice and the media use of the Arabic term 'taharrush gamea'[16] to categorize the assaults.

Power Relations and the Constructions of Gender and Race

The idea of a dichotomous division of the male and female sexes as it is now common in Western society has some of its origins in the bourgeois society of the 18th century. During the Enlightenment and related to sociocultural changes

13 Friedhelm Solms: Internationales Konfliktmanagement nur mit militärischen Mitteln? In: Id. / Gerd Krell / Reinhard Mutz (eds): *Friedensgutachten 1994*. Hamburg: Lit 1994, pp. 94–110, here p. 96.

14 Christine Künzel: Einleitung. In: Ead. (ed.): *Unzucht – Notzucht –Vergewaltigung. Definitionen und Deutungen sexueller Gewalt von der Aufklärung bis heute*. Frankfurt am Main: Campus 2003, pp. 9–18, here p. 18.

15 Marcus: Fighting Bodies, Fighting Words, p. 392.

16 Also known as 'taharrush gama'ei', the term can be translated into 'sexual harassment' or 'group harassment'. It is mostly used in the Arabic world and in Western media since the 2005 demonstrations on Tahrir Square in Cairo, when many women were facing mass sexual assaults in public. See, for example, Farhana Mayer: The Sexual Attacks on Women in Europe Reflect a Misogynistic Mind-Set That Must Be Dismantled. In: *The New York Times*, 14.01.2016. http://www.nytimes.com/roomfordebate/2016/01/14/pulling-in-the-welcome-mat-as-fear-of-attacks-rise/the-sexual-attacks-on-women-in-europe-reflect-a-misogynistic-mind-set-that-must-be-dismantled (accessed 10.04.2016); Alex Shams: Neither Taharrush Gamea Nor Sexism Are Arab 'Cultural Practices'. In: *Huffington Post*, 21.01.2016. http://www.huffingtonpost.com/alex-shams/sexism-isnt-an-arab-cultural-practice_b_9022056.html (accessed 11.04.2016).

accompanying industrialization, life was increasingly separated between the public and private sphere, as well as dualist categorizations like nature and nurture, emotion and reason. Simultaneously, binary gender roles and gender characters were strengthened. Certain features of these dichotomies were associated with each other – women began to represent nature and emotion, whereas men were considered to represent culture and reason.[17] These associations are still used to explain or justify certain behaviors and processes. As a result, socially expected and accepted behaviors differ between men and women – different gender roles, which determine the fates and rights of each individual, seek to form orderly societies.

In her post-structuralist approach, Judith Butler regards gender identity as a cultural and discursive construction, but also attributes the aforenamed dichotomies like nature and nurture to it. In *Bodies That Matter*, she argues that neither gender nor sex is natural, but naturalized and that both categorizations are intelligible and repeatedly created and redesigned by human beings.[18] The body – and, based on it, gender – is produced by language and action, constituted through regular repetition and citation. Certain behaviors, motions, roles, appearances, etc. are directly or indirectly and consciously or unconsciously taught, performed, shared and passed on through language and the body itself. Gender becomes dynamic and performative and follows normative regulations.[19] It becomes a discursive categorization, it is (re)created and the binary gender order is constantly (re)produced and materialized. Masculinity and femininity alike are not necessarily equal to biological man- or womanhood respectively, but are dynamic processes of negotiation and must be demonstrated repeatedly.[20] The unity of gender identity and biological sex must constantly be produced, and gender is practiced.[21] Power relations are inscribed in the body and simultaneously form the body. Hence, race can also be seen as a social construct. Whiteness, for example, is not a biological condition, but the position of a

17 For an overview about the history of gender, see, for example, Karin Hausen: Die Polarisierung der „Geschlechtscharaktere". Eine Spiegelung der Dissoziation von Erwerbs- und Familienleben. In: Werner Conze (ed.): *Sozialgeschichte der Familien in der Neuzeit Europas*. Stuttgart: Klett 1978, pp. 363–393; Claudia Honegger: *Die Ordnung der Geschlechter. Die Wissenschaften vom Menschen und das Weib 1750–1850*. Frankfurt am Main: Campus 1991; Thomas Laqueur: *Making Sex: Body and Gender. From the Greeks to Freud*. Cambridge: Harvard UP 1990.

18 Judith Butler: *Bodies That Matter*. London / New York: Routledge 1993.

19 Ibid., pp. 12–16.

20 Franziska Becher: *Macho, Softie, Metro – das Männerbild in Publikumszeitschriften. Eine vergleichende Inhaltsanalyse*. Saarbrücken: VDM 2006, p. 29.

21 Judith Butler: *Gender Trouble. Feminism and the Subversion of Identity*. London / New York: Routledge 1990.

privileged person, especially within European and North American societies. In *Orientalism*, Edward Said showed that the concept of 'the other' was a colonial and European invention to create and define a white norm.[22] Colonial European travel reports played an essential role for the construction of race. Within the reports, the alien other was constituted. Bodies of color underwent a white imperial inscription,[23] becoming part of a hegemonic Western and colonial discourse. 'The other' was described; it became "the site of dreams, images, fantasies, myths, obsessions and requirements"[24], whereas whiteness remained mostly unnamed, unmarked and still seems unseen, all the while defining individuals. The construction of race becomes even clearer by further examining these colonial times; here, the 'status' of whiteness could be denied to European men when having a love affair with a woman of color.[25] Thus, whiteness can be lost – it is not a rigid and integral part of the body or subject. Race cannot be considered as a fact or fixed category. It must be re-established constantly.[26] Without negating that skin color can have different pigmentations,[27] the categories of 'white' and 'colored' can be seen as binary ascriptions connected with historical stereotypical attributions. Race thus becomes a social and political construction rather than a biological fact.

Aggression vs. Peacefulness: Stereotypes and Hierarchies

In order to be seen as a woman or a man within society, there are purported rules to follow and expectations to meet. Stereotypes are related to these normative expectations and assumed characteristics. Even though stereotypes are flexible while depending on location and time, they seek to give the individual no social choices while being ingrained in society.[28] As part of the dichotomous division of nature and nurture, body and mind and emotion and reason, women in Western culture are traditionally believed to be peaceable, caring, sensitive, gentle,

22 Edward Said: *Orientalism*. New York: Pantheon 1978.

23 Obioma Nnaemeka: Bodies That Don't Matter. Black Bodies and the European Gaze. In Maisha Eggers / Grada Kilomba / Peggy Pesche / Susan Arndt (eds): *Mythen, Masken und Subjekte. Kritische Weißseinsforschung in Deutschland*. Münster: Unrast 2005, pp. 90–104, here p. 90.

24 Homi K. Bhabha: The Other Question. Homi K Bhabha Reconsiders the Stereotype and Colonial Discourse. In: *Screen* 24,6 (1983), pp. 18–36, here p. 24.

25 Anette Dietrich: *Weiße Weiblichkeiten. Konstruktionen von „Rasse" und Geschlecht im deutschen Kolonialismus*. Bielefeld: Transcript 2007, p. 370.

26 Eske Wollrad: Der Weißheit letzter Schluss – Zur Dekonstruktion von ‚Weißsein'. In: *polylog. Zeitschrift für interkulturelles Philosophieren* 8 (2001), pp. 77–83, here p. 79.

27 Melanie Groß: *Geschlecht und Widerstand. Post – queer – linksradikal*. Sulzbach: Helmer 2008, p. 62.

28 Michael Kimmel: *The Gendered Society*. New York / Oxford: Oxford UP 2000, p. 3.

irrational, emotional and prudent.[29] Consequently, and in dualist contrast, masculinity represents the mind and culture and bears stereotypical associations with reason, rationality, activity, courage and strength. Toughness and aggression are also regarded as typical male behavior and often biologically justified (by certain hormones, for instance).[30] These social attributions not only imply gender myths, but support them. In order to be regarded according to one's gender, one must follow certain stereotypical patterns of behavior and appearance. Even so, explicit consistency between femininity and womanhood – or masculinity and manhood – is not necessarily a given.

In *Gender and Power*, Raewyn Connell defines multiple hierarchical types of coexisting masculinities and femininities. With a marginalized, a cooperative, a subordinated and a hegemonic type, four kinds of masculinity can be distinguished.[31] Connell's idea of marginalized masculinity in modern Western societies mostly includes men of color. Homosexual men and househusbands are added to the subordinated type, whereas white, heterosexual, European or North American middle class men can be described as the hegemonic masculine. This type is the most culturally accepted and is considered ideal by men and women alike.[32] It is an image of masculinity that is also reproduced repeatedly by all forms of mainstream media. Here, it becomes clear that masculinity intersects with other categories of identity and systems of power relations like race and ethnicity.

Likewise, Connell defines different types of femininity. The idea of an emphasized femininity mostly corresponds with hegemonic masculinity. However, Connell emphasizes that a truly accurate correspondence of femininity to hegemonic masculinity cannot exist, since all forms of femininity in Western societies are constructed in the context of the subordination of women to men.[33] Femininity is subordinated to masculinity and thus devalued,[34] and the construction of masculinity and femininity is therefore asymmetric. Emphasized femininity is described as overemphasized femininity. Connell points out that this form of femininity is specially performed for a male-dominated world and names Marilyn Monroe as an example par excellence, but at the same time a satire

29 Kimmel: *The Gendered Society*, p. 27.

30 Wilfried Gottschalch: *Männlichkeit und Gewalt. Eine psychoanalytisch und historisch soziologische Reise in die Abgründe der Männlichkeit.* Weinheim / München: Juventa 1997, p. 32.

31 Raewyn Connell: *Gender and Power. Society, the Person and Sexual Politics.* Stanford: Stanford UP 1987, p. 110.

32 Ibid., p. 187.

33 Ibid.

34 Kimmel: *The Gendered Society*, p. 1.

of emphasized femininity.[35] For Connell, this type of femininity is constructed and performed due to gender inequality and alleged or socially accepted male needs.[36] The female desire to be attractive in a heteronormative world and the general acceptance of child care and marriage correspond to the most socially accepted and presented concept of emphasized femininity. The less a woman complies with so-called male needs, accepted ideals or female stereotypes, the less she can be attributed to the concept of emphasized femininity.[37]

Both concepts, masculinity as well as femininity, are more a pattern of action created in certain situations and relational structures than a permanent character trait.[38] Accordingly, hegemonic masculinity is constituted in relation to ideas of femininity and other designs of masculinity. This results in a hierarchical ranking of different masculinities, as not all masculinities (and femininities) are equally socially accepted.[39]

Historically and discursively, attributes like reason and culture are not only identified with masculinity, but also with whiteness and naturalized by different narratives and visualizations.[40] Western colonial discourse – and especially travel reports – attributed primitiveness and bestiality to men of color and made them into not only exotic and alien objects, but second-class people.[41] Homi K. Bhabha has already pointed out that stereotypes play an essential and discursive role by their constitution of 'the other'. In his essay "The Other Question. Homi K Bhabha Reconsiders the Stereotype and Colonial Discourse", Bhabha describes the stereotype with reference to Franz Fanon as a kind of fetish, being "complex, ambivalent, contradictory".[42] The idea of inferior and superior civilizations made the body of color become the wild, the savage, the foreign and therefore the 'other' body.[43] This hegemonic view often objectifies single body parts, puts them in the center and reduces the whole body to these. In particular,

35 Connell: *Gender and Power*, p. 188.

36 Ibid.

37 Ibid.

38 Raewyn Connell: *Masculinities*, Cambridge: Polity 1995, p. 72.

39 Richard Collier: *Masculinities, Crime and Criminology. Men, Corporeality and the Criminal(ised) Body*. Los Angeles / London / New Delhi: Sage 1998, p. 18.

40 Martina Tißberger / Gabriele Dietze / Daniela Hrzán / Jana Husmann-Kastein: Vorwort. In: Iid. (eds): *Weiß – Weißsein – Whiteness. Kritische Studien zu Gender und Rassismus*. Frankfurt am Main: Lang 2006, pp. 7–12, here p. 10.

41 Nnaemeka: Bodies That Don't Matter, p. 90.

42 Bhabha: The Other Question, p. 22.

43 Gabriele Dietze: Critical Whiteness Theory und Kritischer Okzidentalismus. Zwei Figuren hegemonialer Selbstreflexion. In: Tißberger / Dietze / Hrzán / Husmann-Kastein (eds): *Weiß – Weißsein – Whiteness*, pp. 219–248, here p. 221.

sexualized stereotypes of the animalistic, compulsive and sexual aggressive other became central here: as Franz Fanon suggest, the other – for him, namely the black male – is "fixated at the genital."[44] In contrast, the white body is seen as civilized and cultural. Sexuality, gender and race, as well as sexism and racism, are thus strongly connected.

Rape Facts vs. Rape Myths

The information sheet *Sexuelle Gewalt in Deutschland* (Sexual Violence in Germany), published by the German association for women rights Terre des Femmes, makes clear that the majority of acts of sexual violence in Germany are committed by men.[45] In Germany, almost one woman out of seven has experienced at least one criminally relevant form of sexual violence (e.g. rape, attempted rape or sexual assault).[46]

The amount of denounced acts of sexual violence counts less than five percent of all reported cases in Germany. On average, 8,000 rapes per annum occur in Germany, but only 13 percent of the denounced cases result in convictions. Generally, sexual violence is among the least reported and least solved crimes. Therefore, a large number of unknown cases can be assumed.

Rape myths describe different stereotypical assumptions and beliefs with regard to sexual violence, particularly in relation to victims, perpetrators and the act of rape itself. They are recited and institutionalized by cultural fields such as music, television, advertising, literature and language. Rape myths can serve to deny sexual violence, to trivialize, reinterpret or excuse it – for example, by putting a rape crime into question and incriminating victims of false accusation.[47] They relate to notions of the definition of rape and refer to the causes and consequences of sexual violence. Assumptions placing part of the blame on the victim and thus excusing the crime make a stereotype become a rape myth.[48] Typical rape myths are, for example, "women incite men to rape", "only 'bad' women

44 Franz Fanon: *Black Skin, White Masks*. London: Pluto 1986, p. 165.

45 Terre des Femmes – Menschenrechte für die Frau e.V. (ed.): *Sexuelle Gewalt in Deutschland*. https://frauenrechte.de/online/images/downloads/hgewalt/Sexuelle-Gewalt-in-Deutschland.pdf (accessed 10.04.2016).

46 Bundesministerium für Familie, Senioren, Frauen und Jugend (ed.): *Lebenssituation, Sicherheit und Gesundheit von Frauen in Deutschland*, 2004. http://www.bmfsfj.de/RedaktionBMFSFJ/Abteilung4/Pdf-Anlagen/kurzfassung-gewalt-frauen,property=pdf,bereich=bmfsfj,sprache=de,rwb=true.pdf (accessed 10.04.2016).

47 Gerd Bohner: Vergewaltigungsmythen. http://www.uni-bielefeld.de/psychologie/ae/AE05/Bohner_Wien_1999.pdf (10.04.2016).

48 Nicola Brosi: *Untersuchung zur Akzeptanz von Vergewaltigungsmythen in verschiedenen Bevölkerungsgruppen*. Unpublished Dissertation, LMU München, 2004, p. 10.

get raped", and "rapists are deranged".[49] Rape myths are closely linked to gender roles and gender stereotypes, to myths and ideas about sexuality and the acceptance of violence within interpersonal relationships.[50] They can be contradicting and differentiated between victim-related rape myths and perpetrator myths.[51] Statements like "when a woman says no, she means yes" and stereotypical suppositions that rape can only happen if a woman wants it or allows it to happen imply assumptions about the 'right' behavior during rape, such as loud screaming or physical resistance.[52] Furthermore, ideas of 'right' behavior that could avoid getting raped by tracing the source of the violence to the victim's clothing, or the consumption of alcohol, or certain acts that are considered frivolous, irritating or stimulating a potential perpetrator are common during instances of victim blaming.[53]

Perpetrator myths generally relativize guilt by justifying different types of rape. By considering rapists insane, a pathologization of the perpetrator occurs. This also entails that 'real' rape mostly happens outside, at night on the streets, and committed by strangers in an ambush.[54] But since the majority of offenders do not rape indiscriminately and perpetrators and victims, in most cases, already know each other, the myth about men not being able to control their sexuality is common. In a broader sense, this involves assumptions that rape only happens to young and pretty women and that it occurs spontaneously, impulsively, and with passion or uncontainable sexual arousal.

The Grammar of Violence

Rape myths are an example of the language of rape and grammar of violence as described by Sharon Marcus. From a poststructuralist approach, the language of rape "shapes both the verbal *and* physical interactions of a woman and her would-be assailant"[55]. By the language of rape women are exposed to a constant threat of becoming victims of sexual violence.[56]

49 An extensive list of rape myths in contrast to the actual facts can be found on the homepage of the University Minnesota Duluth: http://www.d.umn.edu/cla/faculty/jhamlin/3925/myths.html (accessed 31.03.2016).

50 Brosi: *Untersuchung zur Akzeptanz von Vergewaltigungsmythen*, p. 11.

51 Bohner: Vergewaltigungsmythen.

52 Brosi: *Untersuchung zur Akzeptanz von Vergewaltigungsmythen*, p. 13.

53 Bohner: Vergewaltigungsmythen.

54 Ibid.

55 Marcus: Fighting Bodies, Fighting Words, p. 390.

56 Emilie Buchwald / Pamela R. Fletcher / Martha Roth: Preamble. In: Eaed. (eds): *Transforming a Rape Culture*, p. xi.

Rape consists of a script that is formed by language. The script of rape is applied before and after rape happens, but also during the crime and act itself. So it is not only the crime, but the very talking about sexual violence and rape that influences people's behavior and structures everybody's life. It gives every individual a certain role and meaning due to the grammar of violence.[57] This grammar describes rules of and positions within sexual violence and attributes certain roles within the rape script, which "continually scripts these inequalities anew"[58].
The gendered grammar of violence makes women automatically affected by rape and defines them as not only objects of violence, but subjects of anxiety. The female body becomes a vulnerable internal space, lacking force, penetrable and destructible.[59] Men, in turn, also become objects of violence, but active objects who act with the intent of violence.[60] They become objects of "the feminine fear"[61] – the reason why women walk to the other side of the street at night when faced with an oncoming figure.
The language of rape and a gendered grammar of violence also contribute to the anxiety of white women being raped by men of color. These men are stereotypically perceived as particularly dangerous and unrestrained, yet sexual violence by white men against all types of women (white and of color) is seen as "normal" and inevitable: "Between men of different races, this grammar predicates white men as legitimate subjects of violence between all men and as subjects of legitimate sexual violence against all women"[62].
Marcus attributes to rape considerable power; on one hand, men rape women because they are women or they are being read as women. On the other hand, through rape men simultaneously degrade another person and make them women or feminine subjects. With rape, an offender wants to instill a feeling of weakness, passivity and inferiority in the victim. Analyses of rapes of men by men (in prison, for example) make it even more clear that rape functions as a violent ascription of gender, establishing difference and hierarchy.[63] Here, not multistage hierarchies are created, but two dichotomous classes of people

57 Marcus: Fighting Bodies, Fighting Words, pp. 388–389.

58 Ibid., p. 391.

59 Ibid., p. 395.

60 Ibid., p. 393.

61 Ibid., p. 394.

62 Ibid., p. 392.

63 Gelinde Smaus: Vergewaltigung von Männern durch Männer. In: Künzel (ed.): *Unzucht – Notzucht – Vergewaltigung*, pp. 221–242, here p. 240.

are made, of which women or those made-women become bottommost.[64] Rape becomes a form of language, legitimizing behaviors, manifesting social structures and gender roles as well as racial hierarchies; it creates unequal power dynamics.[65] Sexual violence and rape in particular can therefore be seen as a process, constituted by narratives that describe and (re)create realities.[66]

"An Arm's Length" and "Taharrush Gamea": Doing Gender and Racial Othering

The social stereotype of women (as well as children) consists of them being defenselessness, passive and innocent. When Cologne's Mayor Reker urged women to keep a sufficient distance from strange men, she used these stereotypes and also assumed a potential victim status to every woman in Cologne. Reker contributed to the narrative of rape and sexual violence and declared women as subjects of fear. Here, the discourse of rape subliminally instills terror in women, making them an "endangered species".[67] From a young age, girls learn that they should be careful and that something horrible could happen to them if they are not. A victim mentality is thus indoctrinated.[68] As part of the language of rape, men are almost never told 'not to rape', whereas girls are often warned 'not to get raped' and are given advice on travelling home safely. In doing so, male aggression becomes accepted and seen as normal.[69] The mayor's statement also reinforced this expectation.

While psychologists like Roswitha Burgard stress that the consequences of rape are so massive that all women "should put their conditions (nightmares, insomnia, etc.) in the context of their rape"[70], Mithu Sanyal points out that these assumptions generally limit women's (re)actions and feelings.[71] Rape is always described as the worst thing that can occur to a woman. Women become

64 Ibid., p. 236.

65 Marcus: Fighting Bodies, Fighting Words, p. 391.

66 Ibid., pp. 387–388.

67 Mithu Sanyal: Vergewaltigung gibt es nicht. In: *Missy Magazin* 4 (2011), pp. 46–50, here p. 47 (trans. Sylvia Sadzinski).

68 Brownmiller: *Against Our Will*, p. 224.

69 Michael Kimmel: Men, Masculinity, and the Rape Culture. In: Buchwald / Fletcher / Roth (eds): *Transforming a Rape Culture*, pp. 139–158, here p. 155.

70 Roswitha Burgard: Kriegszustand zwischen den Geschlechtern. Das Bild des Menschen. In: *Psychologie heute* 20,8 (1993), pp. 28–30, here p. 30 (trans. Sylvia Sadzinski).

71 Sanyal: Vergewaltigung, p. 48.

subjected to constant danger and have to live with a persistent, latent anxiety.[72] Between 35 to 70 percent of all raped women suffer from post-traumatic stress disorders.[73] Although this range indicates that not *all* women are traumatized and distraught after a rape, many of them are; their experiences vary greatly, and the aftermaths of said experiences are dependent on the individual. Sanyal stresses that not only the constant, prodding fear of sexual assault intimidates women, but so does the idea that rape is devastating and traumatizing throughout an entire lifetime.[74] Socially, there are no self-empowering identities offered to women after rape[75] – instead, there is a clear idea of how a woman has to behave and must feel after becoming a victim of rape. While earlier, as Sanyal shows, suicide was legitimized by Roman myths as a result of rape, depressive behavior is now expected.[76] A permanent social attribution of women as (potential) victims of rape renders them powerless and helpless. One is rarely a survivor, but rather forever a victim.[77] The declaration of women as victims is like a branding that never goes away, a state that cannot be overcome. It is like a category of identity, which can be understood as a stigma. It reduces a woman based on her sex, makes women penetrable, vulnerable, assailable and powerless.[78] The passivity that accompanies the victimization of women in the context of sexual violence also affects the idea of female sexuality. Female sexuality becomes something internal, something that must be sheltered.[79] This view supports the stereotypical and normative passivity of women. It often leads to the normative expectation that women need to act coyly, that somebody always needs to 'seduce' them and that they cannot enjoy their sexuality actively, deliberately or openly. Rape as a discourse situates women by gender as either already raped or as fundamentally vulnerable to rape – something that characterizes a women's life.

The rape script determines certain fixed behaviors and makes men follow a certain script, as well. Here, emotionality and weakness are not allowed. With rape myths and the general discourse of rape, men are reduced to an instinctual

72 Marcus: Fighting Bodies, Fighting Words, p. 387.

73 Andrea Mohr: Beeinträchtigungen der seelischen Gesundheit in Folge einer Viktimisierung durch Gewalt und Aggression. In: *Journal für Konflikt- und Gewaltforschung* 5,1 (2003), pp. 49–69, here p. 56.

74 Sanyal: Vergewaltigung, p. 47.

75 Ibid., p. 48.

76 Ibid.

77 Brownmiller: *Against Our Will*, p. 249.

78 Marcus: Fighting Bodies, Fighting Words, p. 398.

79 Ibid.

sexuality. Men are made mindless; they become instinct-driven animals.[80] By giving men the power to rape, other roles are simultaneously denied to them. Stereotypically, men have to be strong and courageous. They are socially devalued if they do not correspond to a certain type of manhood, to the notion of the 'right' man – to Connell's concept of hegemonic masculinity.

An engagement with sexual violence against men and boys is still only marginally taking place. It does not fit into the traditional patriarchal concept of men as strong aggressors and therefore remains private and mostly ignored on a social scale. Violence against men is connected with different constructions of masculinity, and this is where Connell's idea of hegemonic and subordinated masculinity applies; women and girls are denied the right to aggression, whereas boys and men are denied as victims.[81] The counterpart of the woman, who always needs to act coyly and then devoted, is a willing man[82] who is always dominant, demanding, and assertive – one who is not just always willing, but someone who is always able to fulfill the expected role. While female sexuality is set aside, female intimacy is accepted, and men are still asked to suppress their emotions. If they deal with feelings like powerlessness and helplessness or express fears and weaknesses, their feelings are discarded or denied;[83] anger and aggression thus appear to be the only legitimized feelings for men.[84]

The language of rape, as well as rape myths and the script of rape, define men as perpetrators, but also as guardians who can protect or rescue women from other evil men.[85] This image is also based on the stereotype of the active, strong and courageous man. It reinforces the idea of the passive and vulnerable woman, who is dependent on the man. Additionally, it excludes other concepts of masculinity completely or otherwise devalues them. Men are afraid of being rated as weak by other men and of not being perceived as male, but rather female, and thereby being socially devalued and inept.[86] Consequently, the rape discourse creates an image of the 'real' man and emphasizes stereotypes. In addition, not all men can be heroes; the debates after NYE 2015 imply that this role is only reserved for white, German men.

80 Kimmel: Men, Masculinity, and the Rape Culture, p. 156.

81 Lothar Böhnisch: *Die Entgrenzung der Männlichkeit. Verstörungen und Formierungen des Mannseins im gesellschaftlichen Übergang*. Opladen: Leske & Budrich 2003, p. 143.

82 Sanyal: Vergewaltigung, p. 48.

83 Böhnisch: *Die Entgrenzung der Männlichkeit*, p. 144.

84 Kimmel: *The Gendered Society*, p. 244.

85 Brownmiller: *Against Our Will*, p. 189.

86 Kimmel: Men, Masculinity, and the Rape Culture, p. 145.

The victimization of women and the identity of men as perpetrators becomes a (stereotypical) process of constructing gender.[87] The debates after NYE 2015 were also accompanied by racial stereotypes. By constantly outlining the origin and appearance of the accused, racial othering was practiced. Additionally, journalists started to use the term 'taharrush gamea' in order to describe and categorize the happenings during NYE 2015. By claiming that "the phenomenon taharrush gamea has arrived in Germany"[88], sexual violence was Islamized and 'othered'.

The Arabic term, meaning 'sexual assault' or 'gang harassment', helps to establish the sexist crimes that happened on NYE as a genuine oriental or Arabic phenomenon. It excludes sexual violence as a German problem as well. It implies that this is something that normally takes place somewhere, outside Europe and the West entirely. It further implicates that the issue is a cultural matter that might be 'normal' elsewhere, somewhere 'over there' in the East, but not 'here'. Archetypical dichotomies that contribute to an Orientalist discourse are thus applied; they manifest Orientalism and define the West as the only civilized place. In his eponymous work, Said points out that sexuality and violence have always been the most important means of constituting a conception of the Orient. The harem on the one side and the warrior with a sword on the other were at the center of European fantasies of the East, simultaneously fascinating and frightening. After NYE 2015, 'the Orient', thanks to the usage of the term 'taharrush gamea', became more unsettling, as it was conceptualized as a threat to white Western women either arriving in Germany or living there already, even though Bhabha, referring to Said, points Germany out as "a unified racial, geographical, political and cultural zone of the world."[89] A division of the West and the oriental East is reestablished by this debate, and the construct of race is practiced. The use of the Arabic word for sexual assault also makes clear how the language of rape functions: it "seeks to induce in white women an exclusive and erroneous fear of non-white men as potential rapists and legitimizes white men's sexual violence against all women as well as their retributive violence against non-white men in the name of protecting or avenging white women"[90]. Sexual

87 Collier: *Masculinities, Crime and Criminology*, p. 4.

88 Martin Lutz: Das Phänomen „taharrush gamea" ist in Deutschland angekommen. In: *Die Welt*, 10.01.2016. http://www.welt.de/politik/deutschland/article150813517/Das-Phaenomen-taharrush-gamea-ist-in-Deutschland-angekommen.html (accessed 01.04.2016) (trans. Sylvia Sadzinski).

89 Bhabha: The Other Question, p. 23.

90 Marcus: Fighting Bodies, Fighting Words, p. 390.

assaults and rape seem to be assessed as worse when done by men of color than by white men. Even though stereotypes define men of color as uncivilized and backward, their violence is not seen as legitimate as the aggressions of white men. Taking into account Connell's concept of marginalized masculinity, men of color seem more likely to be punished and devalued for their aggressions. Referring to the U.S., Marcus claims that "culture tends to label most initiatives by men of color against whites as 'illegitimate violence'. Intra-racial male violence against women does not challenge social inequalities and hence is commonly thought to be legitimate"[91].

The example of the compulsive, instinctive and almost animalistic Oriental incidentally defines Western men as civilized, sophisticated and totally in control of their sexual urges. This also enforces Bhabha's idea that the others should be "almost the same but not quite [white]"[92] in order to still be able to distinguish the white and supposedly civilized men from the wild 'others'.

Conclusion

Following Sharon Marcus, rape and sexual violence were understood as social phenomena and problems, but also as narratives. It has become clear that current discourses of rape and stereotypical attributions and myths of sexual violence simultaneously manifest and (re-)create stereotypical and dichotomous ideas of gender and race by producing notions of femininity and masculinity, as well as by racial othering. Within the discourse of rape, Connell's concept of emphasized femininity is seen as a trigger for male misbehavior. Rape – and even the discourse about rape – create a binary understanding of identity. There are always just two positions: the victim or the perpetrator, the man or the woman, 'us' or 'the other'.

In summary, "rape is not only scripted – it also scripts"[93]; rape and sexual violence follow certain rules and methods. They feminize and masculinize people and establish a hierarchical understanding of not only gender, but race.

91 Ibid., p. 392.

92 Bhabha: *The Location of Culture*, p. 122.

93 Marcus: Fighting Bodies, Fighting Words, p. 391.

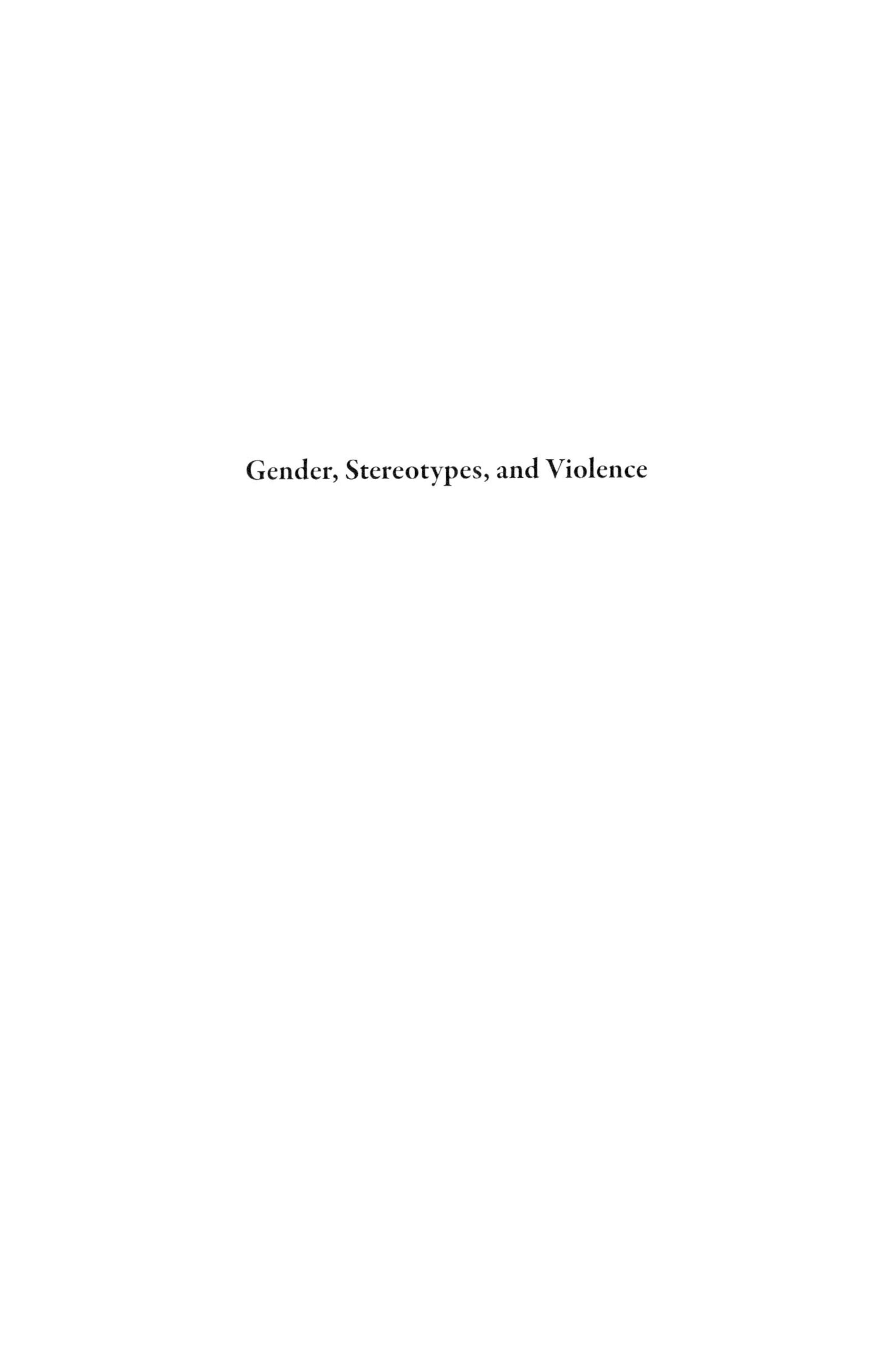

Gender, Stereotypes, and Violence

Gender-based Violence in Serbia

Media, Stereotypes, and Celebrities

Bojan Perovic

Introduction: Violence against Women in Serbia

The politics of media representation heavily influence the ruling narratives about women in the community; the process of representation and identity creation is a massive part of media culture.[1] It is not only important to examine how the media represents the world, but also the nature of the identities, cultural values, and social relations that it establishes. The image of women in the media relies on societal standards and is heavily based on society's historical, cultural and institutional frameworks. Therefore, deconstructing media narratives about women tends to be a diagnosis of society itself, and different types of media can be employed to fully deconstruct media narratives about women.

Serbia has undergone immense political, social, economical, and cultural reform over the past twenty years. Serbian society's transition was characterized by wars, post-conflict crises mostly marked by an inability to deal with past war crimes, and, more recently, the prospect of joining the European Union. After initiating the reform process after the year 2000, Serbia began to intensify its efforts to pay special attention to empowering women. Building institutional mechanisms for promoting gender equality and considering gender perspective in major national strategy documents is a reflection of such reform efforts.

The first efforts in overcoming such stereotypes were paradigmatic and included the introduction of quotas for females in politics, which, taking into account its background, was an insincere and manipulative endeavor. Only 1.7 percent of women were elected in the first multiparty elections for Serbian Parliament in 1992. Under President Slobodan Milosevic's regime, the largest proportion of women in parliament was 5.5 percent. Following democratic changes in 2000 and in subsequent elections, the representation of women in politics now stands at around 11 percent, with six and seven percent in the national parliament and local assemblies respectively. But the actual purpose of enforcing quotas (2002) was completely different from its original aim of strengthening and empowering

1 Douglas Kellner: *Media Culture: Cultural Studies, Identity and Politics between the Modern and the Post-Modern*. London: Routledge 2003, p. 434.

women and overcoming stereotypes; instead, they were used to overcome ethnic tensions in southern Serbia. As Zorica Mrsevic stresses, the main reason for introducing the quota system was not to provide women with a better way of securing political representation and taking on decision-making roles, but rather to establish a more pacified and cooperative atmosphere in future local representative bodies.[2] This was to be done by increasing the number of women in these fora who were believed to be less belligerent and less vengeful.

The relationships between policy, ideology, power, and socio-cultural norms in the context of the media are important parts of transitional discourse. Generally speaking, the roots of gender-based violence are the accepted cultural and social customs regarding male and female behavior, prejudice based on the alleged superiority of one sex over another, and the traditional roles of women and men. These social constructs cause sexism on many levels, particularly in the public sphere. Media representations (and interpretations) of reality occur on a certain social plane and are historicized by changes in contemporary public perception. Serbian journalism faces a great deal of uncertainty and struggle, embraces power, and depends on social crisis to function qualities that imply a lack of balance in reporting. Media groups' reporting policies are seldom clearly defined, and accepted codes of conduct in journalism are often infringed upon in practice. The existence of legal regulations and ethical codes in journalism are therefore not a guarantee of responsible and ethical reporting.

The problem of violence against women has garnered more media attention, but a stereotypical and sensational approach to the problem continues.[3] Since the media tends to dictate public opinion in a serious way, this reality is more than disturbing. It is important to note that according to leading international human rights organizations, freedom of media in Serbia faces enormous problems. Serbian journalists face threats, harassment, and intimidation, as well as interference from other bodies, particularly political ones.[4] The government even interfered in media freedom through selective media subsidies and advertising.[5]

2 Zorica Mrsevic: Implementing Quotas: Legal Reform and Enforcement in Serbia and Montenegro. In: Francesca Binda / Julie Ballington (eds): *The Implementation of Quotas: European Experiences*. Stockholm: International Institute for Democracy and Electoral Assistance 2006, pp. 32–57, here p. 48.

3 Jelena Visnjic: "Killing Me Softly": Izvestavanje stampanih medija o zenama zrtvama nasilja [Print Media Reporting on Women Who Suffered Violence]. In *Genero* 16 (2012), pp. 141–156, here p. 149.

4 Human Rights Watch: *World Report 2015*. https://www.hrw.org/worldreport/2015/country chapters/serbia/kosovo#5b498e (accessed 12.03.2016).

5 Amnesty International: *Annual Report 2015–2016 Serbia*. https://www.amnesty.org/en/countries/europe-and-central-asia/serbia/report-serbia (accessed 01.03.2016).

Little has been done to challenge the stereotypes about women that still exist today, but gender and media activists around the world strive to monitor the media's portrayal of women and find strategies to challenge gender stereotyping in the media. Society's prevailing notions about gender are strongly dependent on the media, since the concept of representation is central to the media itself. Although having a potentially crucial role in challenging stereotypes, the media has more often been part of the problem rather than the solution.

The media in Serbia does not offer a balanced image of women's diverse lives and their contributions to human progress, and they often reinforce harmful stereotypes about women's roles in society. Sociocognitive research on gender stereotypes demonstrates that the relationship between stereotyping and ideology can be explained by a collective aspiration to maintain the status quo.[6] The media represents one of the most significant social factors in modern society, and it has played a key role in transmitting values because of its informative, communicative, and symbolic way of relaying messages. Once founded out of a need to connect the public and private sphere, the use of media has presented and reflected the public's attitudes, wishes, fears, and dominant values, whether in all or some of its parts. Since their very foundations, daily newspapers, journals, and weekly magazines have had to not only inform, but emancipate the public and establish its dominant ideals. Images of women in Serbian media do not accurately reflect reality. The present (i. e. absent) amount of women in the public sphere speaks to how much the public values having women in positions of power, and the quality of many articles about this issue is disputable. Typically, the media portrays women as obsessed with cleaning, marriage, and preparing food. Although the daily and weekly press acknowledge progress and modernization in other spheres, its attitudes about women's lives remain stuck in the 1970s.[7] The general portrait of women in the media is important because it arguably paints gender-based violence as something sensational-something to fill front pages. There are many views on this issue, and in this work they will be divided into several groups through which the attitude of the media in cases of violence against women will be shown.

Violence against Ordinary Women

Gender-based violence against women refers to violence directed at a woman merely *because* she is a woman or violence that disproportionately affects women.

6 Conway Pizzamiglio: Status, Communality and Agency: Implications for Stereotypes of Gender and Other Groups. In *Journals of Personality and Social Psychology* 71 (1996), pp. 25–38.
7 Lidija Vasiljevic: *Gender Equality in and through the Media*. Beograd: Zindok 2008, p. 45.

Violence against women "is understood as a violation of human rights and a form of discrimination against women and shall mean all acts of gender-based violence that result in, or are likely to result in, physical, sexual, psychological or economic harm or suffering to women, including threats of such acts, coercion or arbitrary deprivation of liberty, whether occurring in public or in private life".[8]
The Government of the Republic of Serbia adopted the Anti-Discrimination Strategy, which recognizes that gender-based violence is widespread and that the system of protection and support for victims of gender-based violence is insufficiently developed, existing protection is inefficient, and the existing legal regulations need to be amended, consistently implemented, and further improved. One of the main goals is to prevent discriminatory practices in public media and advertising, as well as to adopt adequate regulations on electronic media reporting regarding gender equality that will include measures related to the improvement of the media's role in combating discrimination against women, as well as to introduce gender-sensitive language in media.[9]
Media reports continuously suggested the idea that those who commit violence against women have a right to do so, especially as men. They are raised this way; they understand and realize their rights and roles as real men in society and the family alike, so violence for them is a normal reaction to the stress and frustrations caused by life's adversities. Herein lies the media's negative role; not only do they directly promote violence (albeit not usually) and minimize its consequences, but they spread stereotypes about men and women's social roles. The promotion of stereotypes actually justifies and encourages violence, regardless of intended purpose. Merely reading the headlines can be shocking: "Husband butchers wife: I slaughtered her because she wanted to leave me!"[10], "He strangled his mistress because he found her in bed with another man"[11], "He killed a woman with an ax's grip"[12], "He killed his wife with his bare hands out of jealousy!"[13], "He broke his mother's neck to repay a debt"[14], "Woman tortured

8 Council of Europe: *Convention on Preventing and Combating Violence against Women and Domestic Violence.* http://www.coe.int/en/web/istanbul-convention/home (accessed 29.02.2016).

9 The Government of the Republic of Serbia: *Anti-Discrimination Strategy for 2013–2018.* http://www.ljudskaprava.gov.rs/index.php/yu/naslovna-l/2-uncategorised/114-strategija-za-borbu-protiv-diskriminacije (accessed 11.03.2016).

10 Natasa Stojanovic: Ubica: Zaklao sam je, htela je da me ostavi! In: *Kurir*, 11.03.2014, p. 16.

11 Zadavio ljubavnicu jer ju je zatekao u krevetu s drugim. In: *Alo*, 14.03.2014. http://arhiva.alo.rs/vesti/hronika/uhvatio-ljubavnicu-u-preljubi-i-smrskao-joj-glavu/49128 (accessed 12.03.2016).

12 Jovan Ilic: Ženu ubio drškom od sekire. In: *Vecernje novosti*, 11.03.2014, p. 1.

13 Dejan Ilic: Zbog ljubomore golim rukama ubio suprugu. In: *Kurir*, 13.03.2014, p. 19.

14 Tamara Subota: Slomio majci vrat da bi vratio dug. In: *Blic*, 29.01.2014, p. 17.

and murdered with electricity"[15], "He beat his wife because she did not set the dinner table"[16], "A minor slaughtered women for betting"[17], "Sister slaughtered for money for the kitchen!"[18].

The term "femicide" seemingly originated from the media since it showed up in the *Ms. Magazine* article "Femicide: Speaking the Unspeakable" by Jane Caputi and Diana Russell.[19] The piece is a critical response to the press representation of the 1989 Montreal Massacre. The term "femicide" refers to the killing of women merely *because* they are women.[20] This interpretation is narrowed down, however, as it excludes other types of violence against women (e.g. rape, harassment, mobbing, trafficking, etc.) that threaten women's health but do not pose the threat of impending death. In 2014 alone, 42 reported femicides occurred in Serbia. In the context of these instances in 2014, a UNDP study[21] showed that when it comes to severe cases, Serbian media has adopted the viewpoint that it is difficult to understand how such tragedies can happen and that they are, in general, unpredictable. But paradoxically, media reports also underline the perennial existence of domestic violence, which include repeated instances as reported by victims. The media thus treats homicides resulting from gender-based violence as inexplicable or unpredictable tragedies simply because the factors that led to the homicide are presumably unknown.[22] In 2014, the Ombudsman of Serbia warned that the system of protection of women against violence does not take into account that women are often murdered by family members or partners after existing and prolonged violence. Femicide is almost always preceded by multiple incidents of violence, often by family members, who are left without adequate and timely replies from relevant authorities.[23]

15 Nevena Bozic: Ženu mučio i ubio strujom. In: *Blic*, 28.07.2010, p. 18.

16 Pretukao ženu jer mu nije postavila večeru. In: *Blic*, 23.08.2010. http://www.blic.rs/vesti/hronika/pretukao-zenu-jer-mu-nije-postavila-veceru/ts56hf3 (accessed 12.03.2016).

17 Maloletnik zaklao zenu zbog kladionice. In: *Vecernje novosti*, 04.02.2014. http://www.novosti.rs/vesti/naslovna/hronika/aktuelno.291.html:476539-Uhapsen-maloletnik-koji-je-zaklao-zenu-zbog-para (accessed 13.03.2016).

18 Denis Cekovic: Rodjenu sestru zaklao zbog para za kuhinju! In: *Kurir*, 09.04.2014, p. 17.

19 Diana Russell / Jane Caputi: Femicide: Speaking the Unspeakable. In: *Ms. Magazine* (1990), pp. 2–34.

20 Drew Humphries: *Women, Violence, and the Media: Readings in Feminist Criminology*. London: UP of New England 2009, pp. 117–118.

21 Zorica Mrsevic: *Media in Serbia in 2014 about Gender-based Violence*. Beograd: UNDP 2015, p. 17.

22 National Union of Journalists: *NUJ Guidelines for Journalists on Violence against Women*. https://www.nuj.org.uk/documents/nuj-guidelines-on-violence-against-women/ (accessed 13.03.2016).

23 Ombudsman: *Annual Report 2014*. Beograd: Ombudsman 2015, p. 71.

This represents one of the main disadvantages of the media reporting on violence against women; in the most drastic cases of femicide where media reports continue to deny the existence of this obvious nexus between existing violence and the invariable murder. What follows is the inadequate and untimely treatment from the institutions that go under the media radar, which seems oriented toward the creation of entertainment even from the most tragic events. Femicide in Serbian media does not usually reflect the result of years and years of male violence, and even when this practice is recognized it is not identified as the cause of femicide; rather, it is often ignored while emphasizing that the killer is a good and respected man, as is illustrated here: "Antics are known for firing guns when celebrating. No one took that as a bad thing, because they were good and worthy people; they tilled over tens of hectares and it was their relief from their daily duties."[24] This manner of presenting abusers and murderers further contributes to the normalization of domestic violence and as something that happens regularly and in the best families, rather than abnormal and deserving of condemnation.[25]

Although there are guidelines stating that journalists should be mindful of the lack of convincing evidence for a cycle of violence and should avoid making simplistic connections between male violence against women and their childhood experiences of violence,[26] the tabloidization of reports on femicide in Serbia is reflected in researching a history of domestic violence, which is then identified as the cause of the violence. Take, for example, these references to cases of violence against women: "Locals say that the late Andrea was also a rape victim. Andrea and her daughter H. L. experienced similar fates. As a teenager, Andrea was sexually abused by her father, who was imprisoned for four and a half years"[27], and "The dark secret of the Djuric family: Makivija Djuric, mother of Dragan Djuric who killed Tijana Juric, tried to kill her colleague 14 years ago by hitting her in the head"[28]. It is important to not refer to abusers as monsters,

24 Muž je ubio dok je posluživala goste. In: *Blic*, 26.05.2014. http://www.blic.rs/vesti/hronika/muz-je-ubio-dok-je-posluzivala-goste/cedfc9b (accessed 13.03.2016).

25 Mrsevic: Media in Serbia in 2014, p. 22.

26 Zero Tolerance: *Handle with Care. A Guide to Responsible Media Reporting of Violence against Women*. http://www.zerotolerance.org.uk/sites/all/files/files/HWC_V5(1).pdf (accessed 28.02.2016).

27 Izašao s robije zbog silovanja ćerke, pa iskasapio bivšu ženu. In: *Kurir*, 11.12.2014. http://www.kurir.rs/crna-hronika/18horor-u-coki-obljubio-cerku-pa-zenu-zaklao-nozem-clanak-1633810 (accessed 13.03.2016).

28 Monstrumova majka Makavija htela da me ubije kao psa. In: *Kurir*, 12.08.2014. http://www.kurir.rs/crna-hronika/mracna-tajna-duriceva-majka-htela-da-ubije-komsinicu-clanak-1504783 (accessed 14.03.2016).

fiends, maniacs or beasts, as this creates the myth that abusers are noticeably and substantially different from normal men. However, a flagrant violation of all of journalistic ethics occurred during the reporting on the murder of Tijana Juric in 2014, who was killed by Dragan Djuric (sentenced to the maximum punishment of 40 years in prison by Serbian criminal law). Although it is now certain that Djuric is a cruel killer, the presumption of innocence in this case had been violated. As soon as the media got the information about who might be a potential killer, this case became an unprecedented witch hunt for not only Djuric and his family, but also to the family of the murdered girl. Media reports even commented on the details of his private life, his sister's family, his mother's past, the pimples on his face, etc. Media reports raced to fuel a desire for lynching throughout the nation; from the very first day the news broke, Djuric was called a monster, a cold-blooded killer, and an animal ("Is he a man or an animal?"[29]) despite being nothing but a suspect at the time. But firstly, when Tijana Juric was still missing, there were speculations in the media that the girl was kidnapped because of her father's debts and that she fled from home because of "complex family relationships".[30] Her father was forced to justify himself by explaining that he did not borrow the money, which indirectly meant that he had to accept and even justify that his "shady business" was not behind Tijana's disappearance. The public's initial reaction was, as expected, an emotional one. Petitions surfaced seeking the "return" of the death penalty, but this path was initially paved by government officials and fueled by the media. Minister of Justice Nikola Selakovic said that the punishment for Tijana's murder should be between 30 to 40 years.[31] An ordinary citizen could say something like this with no problem, but a government minister who prejudges the outcome of criminal proceedings irresponsibly places pressure on the judiciary. If at first one thinks that the Minister simply made an emotional, clumsy statement, the Minister of Justice immediately confirmed his statement by bitterly noting that Serbia only needed to abolish the death penalty because it was required so that Serbia could join the Council of Europe. As Minister Selakovic then said, "Police arrested

29 Da li je to čovek ili životinja. In: *Telegraf*, 07.08.2014. http://www.telegraf.rs/vesti/1182583-tijanin-otac-da-li-je-to-covek-ili-zivotinja-sa-120-kg-se-izivljavao-nad-detetom-od-47 (accessed 22.02.2016).

30 Tijanin Otac: Ne dugujem zelenašima, neka me spale ako su je oteli zbog toga! In: *Telegraf*, 11.08.2014, http://www.telegraf.rs/vesti/1181098-tijanin-otac-ne-dugujem-zelenasima-neka-me-spale-ako-su-je-oteli-zbog-toga (accessed 14.04.2016).

31 Ministar pravde: Ubici Tijane 30–40 godina, to je dovoljno stroga kazna. In: *Blic*, 07.08.2014. http://www.blic.rs/vesti/hronika/ministar-pravde-ubici-tijane-30-40-godina-to-je-dovoljno-stroga-kazna/fkbjwl8 (accessed 23.02.2016).

the monster that committed this act… Because of this monster – and I regret that Serbia has abolished the death penalty – it is obvious that our society is not mature enough for European norms of behavior".[32] In just one sentence, the Minister of Justice said three things that no minister ever should. Firstly, as a lawyer and a Minister, Minister Selakovic should not call someone a "monster" for allegedly committing a crime; the minister of a state has no right to make such a statement and using a term like "monster". Furthermore, the Minister can surely regret that the death penalty does not exist in private, but in public he should refrain from such scandalous statements; after all, his duty is to defend the Constitution of the Republic of Serbia, which strictly prohibits the death penalty. Thirdly, saying that Serbian society was unprepared for European behavioral norms was an insult to Serbian citizens. Without going into the very core of human rights and democratic societies and the fact that virtually no European country has the death penalty in their legislation, what is important here is that when the top politicians give these impulses to the people, one should not be surprised by adequate reaction of the media, who then eagerly questioned the validity of the death penalty.

The Commissioner for Information of Public Importance and Personal Data Protection[33] highlighted that when it comes to confidential information from an investigation concerning a serious crime, the ones to be blamed are public authorities as they were the only ones with said information.[34] Using this

32 Stefanović: Zbog ovakvog monstruma mi je žao što je Srbija ukinula smrtnu kaznu. In: *Novi magazin*, 07.08.2014. http://www.novimagazin.rs/vesti/stefanovic-zbog-ovakvog-monstruma-mi-je-zao-sto-je-srbija-ukinula-smrtnu-kaznu (accessed 22.02.2016).

33 The Commissioner for Information of Public Importance and Personal Data Protection is an autonomous public authority who exercises his/her powers independently and whose competences are set by Article 44 of the *Law on Personal Data Protection*. For the purpose of exercising the duties within his/her sphere of competence, the Commissioner has two types of power: those relating to his/her capacity of a second-instance authority responsible for protecting the right to data protection in appeal proceedings, and those relating to his/her capacity of a supervisory authority responsible for enforcing the law. The Commissioner's rulings on appeals shall be binding, final and enforceable. Where necessary, the Government shall ensure that the Commissioner's rulings are enforced. The implementation of the *Law on Personal Data Protection* shall be supervised by the Commissioner. The Commissioner shall perform supervision through authorized inspectors. While performing supervision, inspectors shall furnish their official identification documents and shall carry out their supervision duties in a professional and timely fashion and produce records of their enforcement activities. The Commissioner shall also supervise the transborder transfer of data out of the Republic of Serbia and shall approve of the transborder transfer of data. The Commissioner's rulings shall not be subject to appeal, but they may be challenged in administrative proceedings by bringing legal action before the Supreme Court of Serbia.

34 Tužbe čekaju tužioca. In: *Danas*, 01.08.2014. http://www.danas.rs/danasrs/drustvo/pravo_danas/izvestavanje_medija_o_ubistvu_tijane_juric_tuzbe_cekaju_reakciju_tuzioca_.1118.html?news_id=286972 (accessed 24.02.2016).

example, the idea was to show the nexus between unethical journalism, tabloidization, politics and how gender-driven violence was completely sidelined while the media reported on sensational issues, a practice condemned by both journalist associations in Serbia. As stated by the Commissioner for the protection of equality, violence against women – the most dramatic abuse of women's rights – is an indicator of how little has been done to eradicate core causes of such violence. Combating violence against women cannot be successful if this phenomenon is not seen in the context of gender stereotypes, prejudice and discriminatory attitudes, which are already deeply rooted and widespread among professionals who work in the prevention and prosecution of violence against women. Furthermore, many of these stereotypes, prejudices and discriminatory attitudes are part of media reporting on violence against women.[35]

Celebrities and Gender-based Violence

Violence against women in the context of celebrities was not a highly reported topic until recently; in the past couple of years, the issue has saturated the local media. Sensationalist ways of presenting violence against women reflects not only a media company's reporting style, but also sparks the constant monitoring of gender-based violence whose actors are celebrities. Violence by abusers known to the public (or violence committed against celebrity women) has become more common, particularly since 2014. It is perhaps most alarming that news about violence against celebrity women are usually published in the following sections: Showtime, VIP, Fun, Stars, Shows, Hot Stories, etc. Placing this phenomenon in the wider domain of entertainment speaks to how violence against women in the media is trivialized. This banalization is often followed by the unauthorized disclosure of personal data with the aim of evoking reactions from audiences, seeking in violence possible elements of romance, misery, destiny and even comedy (e.g. "She stabbed her ex-husband's lawyer with a barbecue fork after losing custody of the child!"[36]).

Regular headline types include the "dramatic confession with a happy ending", "physical clash of former lovers", "romance interrupted" and "from love to war", while repeated violence is regularly referred to as "turbulent or stormy love"; if the abuser wants to continue an abusive relationship, then he is merely "singing

35 Commissioner for Protection of Equality: *Regular Annual Report for 2014*. Belgrade: Commissioner for Protection of Equality 2015, p. 110.

36 Sindi ubola advokata roštiljskom viljuškom! In: *Alo*, 01.08.2014. http://arhiva.alo.rs/v-i-p/veliki-brat/sindi-ubola-advokata-rostiljskom-viljuskom/62973 (accessed 27.02.2016).

a song to get her back".[37] The very first media lynching in Serbia began with the popular pop singer Ksenija Pajcin, who was killed by her partner, model Filip Kapisoda. He committed suicide immediately after killing the singer in 2010 (thereby committing femicide-suicide). For days, the media relativized the violence that the victim was exposed to. Reports of an alleged pregnancy, abortion, and texts focusing on details of their relationship impermissibly implied the responsibility of the murder as divided between the victim and the perpetrator. Media coverage moved the spotlight away from violence against women and ignored the fact that the victim tried to leave the abusive relationship; instead, the victim and the abuser were presented almost as a "modern Romeo and Juliet in the light of their tragic love" while pathological jealousy was presented as "romantic love". The media ignored that celebrating crimes and therefore writing about "a fatal love that ended tragically" or the "Serbian version of Shakespeare's heroes, Romeo and Juliet" is impermissible.[38] As Pajcin was often described as the most beautiful woman in Serbia, her murder was romanticized because of her beauty ("Ksenija Pajcin: Beauty that cost her life"[39]). In this way, the media actually justified crime and suggested that violence against women can somehow be defended with quasi-arguments. The media did not seek to clarify that jealousy is not love, but rather a form of control of others, and that this type of control is not far in nature from physical violence – which, in this case, was painfully apparent.[40]

This case paved the way for scandalous media coverage of violence against women in the context of celebrities to gain traction. When it comes to cases where a celebrity man who enjoys a positive reputation and popularity is an abuser, their victims are often described as "easy moral" women. This can be identified in at least two cases from 2014 and 2015. When lesser-known model Jovana Nikolic accused her husband, famous pop singer Danijel Alibabic, of domestic violence, she was exposed to a media lynch and had to defend herself: "I did not expect nor did get any financial assistance from Danijel"[41]. Although Jovana Nikolic

37 Mrsevic: Media in Serbia in 2014, p. 47.

38 Zorica Mrsevic: *Kvalitativna analiza medijskog izvestavanja o nasilju nad zenama u Srbiji*. Beograd: UNDP 2013, p. 68.

39 Zivotna prica – Ksenija Pajčin: Lepota koja ju je koštala života. In: *Story*, 26.09.2010. http://www.story.rs/vesti/u-fokusu/11017-%C5%BEivotna-pri%3Fa-%E2%80%93-ksenija-paj%3Fin%3A-lepota-koja-ju-je-ko%C5%A1tala-%C5%BEivota.html (accessed 26.02.2016).

40 Zorica Mrsevic: Žene u Medijima u Srbiji [Women in Serbian's Media]. In: Dragana Popovic (ed.): *Zbornik predavanja sa kursa Politike rodne ravnopravnosti*. Beograd: Genero 2011, pp. 69–95, here p. 73.

41 Jovana Nikolić poslala saopštenje medijima: Danijel me je fizički zlostavljao, ja sam mu bila pokriće jer je homoseksualac! In: *Blic*, 09.01.2014. http://www.blic.rs/zabava/vesti/

had seriously accused her husband of domestic violence, the media found it more important to launch polls about the secondary details of the relationship that had nothing to do with violence, such as the food they ate, and in doing so made a mockery of a domestic violence victim. Headlines included that the pair "ate only sandwiches"[42] while jokes about the case spread among citizens. The case, characterized by a lack of condemnation of violence and celebrities arguing about whom they believed more, became ludicrous, and Alibabic, who was more famous than Nikolic, enjoyed the popularity.

The other case included famous TV host Vladimir Stanojevic, who admitted that he beat his girlfriend Ana Marija. Although Stanojevic admitted the act, media reports focused on the photo his former girlfriend posted on Facebook where her bruises were easily seen. Media comparisons with the Rihanna and Chris Brown case made the headlines instead of violence against women itself. Ana Marija was perceived as an "easy girl" who was probably cheating on Vladimir and provoked him to beat her up. Stanojevic's statement that he "shoved her in the head" became famously quoted back then, and it still is. The pair even appeared together on *Pink*, a morning show, where Stanojevic admitted his guilt on national television.[43] But a few months later, Stanojevic became a participant of the reality TV Show *The Farm* – today, he is a regular TV host on national television despite admitting to having committed violence against women.

In the current media spotlight is former mafia boss Ljubisa Buha, the protected witness in the case of the assassinated Serbian Prime Minister Zoran Djindjic. Throughout the years, Buha became a celebrity, and his wife's accusation of domestic violence turned into something ironic and funny in the media coverage. Some of the headlines included: "Buha's wife 'beaten' by shower"[44] and "It's not Buha, it's the shower door stalls"[45]. The culmination of media reporting on this case occurred when Buha brutally beat his wife in front of a considerable number of people, including members of his official security. He was finally

jovana-nikolic-poslala-saopstenje-medijima-danijel-me-je-fizicki-zlostavljao-ja-sam/xq3np70 (accessed 25.02.2016).

42 Jovana Alibabić: Kod Danijela sam jela samo sendviče, nisam imala od čega da skuvam ručak! In: *Kurir*, 16.01.2014. http://www.kurir.rs/jovana-alibabic-kod-danijela-sam-jela-samo-sendvice-nisam-imala-od-cega-da-skuvam-rucak-clanak-1180743 (accessed 26.02.2016).

43 Video available at: https://www.youtube.com/watch?v=SK-HZKGwIRg (accessed 14.03.2016).

44 Čumetovu ženu "tukla" tuš kabina. In: *Alo*, 26.7.2014. http://arhiva.alo.rs/vesti/hronika/cumetovu-zenu-ipak-tukla-tus-kabina/62318 (accessed 01.03.2016).

45 Nije Čume već vrata od tuš kabine. In: *Večernje novosti*, 26.07.2014. http://www.novosti.rs/vesti/naslovna/hronika/aktuelno.291.html:502655-Nije-Cume-vec-vrata-od-tus-kabine (accessed 01.03.2016).

arrested, but, as stated by many, on the sole grounds of having threatened the police; seeing as the Minister of Police said that Buha would no longer be a protected witness shortly after the incident, this theory is credible. The amount of coverage about Buha's defense was immense and, according to Mrsevic, consisted of typical justifications of violence by family abusers ("my wife is crazy"; "she wants to kidnap our child and she threatened to commit suicide"; "she's mentally ill and has a diagnosis"; "she made it all up out of jealousy", etc.).[46]

Reality TV Shows and Gender-based Violence

Serbia has a total of six national broadcasters. These include the country's public television network, Radio Television of Serbia (RTS1, RTS2, and RTS3), as well as private networks Prva, B92, Pink and Happy TV. All televisions with national frequencies are obligated to have varied programming (informational, educational, cultural, scientific, sports-related, entertaining, etc.). This means that TV stations break the rules if one type of program dominates, which in this case is reality and entertainment television. The tendency to reduce program diversity on commercial television stations with national coverage has been noticeable for years, and by reducing program diversity the respect for media pluralism is breached, despite having a core place in European media legislation. If four of the six national TV channels predominantly broadcast reality shows, one can speak of a serious disruption in the obligations of TV stations to offer diverse media content.[47]

The Regulatory Authority of Electronic Media (REM) is obliged to take special care that media service providers comply with the obligations relating to program content provided by the *Law on Electronic Media* and the conditions under which they were issued the license, which is particularly related to the type and character of the program.[48] REM can punish broadcasters, including imposing temporal bans on their broadcasts or revoking their license if the broadcaster violated any of its obligations relating to content, which is referred to in Articles 47 to 71 of the *Law on Electronic Media*. This means that the station can be punished if, for example, it does not contribute to raising the general cultural and educational level of citizens (Article 47, paragraph 3) or does not respect human rights and dignity, including the protection of children and

46 Mrsevic: Media in Serbia in 2014, p. 50.

47 Maja Divac: Zašto REM toleriše prostakluk i nemoral u rijaliti programima? In: *Cenzolovka*, 07.09.2015. https://www.cenzolovka.rs/misljenja/zasto-rem-tolerise-prostakluk-i-nemoral-u-rijaliti-programima/ (accessed 10.03.2016).

48 *Sl. glasnik RS* [*Law on Electronic Media*], br. 83/2014. http://www.paragraf.rs/propisi/zakon_o_elektronskim_medijima.html (accessed 12.03.2016).

minors (Article 50, 68). The purpose of this short introduction is to demonstrate that there are tools that can be used to prevent what will be described in the following paragraphs. Entertainment industry figures and sports stars have long been at the center of celebrity culture, but business tycoons and politicians have also become celebrities. Celebrity culture is also such that there is a class of faux celebrities; in Serbia, gangsters, criminals, people famous for being famous and being in the media have, in recent years, become reality show stars.[49] In these programs qualified as entertainment, violence is so dominant that it is sufficient to note that only in the reality program *The Couples* (Happy TV) brutal physical violence against women constantly occurs. At this time we will mention only concrete cases of physical violence against women reported by the media in the past few months: "Miki hit Dalila in The Couples"[50], "Zmaj hit Vesna and Jelena"[51], "Miki hit Ruzica in the head"[52], "Gastoz punched Miljana and Ruzica"[53], "Hasan Dudic yanked, punched and kicked Jelena Golubovic!"[54], "Era punched Sladjana"[55] and "Zeljko punched Ruzica Veljkovic"[56]. It is important to observe that this is only one reality show program, and these are the headlines from the past few months – violence against women in Serbia is thus approaching an institutionalized level and is somehow widely accepted. Hollow warnings and inadequate penalties were part of what led to violence being allowed in such programs, but it is chiefly used as a means of achieving better ratings.

The most popular commercial Serbian channel is TV Pink, and it is the leading station for television viewers under 55 years of age. It is typical, highly commercialized television with an enormous amount of entertainment programs

49 Douglas Kellner: Barack Obama and Celebrity Spectacle. In: *International Journal of Communication* 3 (2009), pp. 715–741, here p. 716.

50 Prekinut program: Miki u Parovima udario Dalilu. In: *Blic*, 09.03.2016. http://www.blic.rs/zabava/vesti/prekinut-program-miki-u-parovima-udario-dalilu/04rwvse (accessed 15.03.2016).

51 Nasilje i u Parovima: Zmaj udario Vesnu i Jelenu. In: *Blic*, 08.10.2015. http://www.blic.rs/zabava/vesti/nasilje-i-u-parovima-zmaj-udario-vesnu-i-jelenu/kd18d2r (accessed 14.03.2016).

52 Je l' te udario pesnicom? In: *Mondo*, 10.02.2015. http://mondo.rs/a874071/Zabava/TV/Parovi-Miki-udario-Ruzicu-u-glavu.html (accessed 14.03.2016).

53 Gastoz pesnicom udario Miljanu i Ružicu! In: *Telegraf*, 15.12.2015. http://www.telegraf.rs/jetset/1906847-program-prekinut-haos-u-parovima-podivljali-gastoz-udario-pesnicom-ruzicu-i-miljanu-foto (accessed 15.03.2016).

54 Hasan Dudić počupao, udario i šutnuo Jelenu Golubović! In: *Telegraf*, 12.04.2015. http://www.telegraf.rs/jetset/1518600-hasan-dudic-izbacen-iz-parova-jelenu-je-pocupao-udario-sakom-i-sutnuo (accessed 15.03.2016).

55 Era udario Slađu, a onda ga ona DOKRAJČILA! In: *Telegraf*, 09.01.2016. http://www.telegraf.rs/jetset/1942000-nova-tuca-u-parovima-era-udario-sladju-a-onda-ga-ona-dokrajcila-video (accessed 12.03.2016).

56 Željko udario Ružicu Veljković u glavu! In: *Alo*, 23.11.2015. http://www.alo.rs/zeljko-udario-ruzicu-veljkovic-u-glavu/20081 (accessed 16.03.2016).

(featuring reality shows, music talent competitions, and Latin American telenovelas) and a small segment of news.[57] The reality show *The Farm* is aired in Serbia on RTV Pink, while the second most watched show is *The Couples*, aired on TV Happy. The year 2015 was the year of reality shows in Serbia, with the new seasons of these featuring plenty of violence, misogyny and hate speech. The whole picture of the admissibility of violence against women can be shown in but one example. The biggest star of the 2015 reality TV scene was *The Farm*'s participant called Kristijan Golubovic (46), a gangster and a man who spent more than 20 years in prison. His participation was marked by violent behavior, intimidating other participants (especially women), swearing at others and physical attacks. One of the two journalist associations in Serbia, the Independent Association of Serbian Journalists (NUNS), requested that REM "urgently and most severely punish"[58] the television program for its sheer violence. As stated by NUNS on this occasion, Kristijan Golubovic's stay in this program was characterized by violence mostly committed against women, but it was only after his physical attacks against male participants of *The Farm* that TV Pink decided to disqualify him.[59] Shortly after his disqualification, Golubovic returned to the show just to spread fear among other participants, especially to female celebrities. It is inconceivable how the authorities could allow this type of behavior. While the show was broadcast, Municipal Public Prosecutor Dragan Jovanovic required that REM ban *The Farm* within 48 hours. A day before, by order of Prosecutor Jovanovic, the police questioned Kristijan Golubovic about endangering the safety of other participants Maja Nikolić, Alen Mukovic and Rade Lazic, and for doubting that Golubovic caused serious bodily injuries to ballerina Jelena Milosevic but this lonely action of local Prosecutor had no legal epilogue.[60] The Golubovic case is extreme, but by no means the only example of such violence against women. Since they rake in high ratings and do not seem to attract the attention of the authorities, violence against women in reality TV happens on a daily basis.

57 Jovanka Matic / Larisa Rankovic: Media Landscape Serbia. In: European Journalism Centre. http://ejc.net/media_landscapes/serbia (accessed 15.03.2016).

58 NUNS traži od REM-a: Najoštrije kaznite televiziju Pink. In: *N1 info*, 26.11.2015. http://rs.n1info.com/a112701/Vesti/Kristijan-Golubovic-izbacen-sa-Farme.html (accessed 14.03.2016).

59 Ibid.

60 Tužilac traži zabranu emitovanja Farme. In: *UNS*, 05.11.2015. http://www.uns.org.rs/sr/desk/media-news/34486/tuzilac-trazi-zabranu-emitovanja-farme.html (accessed 16.03.2016).

Conclusion

In its concluding observations on the combined 2nd and 3rd periodic reports of Serbia, the United Nations Committee on the Elimination of Discrimination Against Women (CEDAW) remained concerned about the persistence of deep-rooted stereotypes in the media and the recent trend of reestablishing traditional roles and responsibilities of women and men in the family and society, which undermine women's social status and participation in public life. They therefore recommend that Serbia should further strengthen its efforts to overcome stereotypical attitudes regarding the roles and responsibilities of women and men in the family and in society and implementing measures to eliminate gender stereotypes, all the while promoting positive images and substantive equality of women.[61]

An analysis of the media coverage on violence against women is the first line of resistance against the stereotyped and misogynist media construction of the phenomenon of violence against women in Serbia, and such analyses shed light on the realities of violence against women in Serbia and how inadequately institutions respond to this violence. The analysis showed that editors and journalists should be trained in understanding the key characteristics of violence against women. The media aren't bound to, nor can they be experts in the field of gender relations, gender theory and gender-based violence, but what can be expected from them is the factually correct, non-stereotyped and non-discriminatory coverage of specific events and the providing of space for analytical contributions of both women and men.[62] Monitoring the media's portrayal of women and finding strategies to challenge gender stereotyping in the media have been longstanding concerns of gender and media activists throughout the world.

Media development has not been properly discussed in the decision-making process – the rich experiences of other countries and the help of international organizations have only been partially used to remedy the problem. Considering the influence of the media, it is a necessary tool in regulating and improving reports on violence against women. Through investigative and responsible journalism, a deeper understanding of said violence, and cooperation with all actors in the community working to suppress and reduce violence, it is possible to set standards for the protection of victims and continually build public awareness on the unacceptability and punishability of violence, particularly against

61 UN Committee on the Elimination of Discrimination Against Women (CEDAW): *Concluding Observations on the Combined 2nd and 3rd Periodic Reports of Serbia, 30.07.2013, CEDAW/C/SRB/CO/2-3*. http://www.refworld.org/docid/52f3883b4.html (accessed 18.03.2016).

62 Zorica Mrsevic: *Integrisani odgovor na nasilje nad ženama u Srbiji*. Beograd: UNDP 2014, p. 5.

women. Training to educate journalists, reporters and editors on gender equality in media as well as increasing the number of men included in gender equality issues is of enormous importance. However, the creation of public opinion and building good media reporting practices (which still lose out in favor of sensationalism, entertainment, stereotyping and discriminatory mechanisms) is a long process that requires the cooperation and coordinated action of all social actors and decision makers who deal with the problem of violence. Reporting on violence against women in an analytical, factually correct way has the capacity to eradicate stereotypes, and doing so is the only possible way for both the victim and society to leave the vicious circle of violence.

Gendered Epistemology and Harassment

The Case of Dr. Olivieri

Andrew Fuyarchuk

Although Canadians celebrate a tradition in which the instituted social imaginary is routinely subject to cross-examination and held accountable for the effects of its decisions by a tribunal of concerned citizens,[1] the way in which knowledge has been procured about those who have stood up to injustice continues to produce distortions. The universalizing and gendered ways in which the voices of concerned citizens have often been translated into manageable terms do not engage those citizens, and they instead transform their concerns into a threat – responsible citizens into a disease fit to be purged. Canada's legal, political, economic and educated professionals and the epistemic practices they routinely employ to understand others have often denigrated, discredited and defamed responsible citizens to degrees of loss, abuse, frustration and confusion that should not be kept hidden. The story of Doctor Nancy Olivieri is a prime example. She was stigmatized by administrators and doctors at the Hospital for Sick Children (HSC) for having broken a confidentiality agreement with Apotex. When her experiments in the early 1990s demonstrated that the trial drug deferiprone (L1) produced by Apotex posed unexpected medical risks, she did not abide by the terms of the restrictive covenant with the company. Instead, she advised her patients of the dangers of using the drug and published her findings in the *New England Journal of Medicine* in 1998.[2] Apotex answered swiftly by ejecting her from the research program, cancelling the study she was running and threatening to sue her.[3] Amidst the furor, she lost her position as head of

1 The tradition is carried forward by such institutions as the Ontario Human rights Commission, non-governmental agencies such as Amnesty International, and the media, e.g. CTV's *W5* and CBC's *Go Public*. For a definition of "instituted social imaginary", see Lorraine Code: *Ecological Thinking: The Politics of Epistemic Location*. Oxford: Oxford UP 2006, p. 30. She explains that the imaginary consists of an interlacing of structures (ethical, social, cultural) and unarticulated beliefs that do not belong to anyone and yet we all participate in a given imaginary, work within it, and use it to interpret experiences and form a world. Citing Cornelius Castoriadis: *Philosophy, Politics, Autonomy: Essays in Political Philosophy*, ed. by David Ames Curtis. New York: Oxford UP 1991, p. 62.

2 Code: *Ecological Thinking*, p. 241.

3 Miriam Schuchman: *The Drug Trial: Nancy Olivieri and the Science Scandal that Rocked the Hospital for Sick Children*. Toronto: Random House 2005, p. 1. The 1993 contract with Apotex

the hemoglobinopathy program at the HSC until early 1999, and although she returned to that office within a year,[4] she continued to suffer less overt, more sublimated forms of aggression, such as reductions in material resources to support her work. Worse yet, Olivieri's character was maligned and her research and achievements discredited. Even her close colleagues, such as Dr. Gideon Koren, turned against her. Nevertheless, in the midst of this deleterious dilemma, her appeals were heard and supported by people outside the growing consolidation of vested interests and its bandwagon effect in Toronto. Scientists in the UK and the Research Ethics Board at HSC stood behind her work and her decision to inform the public of her findings. The President of the HSC even disciplined Dr. Koren for "gross misconduct".[5] In 2001, the College of Physicians and Surgeons ruled that Olivieri had provided patients with a reasonable standard of care.[6] Both the University of Toronto and the Canadian Medical Protective Association supported her,[7] but the incident did not go without a public hearing. It was investigated by the Canadian Association of University Teachers (CAUT), whose analysis was published and titled *The Olivieri Report* (2001). The *Report* includes recommendations about how to prevent a conflict between corporate funding and academic freedom of research from arising in the future.

Even so, it is unclear that those who sided with Olivieri and the authors of the *Report* recognized the historically embedded social structures that contributed to her predicament. This question has been undertaken by Lorraine Code in *Ecological Thinking* (2006) in relation to the "sexualized politics of knowledge that sustain hierarchies of credibility [...] in ways detrimental to open, democratic epistemic practices"[8]. Her research has been instrumental in developing an explanation as to (1) how science is entangled in social structures that are prone to silence scientists, specifically women who have been dubbed "Whistle Blowers"; (2) how, in the course of doing so, the socially instituted collective undermines itself and thus (3) transfers credibility to the target figure.

had a confidentiality clause, but not the 1995 contract. Jon Thompson / Patricia Baird / Jocelyn Downie: *The Olivieri Report: The Complete Text of the Report of the Independent Inquiry Commissioned by the Canadian Association of University Teachers*. Toronto: Lorimer 2001, p. 5.

4 Code: *Ecological Thinking*, p. 243.

5 Thompson / Baird / Downie: *The Olivieri Report*, p. 12.

6 Schuchman: *The Drug Trial*, p. 359.

7 Thompson / Baird / Downie: *The Olivieri Report*, p. 8.

8 Code: *Ecological Thinking*, p. 252.

There are two principles that guide this study. The first is stated by Jim Cheney and Anthony Weston. They write: "Theory is not inconsistent with storied understanding of self, community and world. Indeed, as philosophers and sociologists of science have amply demonstrated, theories are fully intelligible only when embedded in stories".[9] The story of Dr. Olivieri, albeit informed by my creative reconstruction of it, yields a theory about how science can function to not only suppress science, but harass and harm scientists. Second, in agreement with Adrienne Rich, women's place (for her, the body of a "white Western feminist") relative to a socially instituted imaginary is taken to be distinctly different from that of most men.[10] Women speak from the margins, from the side of those who are often adversely affected by the uniformity of social values and norms. This, in turn, enables them to see possibilities that those who identify with the moral majority do not. Working with these two principles, Part One argues that practitioners of naturalized epistemology place a female "Whistle Blower", or one who from an awakened conscience resists regulatory norms that have become morally corrupting, in the precarious position of having their concerns formally acknowledged but ignored in substance.[11] While "naturalized epistemology" gives those persons a voice within instituted norms, it also robs them of their significance by transforming their voices into terms that function to justify an instituted imaginary's perception of itself. This follows from a contradiction internal to an underdeveloped version of naturalized epistemology exemplified in the work of the renowned thinker, Willard Van Orman Quine, and in the institutionalized regulatory response to Olivieri's findings. After having explained the correlations between said epistemology and the system's response, a case is made for the negative consequences functioning to vindicate both the ethical and epistemic veracity of her location. This, in turn, creates a space in which a "Whistler" might creatively transform a negative stigmatization into desirable outcomes.

Part Two develops the hopeful side of the verdict for women who challenge scientism by arguing for the de-centralization and fragmentation of epistemic practices sequestered within a closed and controlled marketplace of

9 Jim Cheney / Anthony Weston: Environmental Ethics as Environmental Etiquette: Toward an Ethics-based Epistemology. In: *Environmental Ethics: An Interdisciplinary Journal Dedicated to the Philosophical Aspects of Environmental Problems* 21,2 (1999), pp. 115–134, here p. 129.

10 Adrienne Rich: Notes Toward a Politics of Location (1984). In: Adrienne Rich: *Blood, Bread, and Poetry: Selected Prose 1979–1985*. New York: Norton 1999, pp. 210–231.

11 See Thomas Faunce: Developing and Teaching the Virtue – Ethics Foundations of Healthcare Whistle Blowing. In *Monash Bioethics Review* 23,4 (2004), pp. 46–49.

ideas, sheltered from public scrutiny. Through such democratizing reforms as described by Code,[12] a "Whistler" is reconfigured into a responsible citizen given one additional condition. Code's proposals focus on the side of the institutionalizing imaginary rather than on the side of the responsible citizen – that is to say, she elaborates on the structural conditions for advocacy in a democratic forum rather than upon what is required of the responsible citizen-scientist. With a view to the latter, in order to resist being assimilated into institutions of advocacy and preserve a degree of responsibility to their constituents, it is necessary for a "Whistler" to position themselves in the zone between institutionalized epistemic practices and "Outsiders". From that middle location, they are in a position to employ the art of tact in order to create harmony out of a situation riddled by discord, which Code does not specify and instead presupposes in her interpretation of media images of Dr. Nancy Olivieri.

Without quite realizing it, Quine initiated a methodological step that validates Olivieri's state as a female fieldworker wrestling with entrenched forms of power and privilege masquerading under the banner of value-neutrality. He inclines toward reversing the position of an idealized knower (mathematician) by inquiring into the conditions in which knowledge is produced.[13] That is to say, he challenges the assumption of an idealized knower whose knowledge has no relation to the way in which it is produced by turning the assumption on its head. According to Quine in *Natural Kinds*, what a scientist does matters to epistemology.[14] Hence, the naturalized epistemological movement he inaugurated in the late 20th century "set out to explicate its real-world ('natural') conditions"[15]. As Code points out, this move toward an inquiry into the conditions in which knowledge is produced bodes well for feminists in two ways. First, Quine's move validates the relevance of a practitioner's voice to epistemology. For women excluded from an "inner circle" of executive roles chaired by men, "naturalized epistemology" promises to create a space for their perspectives to be taken into account. Second, as a result of creating a role for women in the formation of knowledge, the biases inherent to institutionalized sciences are critically

12 See Code: *Ecological Thinking*, pp. 237–277.

13 The pretense toward objectivity in science stems, in part, from René Descartes' method of doubt. Through a systematic distrust of human relationality and the senses he aspired to a location for knowing in all domains of inquiry comparable to that of a mathematician. It follows from this location that human relationality is an impediment to clarity of thoughts and distinctness of ideas. For the same reason, that location represents a threat to the well-being of a "Whistle Blower" and to the good of society at large.

14 Willard Van Orman Quine: Natural Kinds. In: Hilary Kornblith (ed.): *Naturalizing Epistemology*, 2nd ed. Cambridge: MIT Press 1994, pp. 41–55.

15 Code: *Ecological Thinking*, p. 71.

challenged. The working life of women in the area of health care and biodiversity, for instance, studied by Karen Messing and Vandana Shiva respectively, are windows into the effects of standardized policies on those often most adversely affected by them. Their investigations include empirical evidence from the field of women's work that can be used to test the truth-value of the said policies and, moreover, independently of influence by such organizations as the IMF, the World Bank and Monsanto.[16] When incorporated into institutionalized forms of knowing, the work of Messing and Shiva might yield a higher degree of objectivity than can be achieved under the pretense of neutrality and the social isolationism commensurate with it. In other words, the sense of objectivity based on value-neutrality depends on marginalizing questions about the conditions under which knowledge is produced. These conditions are opened up by Quine's argument with the result that objectivity is potentially reconfigured to include an intra-subjective dialogue between those with privileged access to information and concerned citizens.[17]

This promising turn in epistemology instigated by Quine in 1969, however, undermines itself in a way that is out of sync with the political location of "Whistle Blowers" and thereby places them in a precarious situation. Although naturalized epistemology points in the direction of explaining how knowledge is situated and nestled in social-political commitments and in relation to hierarchies of power (i. e. institutions of knowledge production), it also retains dimensions of an idealized knower that undermines this trajectory as well. Quine argues that humans have an "innate flair"[18] toward classifying propositions into categories of family resemblance, and this consequently opens up space for an evolutionary account. He writes:

16 Lynette Hunter reports that relative to men, women "can be more engaged and engaged with different things. Women in science can more sharply expose its assumptions because they are not part of the prior agreements; hence they can be more objective" (Lynette Hunter: *Critiques of Knowing: Situated Textualities in Science, Computing and the Arts.* New York: Routledge 1999, p. 163). Londa Schiebinger is more specific. She highlights the distinct ways in which women acquire knowledge, including caring, holism, maternal thinking, value-contexts, and connections that are comprehensive, synthetic, cautious, careful and detailed. Londa Schiebinger: *Has Feminism Changed Science?* Cambridge: Harvard UP 1999, pp. 4–5, 10.

17 In contrast to "inter-subjectivity", which refers to an exchange of information between speakers that retain their independence from one another, "intra-subjectivity" implies that the understanding (and disposition implicated in it) of the speakers is modified not only by one another, but by an indefinite array of relations that converge and from whose coalescence understanding of a topic is formed. See "Intra-actions" an interview of Karen Barad by Adam Kleinman. In: *Mousse Magazine, Special dOCUMENTA* 13 (2012), pp. 76–81, here p. 77.

18 Quine: Natural Kinds, p. 41.

> Our experiences from earliest infancy are bound to have overlaid our innate spacing of qualities by modifying and supplementing our grouping habits little by little, inclining us more and more to an appreciation of theoretical kinds and similarities, long before we reach the point of studying science systematically as such.[19]

Whence did the innate disposition to theoretical kinds become modified over the course of time? In part, Quine is looking toward the disciplines of psychology and cognitive science for an answer. In order to know how we know what we claim to know, it is helpful to consult theories about the development of the mind from a psychological and cognitive scientific perspective. However, there is evidence of them retaining the very conditions for knowledge that represent a barrier to women and, with that, to the prospect of achieving objectivity in science. Consider the androcentric bias inherent to research by renowned psychologists. Lawrence Kohlberg's theory of moral development presupposes that autonomy and "principled moral reasoning" are the highest stage of maturation. Although this does not disqualify it, as Code points out via Carol Gilligan, the values that drive his empirical method are male-centered.[20] Even though for Jean Piaget the mind is embodied and knowing involves sensorimotor control systems, he also valorizes a male-centered perspective by modelling cognition on the autonomous instrumental "abilities to distinguish, arrange, and manipulate medium-sized physical objects".[21] Taking its cue from Quine, the naturalized epistemological movement does not so much reverse value-neutrality in science as it puts forward a smoke-screen for the perpetuation of the idealized knower, determining the outcomes of epistemic practices reflected in "logicality" and universalizing moral maxims such as autonomy privileged by both Kohlberg and Piaget. In short, the naturalized epistemological movement thus understood is denaturalized, tantamount to a variation on the same androcentric bias.

The ramification for a female "Whistle Blower" of a naturalized epistemologist moving toward and then recoiling from taking into account the unequal social conditions in which knowledge is produced is confusion and frustration. For example, on the one hand, the uniqueness of Olivieri's location relative to the idealized knowers has three dimensions: (1) she is a woman employed in a traditional man's job, (2) she selected test subjects outside the North American demographic (from the Middle East and Southeast Asia, from parents of

19 Quine: Natural Kinds, p. 50.

20 Code: *Ecological Thinking*, p. 151. See Carol Gilligan: *In a Different Voice: Psychological Theory and Women's Development*. Cambridge: Harvard UP 1993.

21 Code: *Ecological Thinking*, p. 131. See Jean Piaget: *The Language and Thought of the Child*, trans. from French by Marjorie Warden. London: Routledge & Kegan Paul 1926.

Chinese, Greek and Italian descent),[22] and (3) she was dedicated to studying the long-term effects of the drug (4.6 years) on patients outside a laboratory, with whom she had invested the time to develop a personal relationship centered on their well-being. Clearly, there were no barriers to the natural conditions of her practice stipulated by either the HSC or the University of Toronto. She had abided by the rules of being a researcher: don't lie, don't plagiarize, and report results.[23] Why, then, were the results of her experiments considered suspect? The short answer is that her experiments about the dangers of deferiprone were a threat to the financial interests consolidated in a contract between the hospital and Apotex. This is the side of the problem that is emphasized, as mentioned, by CAUT and that determines the kind of recommendations they developed to prevent similar problems from arising in the future. The preceding analysis of naturalized epistemology allows for an alternative explanation; namely, Olivieri's location defined by her gender and reflected in her practice played a role in how her practices were gauged by perspectives on standards derived from an idealized knower. The latter is evident in universalizing discourse coined in such turns of phrase as "surveys show […] experts have proved",[24] or, in the words of the climate change expert Stephen M. Gardiner, "Let us say that"[25], and "Suppose that a number of distinct agents are trying to decide whether or not to engage in a polluting activity and that their situation is characterized by the following two claims"[26]. By divesting people's words of the complex interaction of practices that differentiate people from one another, Gardiner's discourse errs on the side of being applicable to all test subjects. It follows from this train of thought that deviations from the norm, or claims from the side of the experimental sciences and fieldworkers tailored to temporal conditions outside the moral majority's horizon, will be suspect. Hence, even though there were no stipulations from the side of the hospital to prohibit Olivieri's practices, they were also outside the norm, and they could not be seamlessly translated into terms that conformed to regulatory norms. Her experimental results were inadmissibly admissible, and accepted unacceptably.[27]

22 Code: *Ecological Thinking*, pp. 241–242.

23 Schuchman: *The Drug Trial*, p. 1.

24 Code: *Ecological Thinking*, p. 97.

25 Stephen M. Gardiner: A Perfect Moral Storm: Climate Change, Intergenerational Ethics and the Problem of Moral Corruption. In: *Environmental Values* 15 (2006), pp. 397–413, here p. 398.

26 Ibid., p. 400.

27 Other instances of the same incoherent logic are as follows: due to Canada's changing immigration patterns, "the patient load in Dr. Olivieri's hemoglobinopathy programs grew from approximately 150 to 450" from 1986 to 1998; however, no adjustments had been made at HSC

However, room for modification of the "Whistle Blower's" situation is also created by the ways in which an instituted imaginary contends with the problem. Stated in terms of the epistemology that permitted – yet attempted to interfere with – Olivieri's research, insofar as naturalized epistemology suppresses the sociological conditions for its truth-claims (in particular those that bear upon asymmetries of power and the contributions of women to science, and persist instead to strive for value-neutrality in language and human relations), the epistemology generates consequences that function to call into question its authority. This is indicated by Apotex and Dr. Koren's conduct. With respect to Apotex, when the results of Olivieri's research suggested that long-term use of the drug deferiprone increases the risk of heart disease and early death in 39 percent of her sample population gained traction,[28] Apotex terminated the trials and moved to discontinue the drug in 1996.[29] In doing so, the drug company may have sought to protect itself from being held liable for harming patients, but its initiative took no account of those who were dependent on the drug.[30] Although distribution was resumed, the supply of the drug was irregular, and the health of some patients may have taken a turn for the worse. By desisting from wrongdoing in order to preserve a non-relational, asocial concept of good, the company created conditions for harming patients with whom Dr. Olivieri may have been working.

With respect to Dr. Koren, he was Director for Clinical Research at HSC and had negotiated the arrangement with Apotex for funding the next stage of Olivieri's research.[31] Even though he had initially agreed with her findings, while his research was subsequently being financed by Apotex, he re-analyzed the data and concluded that the drug was effective and safe.[32] His conclusions were eventually called into question when it was discovered that he had written disparaging letters to the *Toronto Globe and Mail* (1998–99) about Olivieri and her associates.[33] He had attacked her professional status, competency and

to reflect the increased demands on her time, energy and resources. Over the course of a year and a half, her medical questions about the decentralisation of the Sickle Cell Disease program at the HSC lowering the quality of patient care were not answered (Thompson / Baird / Downie: *The Olivieri Report*, pp. 225–226). However, they were not rejected either.

28 Code: *Ecological Thinking*, p. 202.

29 Thompson / Baird / Downie: *The Olivieri Report*, p. 5.

30 See ibid., p. 151.

31 Ibid., p. 4.

32 Ibid., pp. 6–7.

33 See ibid., p. 397.

reputation.[34] However, these letters were also anonymous. This suggests that he was attempting to remove himself from a situation while nevertheless being manipulative. By presupposing he was above the law, and acting for the sake of an abstract concept of good that exempted him from taking responsibility for his actions, Koren harmed his colleague and his public reputation.

To recapitulate, when the truth of the matter is framed in universalizing terms abstracted from a situation, well-intentioned people might harm responsible citizens without recognizing it. Robert M. Figueroa and Gordon Waitt tell of a naïve adventurer named Mike who did not see anything wrong with trampling over the Aboriginals' sacred rock known as Uluru. He thought that he had communed with the "indigenous" person in everyone by using a sort of new age spiritual energy.[35] If he were confronted by the people native to the land, he might well have lobbied to have them resettled for obstructing everyone's right to enjoy Australian National Parks. Not unlike the mentality of actors in the Olivieri affair, his orientation toward a detached and abstract concept of the good justified harming others without any cognizance of having done so. In a similar vein, although the *The Olivieri Report* includes recommendations about how to protect the public from a conflict of interest when it comes to disclosures detrimental to funding agencies, it was not considered a resolution to the problem for Olivieri. After the affair with Apotex and the HSC, she remained pessimistic about the prospect of resolving larger issues of public responsibility.[36] Her conclusions were justified. Rather than acknowledge the limits of results generated in ideal laboratory conditions, administrators at HSC rejected the results of her fieldwork. Rather than investigate how her gender may have played a role in explaining the reactions of stakeholders toward her and her claims, CAUT bypassed this question altogether. These oversights that pertain to working conditions – with which many women are intimately acquainted – and to the dignity of women in the workplace suggest that the ground motive for them is androcentrism as expressed in the work of Quine, Kohlberg, Piaget and the idealized knower, as well as in the complicated reactions of Apotex and Koren to the Olivieri case. However, in the course of undermining itself, the socially instituted imaginary creates a space for the "Whistle Blower" to transform the negative aura into epistemologically and morally desirable outcomes.

34 Ibid., p. 399.

35 Robert Melchior Figueroa / Gordon Waitt: Climb: Restorative Justice, Environmental Heritage, and the Moral Terrains of Uluru-Kata Tjuta National Park. In: *Environmental Philosophy* 7 (2010), pp. 135–163, here p. 152.

36 Code: *Ecological Thinking*, p. 249.

Possessing a sense of objectivity that depends on being intellectually and socially detached from the complexity of a situation is not entirely sound, because its proponents are unaware of the conditions and effects of their judgments. The Olivieri affair exemplifies the morally dubious consequences of reactions that flow from agents who believe that distance and detachment best afford them an understanding of a particular situation. A viable response to the problem has been developed by Code, but it is also constrained by her focus on structures. In "Toward Democratic Epistemic Practices", she aims to offset the excesses, to which savants insulated from understanding the effects of their actions are prone, with the "standpoint theory".[37] She concurs with Figueroa and Waitt's notion of "restorative justice" and aims to bring together parties that the socially instituted imaginary is designed to separate from one another, to incorporate a medley of voices into a "face to face" dispute resolution process, and to transform "victims" into participants.[38] Toward this end, Code mentions including such avenues for mediation between an instituted imaginary and the public in newspaper reports, panels of ordinary citizens and the testimony of those adversely affected by generalized rules and regulations.[39] While her proposals for democratizing epistemic practices normally controlled by a socially instituted imaginary go a long way toward redeeming the position of the "Whistle Blower" from its pitfalls, they are, however, directed toward re-arranging the procedures for dealing with others, or with "the Other" (i.e. a "Whistle Blower"). What about "Whistle Blowers" themselves? What is required of them to ensure the results of these democratic practices are successful? Is there a capacity of character and cognition that they require in order to be heard that is analogous to the humility and shame Code expects of the socialized tier of the instituted imaginary? She is not explicit about it and instead alludes to the capacity for tact in her interpretation of Olivieri's relation to the public in the media.

Tact is the art of understanding; it is the capacity to find common ground between otherwise contradictory points of view and weave harmony between them while respecting their differences.[40] It seems to have a place in feminist

37 Hunter writes of "standpoint theory": "It asks, could you do science differently if you did not erase those people outside the institutional representation? And if so, how would you do it differently?" (Hunter: *Critiques of Knowing*, p. 163.)

38 Figueroa / Waitt: Climb, p. 140.

39 Code: *Ecological Thinking*, pp. 271, 273.

40 My reading of tact is informed by Hans-Georg Gadamer. Rather than being a knack for feeling one's way around in one's discipline, I see tact as being the art of striking a mean between two extremes that are in a dialectical tension thereby harmonizing them with one another. This interpretation is based on Gadamer's criticism of Hermann von Helmholtz's version of tact (which

philosophy. Code alludes to the notion when she refers to negotiating reciprocity between knowledge and subjectivity,[41] between medical and experiential knowledge.[42] Maria Lugones presupposes that the notion of tact is at work when she refers to people moving between the tension between "dehumanisation" and "the creative activity of be-ing".[43] These characterisations of moving polarised structures whose interaction forms a fecund interval in which a "Whistle Blower" finds herself located in democratic epistemic practices are, however, limited. Characterizations are best grasped in a specific situation such as that afforded by media images of Olivieri.

The changes in the media images of Olivieri attest to her capacity to work constructively with a public perception of women that was skewed and required an antidote. The male-inflected perspective on her predicament is splashed across the 1998 cover page of *Elm Street*. Next to the sexualized image of Olivieri are the headlines, "The Ultimate Shopaholic", "Sorceress of The Skin", "Holiday Hors D'Oeuvres" and "Dressed to Party".[44] These suggestive titles about the commercial pliability of superficial floozies are complemented by a svelte lady, attired in black clothes with hot red lipstick to match her beach blonde hair. Her randy posture and cocksure tilt of the head say it all. The office she holds is at best an ornament to her feminine allure. This image on the cover of *Elm Street* is in marked contrast with another published two years later in the *Toronto Globe and Mail* in which Dr. Koren is pictured "in a normal professional posture".[45] He is a kindly, trusted doctor; she is a defiant woman. This perspective on a female scientist relative to her male colleagues corresponds to the bivalent either/or exclusivity of value-neutral reasoning ("logicality"). Why, then, did Olivieri cooperate with the photographers for *Elm Street* and turn herself into a

is directed against Johann Wolfgang von Goethe's capacity to find wholeness of meaning where others focused on parts) and on the unwritten dialectic that structures Gadamer's hermeneutics, which I infer from his interpretation of Plato and Aristotle. For his criticism of Helmholtz on tact see Gadamer: *Truth and Method*, 2nd rev. ed., trans. from German by Joel Weinsheimer / Donald G. Marshall. New York: Continuum 2004, p. 5. The dialectical structure of Gadamer's thinking is disclosed in his approach to interpretation, e.g., of Aristotle in relation to Plato. He traces it to Plato in his essay Plato's Unwritten Dialectic. In: Id.: *Dialogue and Dialectic: Eight Hermeneutical Studies on Plato*, trans. from German by Peter Christopher Smith. New Haven: Yale UP 1980, pp. 124–155.

41 Code: *Ecological Thinking*, p. 103.

42 Ibid., p. 114.

43 Maria Lugones: Toward a Decolonial Feminism. In: *Hypatia: A Journal of Feminist Philosophy* 25 (2010), pp. 742–759, here p. 754.

44 See Code: *Ecological Thinking*, p. 255.

45 Ibid., p. 253.

product of the hegemonic social imaginary?[46] It is not clear that she did. Code describes Olivieri's kerfuffle as follows: She had "to navigate across a narrow range of options. She [had] to defy, evade, refuse, ignore, exploit, or reconfirm stereotypes, either of acquiescent or of out-of-control femininity".[47] In contrast to Miriam Schuchman, whose interpretation of Olivieri's emotional state and behaviors is from an androcentric-outsider perspective where Olivieri is said to be erratic, unpredictable and impulsive,[48] Code understands, in the words of Lynette Hunter, that "the real" is messy and "snarled in the nets of the living".[49] Accordingly, Olivieri did and did not cooperate with the male chauvinism of the hegemonic social imaginary. Rather than rebel and reject the latter outright, which is a behavior typified by men whose self-esteem has been damaged, she positioned herself between the "colonizer" and the "colonized", between the medical establishment and her patients, between forces of dehumanization and humanity. From that medial location, she could direct attention to her claims from within and out of the imaginary, and thereby entice people to respond to her location. Indeed, this came to pass. Three years after the *Elm Street* photographs were published, she was seen in a more appropriate venue for her story, the *Ottawa Citizen* (2001), wherein she was portrayed as a plain and simple doctor.[50] This is the achievement of tact that Olivieri inadvertently refers to when she valorizes both courage and grace in the same breath while speaking to graduates at Simon Fraser University in 2006.[51] Her message is bold and perhaps unsettling for graduates willing to lend an ear; during her speech, she quotes Iris Murdoch, explaining that at crucial times in life what we decide is decided for us by how we have lived. On this view, ethics is prior to epistemology and this is why Olivieri posed a threat to the administrative, academic, scientific and corporate factors in Toronto that moved in tandem against her.

We do not often suppose that knowledge is informed, shaped and at times determined by social practices. Naturalized epistemology is a window into this

46 I am consulting Code: *Ecological Thinking*, p. 258.

47 Ibid.

48 Schuchman's depiction of Olivieri is skewed in the middle paragraph of page 15 of *The Drug Trial*. She sees her as being an unruly seductress (ibid., p. 16), "high strung", "hyper" (ibid., p. 18) and in need of a lot of reassurance (ibid., p. 51) rather than vibrant, strong, passionate about her work and twisted by the insensitivity of the hospital and Apotex to her vocation – the well-being of her patients.

49 Hunter: *Critiques of Knowing*, p. 3.

50 Code: *Ecological Thinking*, p. 263.

51 Dr. Nancy Olivieri's Honorary Degree Acceptance Speech in 2006 at Simon Fraser University. https://www.youtube.com/watch?v=yxIaQXSWs6E (accessed 24.01.2016).

possibility but has also shown itself to be constrained by an insufficient reflection on the gender bias inherent to sciences that purport to be neutral with respect to values, situations and practices. Olivieri's case shows that institutionalized forms of knowledge that claim to be detached from the complexity and messiness of situations tend to be androcentric, and that in the course of attempting to include the voice of the other in their decisions, they assert procedural norms that not only distort those voices, but that also stray into behaviors and speech that transgress the laws of a civil society. Harassment and credibility deflation have been used to push citizens dedicated to the public good toward the margins of their own profession. By retelling their stories, a scope is created for checking and correcting the tendency to presume that institutions vested with a mandate to serve the public good are capable of fulfilling it. Democratic epistemic practices as explained by Code are required. However, her vision is centered on structures rather than on the art of negotiating actual problems. As evinced by Olivieri and many women who quietly continue to manage entrenched prejudices in institutions that claim to be free of them, there is good reason to critically reflect on how the sciences can become value-laden nests of subterfuge and injustice by overlooking the ways in which the production of knowledge is gendered.

Sinti and Roma, Stereotypes, and Violence

The Violence of Knowledge in Practices Toward Roma in the Czech Republic

The Historical Echo of Surveillance During Socialism[1]

Victoria Shmidt

There are few explanations of why the Roma were segregated in socialist Czechoslovakia, and this lack of understanding is a considerable obstacle when attempting to prevent such discrimination and aggression; placement into residential care, eviction, sterilization, and the forced removal of children from their families are but some examples of violence that once plagued the Roma in Czechoslovakia. This text discusses the connection between the procedures that limit the Roma people's rights and the arguments in favor of such limitations, which are formulated within the matrix of institutionalized violence. Today, human rights activists focus on changing procedures that regulate access to welfare and struggle to remedy organizational flaws that foster institutional violence,[2] but developing alternatives to these procedures also challenges the ways Roma are perceived and the social practices directed at them. The *pro et contra* arguments matter – especially in the case of a long history of disempowerment as experienced by the Roma in the Czech lands.

Whether the socialist policy toward Roma was part of a consistent plan for segregation or just a 'bad shot' in attempting to integrate them is a hotly debated topic. In 2007, the case of D.H. v. Czech Rep divided the European Court of Human Rights judges into two camps – the majority had agreed that the placement of Roma children into special schools should be defined as segregation, but four judges disagreed and highlighted the necessity to take into account historical contexts, demonstrating perhaps the intention to solve the issue of educating

1 The research was sponsored by Közép-Európai Egyetem (CEU), the International Visegrad Fund and the Grant Agency of the Czech Republic, as part of the project "Child welfare discourses and practices in the Czech lands: the segregation of Roma and disabled children during the nineteenth and twentieth centuries" (GA15-10625S).

2 Carmelo Danisi: How Far Can the European Court of Human Rights Go in the Fight Against Discrimination? Defining New Standards in Its Nondiscrimination Jurisprudence. In: *International Journal of Constitutional Law* 9,3–4 (2011), pp. 793–807; Mathias Möschel: Is the European Court of Human Rights' Case Law on Anti-Roma Violence 'Beyond Reasonable Doubt'? In: *Human Rights Law Review* 12,3 (2012), pp. 479–507.

Roma children. It is reasonable to agree with those who do not see segregation and placement into special schools as one and the same thing, but those who aimed to prove that segregation was based on statistical data (i. e. the amount of Roma children placed in boarding schools for the mentally disabled, which was a key topic in the D. H. case) could not provide a comprehensive analysis of the transformation of special education into a controlling surveillance tool. What, then, made such practices agents of segregation? Discussing the socialist policy regarding Roma can answer this question.

Methodology and Data

In line with the concept of violence of knowledge, which is used "to subjugate and control [...] material bodies"[3], this article investigates how the (re)production of knowledge about 'Others' and the abuse of such knowledge in professional practices are intertwined in the Roma's case. There are three forms of violence relevant to this topic: (1) *the violence of essentialization*, (2) *epistemic violence*, and (3) *the violence of apprehension*,[4] all of which recognize the diverse links between knowledge and its usage in institutional violence. The professionals who (re)produce these forms of knowledge become 'gatekeepers' who either launch violence or warn against it. Grouping various forms of potential violence maps the options that scholars and practitioners can choose to revise their own research approaches on the subject.

Understanding the risk of essentialization (i. e. multiplying prejudices from one common essential trait) prompts professionals to emancipate the obvious connection between universal theories based upon ahistorical labels from the theorization of stereotypes. In the Czech lands, the history of Roma includes several stages of essentialization. They are linked to particular individuals like František Štampach (1895–1969), who published his first book in 1933 about the Roma and their way of life, stressing their resemblance to the lowest castes in India.[5] He remained a key expert on the 'Roma issue' during the Protectorate and the socialist period. The other prominent figure, František Ludvik (1908–1974), applied the concept of special care (*zvláštní péče*) to Roma children as those who should be isolated from the negative influences of their families and

3 Edward Said: *Orientalism*. New York: Pantheon 1978, p. 17.

4 Jeffrey Guhin / Johnathan Wyrtzen: The Violence of Knowledge: Edward Said, Sociology and Post-orientalist Reflexivity. In: Julian Go (ed.): *Political Power and Social Theory: Postcolonial Sociology*. Bradford: Emerald Insight 2013, pp. 231–262.

5 František Štampach: *Dítě nad propastií. Dítě toulavé, tulácké a cikánské, jeho záchrana, výchova a výučba* [Child under Chasm. Nomadic, Migrant and Gypsy Child, Its Education and Upbringing]. Plzeň: Nakladatelství Marie Lábkové 1933, p. 15.

communities. The arguments in favor of an essentialist vision of the Roma shifted from a biological view to a social one. In 1933, Štampach substantiated his skeptical view regarding the integration of Roma, saying in 1953 that "the law of nature is stronger than the law of the state"[6]; he put forward the law of social development, describing the Roma as having the "unenviable position of a backward community"[7]. During Czechoslovakia's socialist period, the intensive developments in care professions and in the social sciences put pressure on previous essentialist concepts and their theorizations – exploring this trend is a primary focus of this article.

The Roma were undoubtedly isolated from the opportunity to produce knowledge about themselves and to describe their experiences. "Epistemic violence" included not only blocking the right to be heard, but also the consistent alienation of the Roma from their language and culture in favor of more 'progressive' lifestyles. The resistance of socialist scholars to this oppression was marginal. Epistemic violence affected and was affected by essentialization. The Roma were unable to participate in developing concepts alternative to essentialistic attitudes, and they were reeducated to resemble the Czechs as much as possible, especially in contrast to their previous lives. Moreover, the arguments in favor of preventing the Roma from producing knowledge stemmed from labelling them as ignorant or deceitful. From a retrospective analysis of socialist policies, the Roma's supposed lack of trustworthiness had, until now, prevented their involvement in producing knowledge.

Both essentialization and epistemic violence occur when certain ideas or knowledge pose a purported risk to the future, and both forms of violence enforce harsh measures in the interest of preventing asocial behavior; Roma children were removed from their families to be socialized, and Roma women were sterilized for being poor. The "violence of apprehension" resonates with the forced assimilation and its core practice: to separate children from their parents.[8] Nevertheless, by the end of the socialist period, the separation of Roma children from their families led to their separation from mainstream society, as well. They remained the majority of students in special schools, especially in the two regions with the highest density of Roma populations: the Northern Czech region and Northern Moravia. Such an obvious deviation from the policy's

6 Ibid., p. 41.

7 Svaz českých spisovatelů: Zápis porady o cikánské otázce a o prvních úkolech v jejich řešení ze dne 29. Srpna 1953 [Gypsy Issue and Primary Tasks Toward Its Solution: The Meeting's Minute, August 29, 1953]. Národní archiv, Praha, SIG. 31.

8 Nira Yuval-Davis: *Gender and Nation*. London: Sage 1997.

intentions calls for revising the links between institutional violence, surveillance and segregation.

Historical analysis remains the key method for establishing connections between institutional violence and pseudo-scientific universal theories.[9] This connection is still glossed over in many studies about the segregation of the Roma in Czechoslovakia. In this article, however, we look at the Roma's socialist past as "the scene of losses that may be narrated as well as of specific possibilities that may conceivably be reactivated, reconfigured, and transformed in the present or future"[10]. The timeline of our analysis consists of four periods:

1. the establishment of the socialist discourse regarding Roma and their assimilation in 1948–1958 through the debates of experts and public campaigns;
2. the formation of surveillance procedures for the Roma during 1958–1968, leading to decentralization;
3. the professionalization of surveillance and care professionals' intensive involvement with the Roma between 1968–1978;
4. the ghettoization and universalization of practices that isolated the Roma from mainstream society during 1978–1989.

By juxtaposing two methods, archival research and oral histories, we aim to reconstruct the multi-level nature of the contemporary policies and practices regarding the Roma. Gathering and exploring archives (e. g. the National Archive in Prague, the State Regional Archive in Karlovy Vary, and the Open Society Archives (HU OSA) in Budapest) assisted in reconstructing and reaffirming the historical reality of the problem, and the authentic experiences of certain professionals and Roma involved in the conflict were obtained.[11] Two professionals (a social worker and a psychologist) who worked directly with Roma during the socialist period, as well as three Roma people who experienced various socialist policies, shared their stories – they were recruited as experts for evaluating the hypotheses stemming from the outcomes of archival research. The narratives provide an understanding of how discourses and procedures, when combined, can deploy institutional violence.

9 Michael Billig: *The Hidden Roots of Critical Psychology: Understanding the Impact of Locke, Shaftesbury and Reid.* London: Sage 2008; Kenneth Gergen: Social Psychology as History. In: *Journal of Personality and Social Psychology* 26,2 (1973), pp. 309–320, here p. 312.

10 Domenick LaCapra: *Writing History Writing Trauma.* Baltimore / London: Johns Hopkins UP 2013, p. 49.

11 Shoshana Felman / Dori Laub: *Testimony: Crises of Witnessing in Literature, Psychoanalysis, and History.* New York: Routledge 1992.

1948–1958: The Continuity of Discourses Toward the Disempowerment of the Roma

In the first decade of socialism, Roma policy lacked coherence. The previous policy toward enforced assimilation was seen as discriminatory and as leading to the Roma's extermination. The socialist discourse opposed the previously hostile attitude toward the Roma typical of the First Republic, the Protectorate and the Third Republic. In communist propaganda, the Roma were seen as the communists' "best friends",[12] and different camps of professionals competed in their agenda regarding Roma. The main difference was their attitudes toward assimilation, which was seen as an acceptable strategy. Those who continued to advance assimilation were eminent experts from the interwar period. In order to link their experience with the new Communist approach, František Štampach and František Ludvik offered to look at the 'Gypsy issue' through the lens of the Pavlovian approach, since "primitive prehistoric forms of behavior are still typical of them [the Roma]"[13]. The other camp relied on Stalinist principles toward small ethnic groups (*maly narody*). The culture and language were accepted as key tools for establishing sustainable positive relations with the Roma, which is now defined as *pospolitost*, a community without any consistent feature of national group:

> In order to improve the involvement with the Roma, we need to use their language. All who work with the Roma must learn the Roma language and try to get Roma as providers of new values. We need to demonstrate to the Roma their own past and traditions, and persuade them that through their customs they exist in a previous stage of human history.[14]

Despite the difference in attitude toward Roma language and culture, both camps shared the vision of the Roma as a group far behind progressive social development. Both highlighted the impact of education on improving the Roma way of life. Even more, those who embraced the Roma language and culture warned against establishing "Roma" schools as a potential risk for increasing nationalism amongst Roma. The socialist experts agreed that the Roma were a heterogeneous community without any attributes of a modern nation – even they talked about them in plural, yet nationalistic ways.[15] The hegemonic collectivity of the 'white' progressive majority responsible for the integration of the backward Roma minority replaced the previous simplistic opposition of 'Czech

12 Z diskusie o národnostej politike [About Nationalist Policy]. In: *Rolnické noviny*, 05.05.1956.

13 Svaz českých: Zápis.

14 Ibid.

15 Michael Billig: *Banal Nationalism*. London: Sage 2010.

vs. Gypsy'. The universal inclusiveness of such a scenario misled not only the Roma, but the general public, too.

The most consistent message to the public was to differentiate the attitudes of the "good, socialized" and "not yet integrated" Roma because of "their incredibly low cultural [...] level".[16] The Roma who began a new life according to Communist ideals were consistently opposed to those "backward creatures" who "aggravated the reputation of Gypsy people through their irresponsible behavior".[17] Such a categorization aimed to increase tolerance among the white majority toward 'the Gypsies'; apparently, not all Roma were seen as hopeless. The main public expectation was that that reeducated Roma would become mediators between mainstream Czech society and the rest of the Roma:

> Gypsies should work in their own way as educators amongst others. We need to give them such opportunity even if we have to accept the inevitable decrease of the professionalism of such educators. But due to obvious difficulties in finding proper *white* teachers we should choose this option.[18]

Remarkably, in the 1953 propaganda film *My friend Fabian* (*Můj přítel Fabian*), filmmaker Jiri Weiss told the story of two Roma, father and son, whose integration was directly linked with the reeducation of the Czech majority about a more tolerant attitude. Even the central argument in the movie aligned with the official discourse, and there were no other Roma characters except two men highly motivated to integrate into mainstream socialist life of the Czech people.

The policies about the Roma mirrored the inconsistency of the experts' positions. The Ministry of Internal Affairs issued a resolution for preventing discrimination against the Roma in 1952, and local authorities were under pressure to meet this objective. However, there were no departments other than the Public Prosecution and the Ministry of Internal Affairs to take the responsibility of dealing with the Roma. The local authorities' complaints during that period highlight the ambiguity of the policy: "on the one hand, we call the state security because there are no other tools. On the other hand, we are scared of being accused for discrimination".[19]

16 Naprávajme krivdu minulých režimov. K otázke likvidácie zaostalosti občanov cigánskeho pôvodu [We Redress the Injustice of the Past. About Elimination of Backwardness of the Citizens of Gypsy Origin]. In: *Pravda*, 01.10.1957.

17 Koloman Mášik: Likvidujeme jeden z neblahých pozostatkov minulosti. Na programe problém cigánskych osád [We Eliminate an Unfair Legacy of the Past: the Agenda of Gypsy Settlement]. In: *Pravda*, 20.12.1956. The quotes were translated into English by the author.

18 Ibid.

19 Svaz českých: Zápis.

The Ministry of Internal Affairs tried to organize the Roma's registration to kick start their systematic surveillance,[20] but the local authorities did not support the initiative. The placement of the Roma who broke the law in the forced labor camps also became well organized in the North of the country, where the amount of Roma had increased. The practice of placing and monitoring inmates in forced labor camps deserves special attention for its consistent two-level selection. The primary selection determined the most fitting jobs for those sentenced and included criteria like age, physical ability, social origin and reason for being placed in the camp.[21] After three months of working at the camp, the secondary selection occurred; authorities divided the inmates into three categories. Those who worked as shock workers (*udarnik*) and who were loyal and obedient had the chance to be placed in the first category, members of which were allowed to visit their families during the weekends. The second category included those who were not socialized but did not resist assimilation. The third category consisted of those who were at risk of escaping. These inmates were monitored more harshly. The Roma who fell under this category had low social statuses and had often already attempted multiple escapes. They were sent to do the hardest types of work and were not even provided with elementary occupational safety measures. The socialist mass media, however, could not keep secret the fact that six Roma workers were killed due to a tunnel collapse during construction in early August of 1956.[22] Because of such incidents, many Roma rejected going to work and tried to escape the camps, but attempts to do so never benefitted them.

Not only categorization, but the procedure of such decision making played a significant role for establishing administrative arbitrariness; both types of decisions about the Roma's placement into camps and the prescription of categories were made by a Board consisting of local Communist Party members, public security presenters and physicians. There were no options to contest the decision. Even those who introduced this system – the Ministry of Internal Affairs – were not satisfied by this obvious lack of transparency. In a few years, when the 1958 law banning the free transfer of Roma codified the discourse of the Czech

20 Tomáš Zapletal: Přístup totalitního státu a jeho bezpečnostních složek k romské menšině v Československu (1945–1989) [The Approach of Totalitarian Regime and Its Securities to the Roma Minority in Czechoslovakia]. In: *Sborník archivu bezpečnostních složek*, 10/2012, pp. 13–84, here p. 18.

21 Ministerstvo vnitra skupina I Sprava TNP Praha III, Sněmovní 1: *Situační zpráva o TBP ke dnu 31. prosince 1949* [The Current Situation Around the Camps of Enforced Labor by August 31, 1949]. Národní archiv, Praha, 4.J.1005 Taj. 50-TNP / 006.

22 Radio Free Europe: *1956 9 Gypsy Workers Killed in Collapse of Lipno Dam Tunnel.* Item 8820/56 1956. Open Society Archives HU OSA 300-30-3.

progressive majority vs. the Roma backward minority, the selection into categories and the administrative order of decision making became the universal response to the 'Roma issue'.

1958–1968: Transforming Universal Inclusiveness into Constant Surveillance

The regular practices of surveillance on the Roma were launched by the *Law about the Permanent Settlement of Nomadic People* (*Zákon o Trvalém Usídlení Kočujících Osob*, 1958). The law dictated that those who did not have permanent address be registered to and stay in their locality, and any free transfer was banned. Restrictions like imprisonment and termination of nomadic people's rights were introduced. The law defined the target group of such measures as a "particular small group of citizens who practice a backward mode of life, nomadism, avoid regular labor and offend the majority of people with criminal activities"[23]. The law asserted the primitive, collective form of community life as a main source of backwardness. Reproducing the opposition of white majority vs. Roma minority, the law suggested the dispersion of the Roma (*rozptyl*), placing one Roma family amongst the Czechs in order to isolate the Roma from the negative influence of their community. The primary task was to stop the practice of settled Roma families taking in nomadic relatives. Such cohabitation was prosecuted, as well as nomadic modes of life. The Roma started being put under surveillance and were unable to change their address or place of work without special permission. This strategy remained active between 1958 and 1989 when more than 4,000 Roma families were dispersed, although the diaspora of even more families had been planned.

The rule of dispersion also encompassed education; no more than one or two Roma children could be placed in the same group in school. The outcomes of such rules are debatable. One Roma interviewee whose family was placed into a small village in the Central part of the Czech lands in the early 1960s describes her tribulations at a mainstream school: "It was the worst period of my life. I was the only Roma there, and we lived as only one Roma family, there were no other Roma families. Because of my black eyes and dark hair, I regularly had to listen to people saying, 'A Gypsy has arrived and it's beginning to stink'."[24] Answering the question of who said it and what was done to prevent it from happening again, she continued:

23 *Zákon o Trvalém Usídlení Kočujících Osob* [The Law about the Permanent Settlement of Nomadic People], 1958.

24 Interview I. D., female, 34, Roma, social educator, born and raised in a Czech village.

> My classmate did, but the teachers just kept quiet, and never prevented such insults. One time my mum decided to stop it when I was beaten by a teacher. She went to school, but the teacher only laughed, and the principal didn't accept my mum; after that, she wrote an official complaint. The teacher stopped beating me, but she told everybody that those who complain will never participate in school performances and excursions. And I was isolated.[25]

Special boards at the regional and district levels were established as the main actors for implementing new regulations. Operating between 1958 and 1990, these boards changed their names several times. While the concept of reeducation remained the same, the description of the target groups had changed: first 'Gypsies' (*Cikans*), then 'citizens of Gypsy origin', followed by 'Roma-Gypsies'. Local boards were obligated to register the Roma by placing them on a special list and by organizing an array of activities aimed at reeducating the Roma. Two years after issuing the law, the central authorities were not satisfied with the Boards' activities, and the Roma's three-level categorization was then introduced.

Dividing Roma families into the most socialized, the moderately socialized, and the unsocialized reinforced the Boards' actions. Categorizing relied on data about the Roma's productivity, the discipline of adult family members (special attention was paid to those adults who were able to be productive yet did not work), children's school attendance, the orderliness and cleanliness of the Roma's houses and flats, and their public behavior. Employers, schools, police and other official bodies were instructed to inform the Boards regularly about the behavior of their Roma workers, students and patients. The regions even mandated that institutions fill out forms about the Roma people according to three-level categorization. For instance, schools evaluated parental care as either sufficient, mediocre or insufficient according to such indices as elementary hygienic skills, dress, and lousiness.[26] Additionally, the families of those in the third category were attended by the Boards in order to evaluate their living conditions and daily routine.

The special profiles of the Roma families were completed by the members of Boards (until social workers became responsible for that). In the local archives, it is possible to find profiles that were completed for more than ten consecutive years. The main indicator for assessing the Boards' activities was the patterns in

25 Ibid.

26 Základní škola Žlutice: *Seznam žaků ZDŠ cikánského původu a péče rodin o tyto děti* [The List of Students of Gypsy Origin and the Family Care for These Children], 1964. Státní archiv Karlových Varů, Inv. 32.

Roma families' transfers from worse to better categories.[27] According to categorical changes among Roma families, the Boards developed new plans for reeducating the Roma.

The procedures for registering and monitoring Roma did not include ceasing surveillance of those Roma who were already deemed to be reeducated. Until the early 1970s, the regulations for releasing Roma from the obligation to be registered were not developed. When one particular Roma asked for such things, the authorities rejected the request and responded apprehensively: "the person spent the major part of his life as a nomadic stranger, and there is no guarantee that after being excluded from the list, he would not start the same backward mode of life"[28].

From the very beginning, the public opinion of the Boards' activity was different from their previous optimistic beliefs about reeducating Roma:

> Reeducation is an extremely difficult and long-term task. That's why the board cannot reeducate recently settled Gypsies without the cooperation of workers at factories, the members of the local branch of the Communist Party, schools, and health care workers. The task to assimilate can be solved exceptionally by collaborative and patient efforts.[29]

Claiming to work together was not just empty rhetoric; the employers resisted the new policy and continued to employ the Roma, failing to cooperate with the surveillance system. Small enterprises (mostly construction companies) avoided monitoring the Roma, as they required their cheap labor.[30] However, the socialist authorities were interested in controlling such enterprises, especially after the liberalization of their regulations in the early 1960s. The surveillance of the Roma provided such opportunities. This conflict of interest was likely one of the reasons behind the increase in unemployment among the Roma in the second half of the 1960s.

27 Rada okresního národního výboru v Karlových Varech: *Instrukce čís. 45 Podklady pro realizace vlád. usněsení čís. 502 1965 K řešení otázek osob cikánského původu* [Guidance N 45 The Grounds for Implementing the Government's Resolution About the People of Gypsy Origin], 17.08.1966. Státní archiv Karlových Varů, Čis. Vnitř.3557 65.

28 Městský národní výbor komise pro ochranu veřejného pořádku Žlutice: *Vyjmuti ze spisu některých osob cikánského původu* [Elimination from the Surveillance List for Some People of Gypsy Origin], 21.09.1962. Státní archiv Karlových Varů, Inv. 32 Sign 052.6-K.

29 Městský národní výbor Nejdek: *Zápis ze schůze komise pro převychovu občanů cikánského původu dne 16.7.1958 (včetně zprávy o činnosti komise v roce 1958)* [The Board for Reeducating the Citizens of Gypsy Origin: Meeting's minute of 16.07.1958 including the annual report for 1958]. Státní okresní archiv v Karlových varech, Inv. 485 Sign 052.6-K.

30 Radio Free Europe: *Cooperation with Gypsies not Much Asked for.* Item 9901 1955. Open Society Archives HU OSA 300-30-3.

While Roma surveillance became more and more widespread, the social intervention around third-category families remained quite fragmented. Both the financial support and restrictions placed on the Roma were atypical of that period. Providing housing needs (the Roma's most demanded service, the majority of whom lived in extreme poverty) was short-lived because of the general crisis in the construction industry, which ended up being one of the main economic challenges for Czechoslovakia until the mid-1970s. The economic crisis also remained the core obstacle for not only developing a benefits system, but establishing institutional systems for the Roma. It is thus reasonable to conclude that their assimilation strategy corresponded with their limited resources, and between institutions' failures to monitor Roma and their fragmented responses, the practitioners who sought to assimilate the Roma became irritated.

The Boards received several requests from practitioners (especially educators) calling for more consistent interventions with Roma children and their families. The main message was to isolate the Roma from the majority. In 1962, the educators at a school in Nejdek, Northern Czech region, asked local authorities to place Roma girls into a special institution because of their premature sexual activity and the total lack of parental control over them. It is easy to recognize the violence in the arguments provided by the practitioners in favor of the girls' segregation:

> [T]he majority of Gypsy girls start their sexual lives at 12–13 years old and they do not accept it as immoral behavior – even their parents do not. How many children would they have by the time they are 30? What will these children bring to our socialist society? We call for advice: should we accept it? Could we place these girls into a special setting in order to limit the negative influence of their family space?[31]

The local authorities reprimanded the educators with socialist rhetoric: "such attitudes of panic cannot be disseminated even when you run into serious problems," they said, and the issue of how to assimilate the Roma and help them adopt new lifestyles still remained.[32]

By the end of the 1960s, Czechoslovak authorities started taking into account the local practices aimed at limiting Roma's access to social facilities, mainstream

31 Základní devítiletá škola v Nejdku (1963). *Dopis školské komisi při MěNV Problémy s dětmi cikánského původu* [The Letter to the Board for Reeducating the Citizens of Gypsy Origin. The Problem with the Children of Gypsy Origin], 1962. Státní archiv v Karlových Varech, Inv. 753 Sign 104 1-A.

32 Městský národní výbor Nejdek: *Odpověď na dopis základní devítileté školy* [The Response to the Letter by the School Administration], 1962. Státní archiv v Karlových Varech, Inv. 753 Sign 104 1-A.

schools and social benefits. The main reason for such changes was the significant policy change to a family-oriented strategy: the state generously increased the benefits for the families with more than three children, allowing women to take maternity leave and give birth to their next child just two years after the previous child's birth. The Roma families became the target group for receiving these benefits.

One of the most prominent cases was to legalize the practice of stopping parental benefits for the Roma, whose children did not attend school regularly. Some regions adopted this practice in the early 1960s and reported its efficiency to the prosecutor:

> [W]e offer only one last possible measure – not to pay parental benefits if the children do not meet their obligation to attend school while the parents do nothing. There is a particular difference between the children who regularly attend school and achieve academic gains and those who avoid education. We get totally different kinds of people![33]

The General prosecutor officially recommended the implementation of this measure more consistently in all regions. The central newspaper, *Pravda*, published an article by Jiri Špiner entitled "Illiteracy is on the way. Skip it!"[34] that demanded this norm be made into law. The 1966 law concerning consequences resulting from neglectful parental care *(Zákon o Některých Důsledcích Zanedbání Péče o Děti č. 177/1966)* introduced such relevant changes. Remarkably, the legal grounds for blocking parents' access to benefits included more reasons than a mere lack of school attendance: addiction to alcohol, criminal activity of any type and any behavior threatening the moral education of the child.

This legal approach reverberated with the increasing pressure for mothers to be solely responsible for their children's conduct. The Boards' reports regarding the third category of Roma families highlighted this trend: "the children are dirty and neglected; the mother lacks the energy to care for six children"[35]. The Boards stressed that Roma women neither worked nor cared for their children, and instead used kindergarten to do those jobs; they displaced their parental obligations on relatives who did not gain their trust. In such cases, the decision to remove children and place them into institutions was seen as a plausible solution. One instance is described as follows: "her oldest daughter lives with her

33 Ředitelství 4. národní školy v Děčině III Staré město Březova ul. 17027: *Dopis ředitele školy 1964* [The Letter of the School Principal 1964]. Národní archiv, Praha, SIG. 31.

34 Jiři Špiner: Negramotnost na postupe. Dokedy? [Illiteracy Is on the Way. Skip it?]. In: *Pravda*, 23.07.1966.

35 Městský Národní výbor Nová Role: *Péče o cikánské obyvatelstvo* [The Care for Gypsy People]. Státní archiv v Karlových Varech, Inv. 383 Sign 561.

friend and the younger son, but the mother does not work at all; we will make all efforts to place the children into institutions"[36]. In the 1960s, such decisions required a lot of work not only due to the resistance of the authorities who were devoted to their assimilation strategy, but also due to the legalities of removing and limiting parental rights. But during the next era, the professionalization of interventions regarding the Roma replaced the legal order by employing administrative measures provided by professionals, and this system made such decisions easier.

1968–1978: The Professionalization of Surveillance

The next period characterizing the policies toward the Roma can be referred to as the period of the helping professions: in 1968, the Ministry of Labor and Social Affairs was restored after more than thirteen years of absence, and social work with Roma families was debated among the officials who were responsible for the 'Roma issue'. Institutionalizing and professionalizing social work with Roma was a direct response to the challenges of new family policies. By focusing on two priorities – the quantity and quality of the population – the Czechoslovakian authorities could more tactfully assist Roma families with more sophisticated measures and more qualified individuals: care professionals. The reliable, first-category Roma families were treated like the 'white majority'. A Roma interviewee, whose family was respectable and comprised a completely integrated household, shared her history of hormonal therapy because she was unable to get pregnant: "I started getting worried after my seventeenth birthday – all around me people had children, and it was by chance that I met a sensitive, sympathetic gynecologist. She first asked me if I had a boyfriend with whom I would like to have children, and eventually, my body actually responded to her treatment."[37] The less socialized, however, became the object of new, tougher strategies aimed at decreasing their natality.

In 1973, two special resolutions established the framework for sterilization. In January, the Ministry of Health issued a resolution about sterilization that established the following key criteria: high risk of giving birth to a "defective" child or high risk that the child would live in "defective"[38] conditions (e.g. bad

36 Ibid.

37 Interview D. R., female, 46, teacher, was born and grew up in ghetto, Roma.

38 Směrnice Ministerstva zdravotnictví České socialistické republiky č. 1/1972 O provádění sterilizace [The Resolution of the Ministry of Health of the Czech Socialist Republic about Implementing Sterilization No. 1/1972]. Věstník MZ ČSR, 19.11.1971.

housing conditions, overly large family, parents with a history of criminal activity), which was congruent with the indices used to describe the third category of Roma families. Both criteria could be seen as an example of the violence of apprehension – not an actual risk, but a possible one became a sufficient reason for sterilization. In October, the supplementary resolution introduced the regulations for repayment for those who were sterilized. However, the amount was not fixed but was to be agreed upon according to "the number of children in the family and number of days spent by the person in hospital in order to compensate the absence of the parent"[39]. There was not only one measure aimed at reducing the number of undesirable children among the Roma; they also received hormonal contraception free of charge, as well as permission to have abortions. The regulation of Roma natality became an aspect of family intervention and the core activity of social workers. In some regions with smaller number of Roma, increasing the number of those who started to use hormonal contraception and decreasing the number of abortions and sterilizations was seen as an undoubtedly positive indicator, while in others (Northern Moravia and Northern Czech region) the increase of sterilization remained an expectation of authorities from social workers.

From the very beginning, social workers were obliged to solve several tasks that would nowadays be connected with case work: regularly tend to Roma families, provide connections between Roma families, health care institutions, employers and educational centers, and manage services catered to intervening with the Roma. While the total number of social workers working with the Roma in 1970 was a mere 14 (and in three regions there were no social workers at all), by the end of 1971 this number had increased more than ninefold. 2,000 Roma families were under the intensive control of social workers (who visited homes more than once a month) by 1978. These families mostly required more financial support and monitoring: "partner is in prison; she is pregnant again without sustainable income, all our savings are spent, she is a former student of a children's home in Nova Role [an institution for children with mental disabilities – V. S.], and her immediate family is third-category with 8 children"[40]. Also, social workers completed the forms for more than one third of all Roma families by the end of the 1970s.

39 Ministerstvo práce a sociální věcí: *Zásady pro poskytování příspěvku při sterilizací (zneplodnění)* [The Main Principles for Paying the Benefit for Those Who Have Been Sterilized]. Národní archiv Praha, Ze dne 30. září 1973 č.j. IV/1-8750.

40 Městský Národní Výbor Nová Role: *Péče o cikánské obyvatelstvo 1977–1988* [The Care for Gypsy People]. Státní archiv v Karlových Varech, Inv. Číslo 383 Sig. 561.

The authorities reported the social work's success with families and noted that for every hundred Roma families, there were 0.4 social workers. Social workers made decisions about parental benefits, limitations on parental rights (e.g. by preparing arguments for judges) and removing children from families. They were also obliged to persuade Roma women to use hormonal contraception and consider sterilization: "we were trained and have a manual with pictures; the trainers told us that there are not any consequences for the... you know... relationship. We were taught to persuade men, too, but when I tried to use it with one Cikan, his wife came next day, and she threatened to beat me"[41].
Risks and threats remain salient in the memories of those who worked with the Roma, although professionals do distinguish the responsible and grateful Roma from those who were described as "dreadful and horrible"[42] and posed threats to others. Such risks often accompanied stories about attempts to assist the Roma. Another interviewee described his students' failed attempt to organize training for Roma based on the Indian epos in order to encourage Roma's identity. She says,

> She did not achieve any visible results, but she shared with me that when they were together in a small house in the mountains where the training was organized [...] they just sat in their room and were drinking, and they were so drunk that they tried to rape her, and then they explained that they were just reproducing what happens in 'normal Roma' families.[43]

Demonizing the Roma is connected with the regular retraining of professionals to equip them with the 'special' skills needed to force the Roma to tell professionals the truth. "it was the purpose of our training, knowing which weak points we should play on [...] if they would not tell me the truth, they would not say it to anyone, and if I would be unable to help them then nobody would"[44]. Regarding the efficiency of training and his most successful case, a psychologist told the story of a Roma boy who was placed into an institution for young offenders:

> The first thing he said to us was that he would escape, and the principal asked me: could we accept this boy, and do we have resources to keep him or not? And we put this boy into a special space [...] in isolation, and then we took him back [...] two weeks later we were going

41 Interview with M. C., female, 73, social worker, worked in the Northern region in 1971–1990, Czech.

42 Ibid.

43 Interview with V. S., male, 75, psychologist, worked at special school in the late 1950s, Czech.

44 Interview with M. C.

> to walk in the park, and it was perfect for his escape [...] but instead I hugged the boy around his shoulders, and we ended up talking for a long, long time.[45]

Being equipped with such special knowledge, the professionals decried other non-Roma and recognized in their behavior toward the Roma either a lack of power or unfairness – obviously toward the state, not the Roma:

> I had to control 'our' people too. Gypsies got 500 crowns every month for purchasing food, and I went to the stores – asking the staff what they bought, as they were permitted to purchase only healthy things, no alcohol, no cigarettes and no sweets. The bill listed five kilos of meat, and I asked my Gypsies whether they really did buy 5 kilos, and they said that it was a small piece. The salesgirls took the meat. I came back to the shop and started an official procedure with public security and the prosecutor.[46]

Fixating on their own uniqueness in working with the Roma can partially explain the fall of the volunteer's movement, which was initiated by the authorities in 1972 in order to improve communication between the Roma minority and the Czech majority. Even though the number of volunteers increased from 22 in 1972 to 789 in 1978, their activities only consisted of irregular meetings with Roma and some elements of group work.[47]

In the 1970s, Roma group work developed more slowly than family interventions, and only 900 Roma were involved in such activities, mostly in the regions with the highest density of Roma population. At the same time, the number of social workers was the smallest in these regions. In 1978, for the first time during the span of their social work with the Roma, care professionals' fees were increased by 50–75 % for their "hard and demanding tasks".[48] Despite this, the recruitment of these professionals remained a policy issue. One social worker attributed her overwhelming work to the low motivation of others to help her do it: "I created all these leisure activities because it was very difficult to find educators who would be glad to be a part of our team – I begged them even when they received a very good fee for working with the Gypsies"[49].

45 Interview with V. S.

46 Interview with M. C.

47 Komise vlády ČSR pro otázky cikánského obyvatelstva: *Informace o činnosti odborových orgánů a organizací mezi cikánskými pracujícími* [The Information About the Activities of Local Authorities Towards Re-educating Gypsy Workers], 22.11.1979. Národní archiv, Praha.

48 Komise vlády ČSR 1979: *Zápis z 27.zasedání Komise vlády české socialistické republiky pro otázky cikánského obyvatelstva, konaného ve dnech 6.a 7. června 1979 v Mostě* [The Commission of Czechoslovakian Socialist Republic Government for Solving the Issue of Gypsy People: The 27th Meeting's Minute, July 6–7, 1979]. Národní archiv, Praha.

49 Interview with M. C.

This lack of human resources played a crucial role once the Roma population grew and when ghettoization started. The number of Roma increased from 53,585 in 1971 to 99,620 in 1978 – more than half were under the age of 15. The previous focus on individual work could not be sustained, and social workers as well as other professionals were involved in the development of large-scale strategies such as ghettoization, the placement of Roma children into residential care settings and forced sterilization.

1978–1989: Large-scale Segregation

Initially, ghettos for the Roma were described as a social experiment. They were organized in several Northern regions where half of all the Roma lived.[50] The Roma were placed into districts with new houses accompanied by a full social infrastructure that was aimed at establishing and encouraging a 'proper' way of life. Remarkably, social workers divided the Roma families into not three, but four categories in the ghettos "in order to specify the re-education plans and reasonable expectations"[51]. The adults were transported to their jobs by special buses, but the children remained in ghettos. In the early 1980s, 98 % of students at schools near ghettos were Roma, and the Roma children in ghettos were placed in special schools more often than in other regions; although the average number of Roma children who were placed in such schools was 16 %, the rates were 27.5 % and 26.2 % in the Northern Czech region and Northern Moravia respectively. The decision to transfer children was made after the first academic year. As one of them recalled, "I attended a normal school with Czechs, and I was the only one who finished it. In the first year there were three more girls, but they were removed just after the first year. For me there was no difference; Nadya wrote better than me, and in general she was not worse than me, but they removed her from our class".[52] The number of children placed into special schools from 1978 to 1989 also increased in these two regions alone. In the ghetto, the amount of Roma children who attended kindergarten was the smallest – not more than 31 %, while in some regions the number of Roma was comparable with the number of Czech children – 60 % (whereas Czech children constituted 75 %).

50 Nina Pavelčíková: *Romové v českých zemích v letech 1945–1989* [Roma People in the Czech Lands in 1945–1989]. Praha: Úřad dokumentace a vyšetřování zločinů komunismu 2004, p. 46.

51 Městský Národní Výbor v Mostě: *Péče o občany cikánského původu na území města Mostu* [The Care for the Citizens of Roma Origin in Most], 04.08.1979. Národní archiv, Praha.

52 Interview with D. R.

The authorities soon recognized the ambiguous results of ghettoization. More socialized families lived in neighborhoods close to the problematic families that caused conflicts, and at the same time, several pandemics of hepatitis B in 1978–1979 raised the issue of elementary hygiene in the ghettos. The most consistent concern was the caring of children. During this period, the new concept of "Gypsy children threatened by their environments" (*cikánské dětí ohrožené prostředím*) was introduced. The typical description of such an environment included various indicators regarding "unhealthy" lifestyles: "We tended to the family at 11:00 a.m. and nobody was cooking at that moment, but the children stayed at home and were not at school; the flat was uncleaned, the children were undressed, the father was convicted but still waiting to go to prison and lives in the flat; his sister lives with them without any registration."[53]

By the end of the 1970s, Helena Malá, a Czech anthropologist, conducted several surveys arguing for the necessity of placing Roma children into residential care institutions. Viewing Roma "backwardness" as a multiple issue, she defined the source as the blocking of their social integration, combined with the concept of social-cultural retardation transferred from generation to generation and aggravated by an "unhealthy mode of life"[54]. The authors directly determined the implementation of social norms by using a particular anthropometric profile based on the average Czech: "they [anthropometric norms] operate as the essentials for successful socialization"[55]. Contrasting anthropometric characteristics of the Roma with those of the ethnic majority, Malá differentiated Roma children between those who were raised in families and those who were raised in institutions. She noted the positive impact of residential care on the anthropometric profile of the Roma children, who were significantly not different from their non-Roma peers in contrast to those who remained at home with the families: "in their physical development, the Roma students who learn in boarding schools for a considerable length of time can be placed between their Czech

53 Městský Národní Výbor Nová Role *Péče o cikánské obyvatelstvo 1977–1988* [The Care for Gypsy People]. Státní archiv v Karlových Varech, Inv. Číslo 383 Sig. 561.

54 Helena Malá: *Problematika současného vývoje a výchovy cikánů a antropologická studie cikánských školních dětí Východočeského kraje* [The Issues of Contemporary Development and Education of Gypsies and Anthropological Studies of Gypsy Children in Eastern Czech Region]. Habilitační disertace, Karlová Univerzita, Praha, 1974. Archiv Univerzity Karlovy.

55 Helena Malá: Význam některých poznatků z vývojové antropologie cikánské etnické skupiny a jejich uplatnění ve výchovně vzdělávací práci učitelů a vychovatelů' [The Outcomes of a Developmental Anthropological Survey Conducted on Gypsy Ethnic Group: Implications for Activities of Teachers and Educators]. In: *Otázky defektologie* 3 (1985), pp. 89–95, p. 94.

peers and Roma children growing up in Roma families"[56]. Highlighting the role of anthropometric features, Malá restated the importance of parenting and directly connected the unhealthy patterns of Roma mothers during pregnancy to the problems encountered by their children in later development.[57]

Due to the modest success of the Roma's socialization and the high birth rate typical of this ethnic group (by the mid-1980s, more than 40 % of the Roma population were under 14, while children made up less than 25 % of the total population in Czechoslovakia), Malá suggested that special boarding schools should remain a long-term strategy for the socialization of the Roma children. Based on František Štampach's 1933 study, Malá arrived at the conclusion that the anthropometric indices of the Roma children became more compatible with their Czech peers – but whose standards, in turn, had changed significantly.[58]

Practitioners who should bring this strategy into practice felt apprehensive about the possible outcomes. One social worker described the obligation to remove children as the hardest part of her job:

> One nurse requested that we remove twins, about 2 years old, from a single mother; she was dumb and deaf, and the nurse's idea was that because she didn't understand anything, she couldn't care, and I passed it to the court. And I was there when the police removed the children. I never forgot how she cried and screamed. I was lucky to avoid feeling guilt, because these twins were adopted very soon by the family of the State security officer (*VB veřejná bezpečnost*). They avoided being placed into an orphanage.[59]

In 1986, Josef Štěpán, the principal of the special school for Roma children in Dětenice and one of the most important experts on the education of the Roma, asked his colleagues: "What helps the defective individual more? Segregation with further socialization in collective institution, or staying in the family with its deep mutual ties?"[60] He offered the solution: boarding schools "in an open and healthy society", which resonated with contemporary arguments in favor of transforming special education – but in socialist Czechoslovakia, it was yet another idealistic plan.

56 Ibid.

57 Helena Malá / Milena Hajnišová: Příspěvek ke sledování tělesného vývoje cikánských novorozenců okresu Kladno a Chomutov [The Report about the Physical Development of Gypsy Infants in Kladno and Chomutov]. In: *Otázky defektologie* 8 (1983), pp. 297–300, here p. 297.

58 Helena Malá: *Výchova, vzdělání a biologický vývoj cikánských děti a mládeži v ČSR* [Upbringing, Education and Biological Development of Gypsy Children and Youth]. Praha: Univerzita Karlová 1984, p. 72.

59 Interview with M. C.

60 Josef Štěpán: Perspektivy speciálního školství (diskuse) [The Perspectives of Special Schools (Debates)]. In: *Otázky defektologie* 2 (1986), pp. 44–48, here p. 47.

One Roma who had gone through four different institutions discloses his ambivalence toward his experience as a child:

> My mother was 15 when I was born, and social services supported her until I was three years old because they believed in her bond with me. But when they started thinking that she was too immature to raise me, they took me away. I was very happy before entering school. It was a good place and there were a lot of toys and games. But when I went to school, I fell ill and spent half a year in hospital. I couldn't pass the final tests, and they sent me to a special school for the mentally retarded. My disease helped – nobody knew what to do with me, because for the children with mental retardation physical activities were ranked first. They sent me to *Jedlichkův ustav*[61]. The psychologist there was extremely good. She tested me, and said to everybody that I am normal but that I need more time. I was placed into a normal school with normal children, so my disease actually saved me from being in school with imbecile children. I was in the school for the mentally retarded for only one month; they had beaten me and there were no lessons for me. And in the new school I was the healthiest amongst others, and I helped them. I think I learned to help disabled people there.[62]

By the end of Czechoslovakia's socialist period, more than 60 % of the children in infants' homes were Roma, and so were over 40 % of students in boarding schools.[63] Similar figures apply to the Northern regions, which were much higher than average. It was in Ostrava – the main city in Northern Moravia and the one with the biggest Roma ghetto – where the case of D. H. versus Czech Republic was launched in 2006.

Conclusion

Although the facts of institutional violence against the Roma had been admitted by the national government, this episode of Czechoslovakia's socialist past continues to remain marginal to public debates. In contrast to the recent yet extensive Western trend of reimbursing those who suffered through residential care, post-socialist countries like the Czech Republic still avoid addressing these parts of their pasts and even fail to provide options for those Roma who experienced residential care. The unmediated violence "may be more likely when there are no accepted modes of symbolizing difference and conflict in an effective manner

61 One of the oldest and most prestigious residential care settings for children with physical disabilities.

62 Interview with P., male, 36, educator, born and raised in the Northern Czech region, ghetto, Roma

63 Ministerstvo kultury ČSR: *Navrch zprávy o aktuálních otázkách žijících cikánských občanů* [The Draft of the Report About Current Issues Regarding Gypsy Citizens], 1985. Národní archiv, Praha.

that enables them to be addressed and, to some extent, dealt with".[64] Precisely, the intractability of practice to place Roma children into special schools, as well as the current resistance of authorities to compensate for the moral sufferings of women who were sterilized, is a clear example of this attitude. Recognizing the history of segregation can offer alternative ways to discuss the issue of violence against the Roma by those who succeeded socialist policies (such as care professionals and local authorities), as well as the Roma who needed to find ways to cope with their experience. "The main reason for viewing the Roma children as a specific group – who require very special attention in education and in growing up – is based on the significant differences in the biological, cultural, and socio-economic conditions regarding the formation of this ethnic group in contrast to the majority of our population."[65] This argument, voiced by Helena Malá in 1984, remained the most popular explanation for the system of special Roma education to this day. Special education was combined with social control of the Roma people. Despite being able to monitor reproductive patterns and limit criminal activity amongst the Roma youth, special education became the most accepted way of solving the Roma issue; this method, however, saw that Roma children would be placed into special schools and be torn from their families. Is it possible to break such a vicious cycle of injustice without a redefinition of the professional attitudes regarding the emancipation from diverse stereotypes linking childhood, ethnicity and education? The answer to this question lies still ahead of us.

64 LaCapra: *Writing*, p. 60.
65 Malá: *Výchova, vzdělání*, p. 85.

Violent Fantasies

The Persisting Stereotypes of European Roma

Biba Hadziavdic / Hilde Hoffmann

In the past few years, international organizations have reported alarming findings about the living conditions of European Roma, whose population of twelve million makes them the largest minority within the European nation-states.[1] Statistical data also show that the majority of Roma in Europe continue to face serious problems of access to academic and vocational training, respective national labor markets, medical care, adequate housing, and political representation (ERTF, UNDP, and FRA).[2] Since the early 2000s, a series of initiatives has come from various European bodies and international organizations: the EU Roma-Summit, the Decade of Roma Inclusion 2005–2015, and the EU Framework for National Roma Integration Strategies by 2020. Each shares the common goal of ameliorating the conditions that Roma face today, including combatting general anti-Romani sentiments and violence against Roma. These political measures have managed to raise awareness among the majority population about the pervasive impact of antiziganism; at the same time, they have produced no substantial improvement for Roma in Europe. The non-governmental international human rights organization Human Rights First published a Hate Crime Survey in 2008; the survey yielded alarming findings detailing violence against Roma throughout 56 countries. The report refers to "expulsion, eviction, dismantling of settlements, destruction of Roma homes and communities, to wholesale incarceration, or the deportation of Roma as a national objective";

1 Referring to the first World Romany Congress (1971), we use the term "Roma" as a collective term for an extremely heterogeneous group of people who themselves use the names Roma, Sinti, Kalderash, and so on. What this group of people has in common is how they are affected by antiziganism. Notably, there have been eight Congresses to date, the most recent taking place in Romania in 2013. Over the span of some 45 years since its inception, the achievements that have resulted directly from these meetings are vast: addressing social and cultural affairs, education, language, recognition of Roma as a national minority, genocide and reparations, and the establishment of the Nation Building Plan for the promotion of the Romani nationalism and representation. The Roma people continue to be at the forefront of the struggle against antiziganism, and are to be largely credited with continuous fight against anti-Roma sentiments and policies.

2 ERTF: European Roma and Traveller Forum (founded in 2004), UNDP: United Nations Development Program, FRA: European Union Agency for Fundamental Rights.

additionally, the report focuses on the "violent manifestations of prejudice and hatred in which private persons are responsible for hate crimes." From set fires to Molotov cocktails, the number of affected people is disheartening.[3] Our paper mainly focuses on discourse and the prevailing stereotypes that lead to manifold forms of violence, including (but not limited to) alleged nomadism, eroticized, gendered, and the nonconformist other, and the myth of music.

To clarify, "antiziganism" refers to society's dominant mindset about those known as "Gypsies"[4], as well as the stigmatization, exclusion, and persecution[5] of those people.[6] The beliefs and concepts characterizing antiziganism (e.g. Roma as nomads, unable to conform to established societal norms, petty criminals, child abductors, shoddy entertainers), which are constantly being reshaped and renewed, are core constituents of the violent phenomena of targeting and excluding Roma.[7] In order to understand the striking longevity of today's exclusionary semantics and mechanisms, one must reflect upon the function that the term "Gypsy" plays within the dominant society that continues to define and perpetuate it. It is no surprise, then, that this structure of prejudice says less about the people who are targeted by antiziganism than it does about the society that stigmatizes them.

3 http://www.humanrightsfirst.org/wp-content/uploads/pdf/fd-080924-roma-web.pdf (accessed 15.08.2016), pp. 1–3.

4 The term "Gypsy" is rejected by most Roma as discriminatory. The composition of social groups who are given this label is in flux, and is not identical with the diverse groups that identify as Roma. Independent of these shifts, many connotations of the word "Gypsy" have now been transferred to the word "Roma". As with other groups, the types of people who identify as Roma vary. As the consequences of these harmful stereotypes endure, we remain actively sensitive, transparent, and consistent with our terminology. We gauge the term "Gypsy" with acute prudence and use it only when directly citing antiziganistic texts, and on rare occasions when trying to illustrate the racial prejudice inherent to such a cultural construct.

5 Markus End / Kathrin Herold / Yvonne Robel: Antiziganistische Zustände – eine Einleitung. Virulenzen des Antiziganismus und Defizite in der Kritik. In: Iid. (eds) *Antiziganistische Zustände: Zur Kritik eines allgegenwärtigen Ressentiments*. Münster: Unrast 2011, pp. 9–22, here p. 12.

6 The ancestors of European Roma are said to have come between the 8th and 10th centuries from India and/or present-day Pakistan and travelled through Persia, Asia Minor, or the Caucasus; by the 13th and 14th centuries, they made their way through Greece and the Balkans towards Central, Western, and Northern Europe. From there, they traveled to America. Both the history of the Roma migration and the history of their living conditions in past centuries are heterogeneous.

7 There is much debate around the term "antiziganism"; various terms such as "romaphobia", "anti-romaism" or "racism against Roma" are also used. Since our focus is on the projective quality of this set of ideas, we have chosen to use "antiziganism", the term related most closely to antisemitism.

The Long History of Antiziganism in Europe

Since the seventeenth century, the representation of Roma has borne significance for German and European concepts of the self.[8] For many centuries, the imagined "Gypsy" served as a foil for self-description and differentiation in Europe's ideological history.[9] The ambivalent position is reflected in literature, art, scientific texts, and political debates.[10] This "inclusive exclusion" played a central role in the formation of European nation-states.[11] Franz Maciejewski describes the historical situation in which European societies first mention "Gypsies" in writing (which was in Germany in 1407) as a time of fundamental social change.[12] The economic transformation entailed a shift from agrarian societies to capital-based ones, and it placed strong emphasis on ideals of work and self-discipline. Cultural changes were also marked by the advent of scientific perspectives on the world. With regard to gender relations, the dominance of the patriarchy was established during this time, along with the separate public and private spheres that were respectively coded as masculine and feminine, alongside a strict moral code with regard to sexuality. The profound changes in cultural values and norms were enforced upon the individual with religious and political fervor.[13] According to Markus End, during this profound shift to capital-based nation-states, the counter-figure known as the "Gypsy" served as a means of discipline, opening a space onto which individuals of the majority

8 Even though a significant part of our research centers on Germany, it is important to note that the processes of exclusion, othering, stigmatization, and stereotyping are pan-European in nature. Starting in the 18th century, "there has been a shared space of discourse within central and eastern Europe, in which knowledge about 'Gypsies' was produced and circulated" (Herbert Uerlings / Iulia-Karin Patrut: ‚Zigeuner', Europa und Nation. Einleitung. In: Iid. (eds): *‚Zigeuner' und Nation. Repräsentation – Inklusion – Exklusion*. Frankfurt am Main: Lang 2008, pp. 9–63, here p. 40.

9 Iulia-Karin Patrut: *Phantasma Nation. ‚Zigeuner' und Juden als Grenzfiguren des ‚Deutschen' (1770–1920)*: Würzburg: Königshausen & Neumann 2014, p. 8.

10 For Literature and Fine Arts, see Klaus-Michael Bogdal: *Europa erfindet die Zigeuner: Eine Geschichte von Faszination und Verachtung*. Frankfurt am Main: Suhrkamp 2011; Patrut: *Phantasma Nation*. For anthropology, law, and politics, see Karl Hölz / Viktoria Schmidt-Linsenhoff / Herbert Uerlings (eds): *Beschreiben und Erfinden. Figuren des Fremden vom 18. bis zum 20. Jahrhundert*. Frankfurt am Main / Bern / New York: Lang 2000; Jennifer Illuzzi: Negotiating the "State of Exception:" Gypsies' Encounter with the Judiciary in Germany and Italy, 1860–1914. In: *Social History* 35,4 (2010), pp. 418–438.

11 Uerlings / Patrut: ‚Zigeuner', pp. 11–12.

12 Franz Maciejewski: Elemente des Antiziganismus. In: Jacqueline Giere (ed.): *Die gesellschaftliche Konstruktion des Zigeuners: Zur Genese eines Vorurteils*. Frankfurt am Main: Campus 1996, pp. 10–25, here pp. 12–25

13 Franz Maciejewski: Das geschichtlich Unheimliche am Beispiel der Sinti und Roma. In: *Psyche* 1 (1994), pp. 30–49, here pp. 42–49; id.: Elemente des Antiziganismus, pp. 12–25.

society could project their failed attempts to live according to prescribed values and rules.[14] The representations and stereotypes against Roma that still appear today, such as "parasitic", "indolent", "undisciplined" and "thieving" are rooted in the contemporary socio-historical processes that introduced and enforced norms and morals during the development of Europe's nation-states. During the formation of territorial states (1650–1750), so-called "Gypsies" became one of the prototypes for the early modern practice of segregation and exclusion (similar to early discrimination against Jews), and soon in most sovereign areas, people designated as "Gypsies" were no longer tolerated. Claudia Breger explains that around 1800 "Gypsies" were increasingly discussed and pictured as projections and dissociations during the collective construction of bourgeois European identity.[15] From the nineteenth century onward, policies of segregation grew harsher against the background of developing nation-states. It is with regard to the figure of the "Gypsy" that the most central essence of nationalism comes into focus. Perception of one's surroundings through a nationalist lens occurs through a binary distinction, in which the 'foreign' must be disparaged and stigmatized. This polarized thinking fixates an external enemy which one imagines as the caricature of the self-image, and without which it is difficult to define the self. Definitions of self and other do not arise independently of one another; rather they stand in a reciprocally constitutive relationship. In the history of European nationalism, as well as in current nationalist discourses of Europe, the Roma people play a special role: in them and through them, the 'Other' is constructed.

Moreover, the perpetual discrimination against Roma – throughout centuries and into the present – is facilitated by the rhetoric of Roma as nationless people, who are thereby first and foremost perceived as not-European. As there might be some individuals who indeed would associate with nation-statelessness, our emphasis in this critique will be on the general argument of the inherent nation-statelessness of Roma as "eternal wanderers", incapable of relating to the conventional lifestyle of the dominant society. It is, among others, the homogenizing feature of discourse about Roma that makes it antiziganistic. Similarly, even if some Roma might live a nomadic lifestyle (as do individuals of various other ethnicities across the world), the contention that Roma are inherently nomadic is racially prejudiced. Additionally, due to the historical circumstances associated

14 Markus End: History of Antigypsyism in Europe: The Social Causes. In: Hristo Kyuchukov (ed.): *New Faces of Antigypsyism in Modern Europe*. Prague: NGO Slovo 21 2012, pp. 7–15, here p. 10.

15 Claudia Breger: *Die Ortlosigkeit des Fremden: „Zigeunerinnen" und „Zigeuner" in der deutschsprachigen Literatur um 1800*. Köln: Böhlau 1998.

with nomadism and Roma, such as the "anti-Gypsy" laws explicitly targeting Roma's alleged itinerant way of life and trades, the issue of nomadism in relation to Roma remains a multifaceted issue that has not yet been studied in all its dimensions.

In his 1996 article "Antigypsyism in the Political Culture of the Federal Republic of Germany: A Parallel with Antisemitism?" and his 2002 book *Germany and Its Gypsies*, Gilad Margalit characterizes and exploits the cultural construct of "the Gypsy".[16] His depictions are archetypical of the scholarly perpetuation of the scientific data that marks Roma as "Gypsies".[17] A critique of Margalit's marginalization of the persecution of Roma allows us to delineate some of the general misconceptions still circulating within the Roma discourse (both in German/European and American scholarship) as it regards Roma's supposed lack of national identity. Margalit portrays "Gypsies" (his term for Roma) as "stateless", "apolitical" and "criminal nomads"; again, his characterization of Roma parallels historical, narrative and ethnographic texts, which in similar fashion typify Roma as uncivilized and uncultured. In order to show that discrimination against Roma lacks racial and religious pretext, Margalit evokes Europeans' preoccupation with the so-called romantic images of "Gypsies". The abundance and forcefulness of the "antigypsy" decrees and edicts passed by the European authorities as early as the fifteenth century – which target and limit the movement, settlement and coexistence of Roma – elucidate the politically, racially, and culturally motivated exclusion of the Roma. Margalit's emphasis on romantic imagery obscures this fact.

In *Zigeunerverfolgung in Deutschland mit besonderer Berücksichtigung der Zeit zwischen 1918–1945*, Mohammad Gharaati outlines the persecution of the Roma. According to Gharaati, the German authorities passed 148 anti-Gypsy edicts between 1500 and 1800 that prevented Roma from acquiring permanent residency and employment.[18] Decades before the rise of National Socialism, German police and various government ministries enacted laws according to which Roma residing in Germany were required to register with the police

16 The primary concentration is on Margalit's article; most of his chief ideas from the article were later elaborated in his 2002 book. Margalit's texts are a part of the discourse embedded in the long tradition of ethnology, ethnography, anthropology and sociology.

17 Gilad Margalit: Antigypsyism in the Political Culture of the Federal Republic of Germany: A Parallel with Antisemitism? In: *The Analysis of Current Trends in Antisemitism* 9 (1996), pp. 1–29, here p. 2; id.: *Germany and Its Gypsies*. Madison: University of Wisconsin Press 2002.

18 Mohammad Hassan Gharaati: *Zigeunerverfolgung in Deutschland*. Marburg: Tectum 1996, p. 32. In addition to the earliest "antigypsy" edicts, the late eighteenth and early nineteenth centuries reveal intense, politically motivated assimilation policies. See Ian Hancock: Chronology. http://www.radoc.net (accessed 15.08.2016).

and unemployment agencies in each district; they were to be fingerprinted and photographed and have their genealogical data recorded. From April to December of 1907, a few years after the establishment of the "Central Office for Fighting the Gypsy Nuisance" ("Nachrichtendienst für die Sicherheitspolizei in Bezug auf Zigeuner", in short called „Zigeunerzentrale", 1899) in Munich under the directorship of the criminal investigator Alfred Dillmann (1849–1924), there were 289 criminal cases filed against Gypsies, the majority of which, 59 cases, were for such trivial offenses as camping or driving a dilapidated car. By considering the historical data that Gharaati presents, we see how so many authors fail to reveal the mendacity inherent in the romanticized depiction of "wandering Gypsies". It is exactly due to the fact that no permanent housing, employment, and education were available to Roma that they were forced to be on the move.

The nineteenth century was the age of categorization, in large part due to the rise of anthropology as a discipline.[19] The scientific knowledge of that time was collected in a book that long exerted the most influential publication on the subject:[20] *The Gypsies: A Historical Essay on the Way of Life and Constitution, Mores and Destiny of this People and on their Origins* by Heinrich Moritz Gottlieb Grellman, published in 1783.[21] As expected, this so-called scientific perspective broadened the divide and accentuated the Roma's otherness by tracing descriptions back to fundamental differences. Based on this, a system of detection and registration developed along with a professional apparatus of persecution. Those labeled as Gypsies were increasingly stigmatized, discriminated against, and physically excluded.

As much as the historical data suggest that Roma have lived in Europe for centuries, the taxonomical description of their culture makes the debate about their nationality and the nature of their cultural production continuous and consistently animated. In the spirit of the Enlightenment, research on Roma continues to be based on observation, collection, classification, and description whereby the researcher's objectivity frequently remains unquestioned. Often, the authority of the researcher is established by an addendum of charts, tables and other

19 See Munasu Duala-M'bedy: *Xenologie. Die Wissenschaft vom Fremden und die Verdrängung der Humanität in der Anthropologie*. Freiburg / München: Alber 1977.

20 See Wolfgang Wippermann: Antiziganismus – Entstehung und Entwicklung der wichtigsten Vorurteile. In: Karl-Ulrich Templ (ed.): *„Zwischen Romantisierung und Rassismus". Sinti und Roma 600 Jahre in Deutschland*. Stuttgart: Landeszentrale für Politische Bildung Baden-Württemberg 1998. https://www.lpb-bw.de/publikationen/sinti/sinti8.htm (accessed 15.08.2016).

21 Heinrich Moritz Gottlieb Grellmann: *Die Zigeuner. Ein historischer Versuch über die Lebensart und Verfassung, Sitten und Schicksale dieses Volkes, nebst ihrem Ursprunge*. Dessau / Leipzig: Dieterich 1783.

statistical data as empirical support of their claims. In *Time and the Other*, postcolonial scholar Johannes Fabian addresses the issue of the de-temporization of the Other in anthropological writing. In his account, the Other is the object of a researcher's study, ontologically and culturally presumed to be different. Additionally, Fabian maintains that the researcher is allowed to disregard temporal relations when studying a presumably unchanging, "primitive" culture. The terms civilization, evolution, development, acculturation and modernization are all notions "whose conceptual content derives from evolutionary time"[22]. Persistently referring to the time of the Other as not belonging to contemporary time, the researcher marginalizes the Other, with the effect of creating a permanent signification of primitive and not-the-same. Partially borrowing from Claude Levi-Strauss, Fabian argues that the taxonomical description of culture becomes ontological when "it maintains that culture is created by selection and classification." The consequent concept of culture is "devoid of a theory, creativity or production because in a radically taxonomic frame it makes no sense to raise the question of production. By extension we never appreciate the primitive as producer".[23] In cultural texts, the examples of portraying Roma as "primitive", as gatherers rather than producers, as people completely incapable of relating to modern society and its economically highly structured system, and as borrowers, if not thieves, are myriad.

The Roma people were seen as revelatory objects of investigation for the burgeoning field of European ethnology. The researchers' own European culture, deemed superior, remained the normative and unquestioned point of departure. The described apparatus of classification and persecution culminated in the 20th century with the Porajmos (Romani genocide committed by the government of National-Socialist Germany and its allies in World War II), after which the systematic persecution and murder of Roma based on racial grounds under National Socialism was recognized only after much hesitation, and much too late (in the 1980s) for reparations to be paid to the survivors.

22 By "evolutionary time", Fabian refers to the secular replacement of the biblical chronology of human existence from a few thousands of years to many tens and hundreds of thousands of years, by the 1850s and 1860s. Anthropologists "filled" this newly expanded scale of human time with stages of development resembling a development along a single line (rather than a figure of a branching tree, for example). According to this new vision, non-Europeans were exemplars of the stages of human development through which civilized Europeans had presumably passed long ago. In their propensity for development, Europeans were allegedly far ahead of their non-European counterparts. Johannes Fabian: *Time and the Other: How Anthropology Makes Its Object*. New York: Columbia UP 1983, p. 17.

23 Ibid., p. 62.

Myths of the Everyday

Much of the knowledge – which was produced over a large time span – is amassed within a framework of a myth. The enormous set of assumptions, notions, images and narratives is no longer regarded in the context of respective historical circumstances; instead, these are perceived as 'natural'. In these recurring patterns and narratives, a counter-figure is conceived in order to express a specific understanding of the self. These ideas of the self, and of that which has been made external and foreign, become the myth. Roland Barthes called these secondary semiotic systems "myths of the everyday"[24]. They are not defined via the object of their message, but through the way in which they are articulated. In this sense, myths of the everyday are not content, but form – not an idea, but a manner of signifying. The means to it is the complete de-contextualization and de-historicized narrative of the object, in order to in the end re-substantialize it at will. That is the actual "principle of myth – it transforms history into nature"[25].

The image of the described counter-figure to bourgeois culture is articulated in mythical narratives that connect "Gypsies" with magic, seductive femininity, innate musicality, kidnapping and thievery. Some myths have proven extremely persistent, even though – or perhaps because – they can never be tested. For example, there is neither historical nor current evidence supporting the accusation of kidnapping, and yet there is a state-run practice of removing Roma children from their homes, ostensibly for the good of the child and of society.[26] As Stefanie Kugler shows, "Gypsy kidnapping" is a literary invention, introduced in Miguel de Cervantes' *La Gitanilla* from 1613.[27] Subsequently, the idea was taken up and propagated in many literary works. What began as a literary myth became 'everyday knowledge', to be reinforced in a great number of cautionary tales for children. Since the second half of the nineteenth century, when there are unsolved disappearances of children, the public tends to suspect people who have been stigmatized as "Gypsies". In 2013 we see two cases with international media coverage that show how powerful the connotation of child abduction still is. In Greece, the police noticed a blonde girl in a Roma family and removed her from her home. In the media, the main focus was the accusation of

24 Roland Barthes: *Mythologies*, trans. from French by Annette Lavers. New York: Hill & Wang 1972, p. 5.

25 Ibid.

26 As can be seen in Maria Theresa's 1773 decrees for Hungary or in the self-representation of the Swiss Aid Organization for Children of the Country Road (Hilfswerk für Kinder der Landstraße), which was active until 1973.

27 Stefani Kugler: Zigeuner als Kinderräuber. Fontanes Graf Petöfy und die Tradition eines Vorwurfs. In: Uerlings / Patrut (eds) *‚Zigeuner' und Nation*, pp. 571–588, here pp. 571–586.

"kidnapping"; the phenotypical difference of blond vs. dark hair functioned as a confirmation. In that case, media coverage brought on public protests and police response. In Ireland, police removed light-haired children from two families due to the suspicion of kidnapping. These accusations were also false.[28] The media coverage of these cases conjured a historical myth and connected it with current resentment toward Roma. The reports about the girl "Maria" in Greece were always coupled with the assumption that Roma exploit children; media reports even speculated about organ trafficking and organized begging. Through this discursive conflation, the racist stereotypes are reanimated, updated, and affixed to real people – the European Roma.

Stereotypical Figures

According to Barthes, myth is both stereotypical and imperative. An array of stereotypes has developed in terms of attributions, narratives, figures and images. Numerous concepts define the function of stereotypes in diverse ways, on multiple levels and in varying contexts. In the social sciences, stereotypes are normalized notions about primarily referencing belonging to some category, such as race, nation, class, gender, etc. These are solidified collective assumptions with largely emotional content that can only be understood in their linguistic and/or figurative representations. They shape attitudes and govern perception.[29] Concepts of stereotype in the studies of language, literature and art focus mainly on its linguistic, textual or metaphorical form. In this context, stereotypes are understood as a structural pattern of representation. It is a question not of human images, but of reductive schematization and conventionalization. In this way, texts (including film and other media) "depend on entire intertextual networks of stereotypes of every kind: stereotypes of figures, plot, conventional story patterns, and stereotypes of visual or auditory production"[30]. Stereotypes become especially potent when aesthetic schemas combine with stereotypical presumptions. In those cases, an entire network of sensory information can be called upon quickly through a conventionalized form. In the study of stereotypes, the interest does not lie in proving or rebutting stereotypes, but rather in the interpretation of their genesis, function, and effects on societal discourses.

28 See Isabell Pfaff: Wenn Vorurteile neu erblühen. In: *Süddeutsche Zeitung*, 06.11.2013. http://www.sueddeutsche.de/panorama/der-fall-des-roma-maedchens-maria-wenn-vorurteile-neu-erbluehen-1.1810445 (accessed 15.08.2016).

29 Social science research on stereotypes dates back to Walter Lippman: *Public Opinion*. London: Allen & Unwin 1922.

30 Jörg Schweinitz: *Film und Stereotyp. Eine Herausforderung für das Kino und die Filmtheorie. Zur Geschichte eines Mediendiskurses*. Berlin: Akademie 2006, p. 84.

Fig. 1–3
Left: Khariton Platonov: *Gypsy woman with a tambourine*, oil painting, 1877.
Middle: Trading card, early 20th century.
Right: Film still from Walt Disney's *Esmeralda*.

"Gypsy Women" and the Amplification of the Stereotype

Ethnic and gender stereotypes are inextricably woven together in the constructs of "Gypsy" and "Gypsy woman". Rafaela Eulberg points out the "parallels in the construction of a feminine identity and a specific Gypsy identity": many of the characteristics ascribed to "Gypsies", such as irrational, intuitive and mysterious, are also attributed in the history of Western ideas to the feminine.[31] Nineteenth-century ethnology describes Roma as a "primitive race" as opposed to members of the dominant society, described as "civilized people". This binary structure is analogous to the notion of women as close to nature and men as the producers of culture. The magical abilities of "Gypsies" and the notion of women's intuition are both set up in opposition to the capacity for logical thought.[32] The recurring image of fortune telling was already an established trope in the early modern era, appearing in various contexts like in paintings (e.g. in the works

31 Rafaela Eulberg: Doing Gender Doing Gypsy. Zum Verhältnis der Konstruktion von Geschlecht und Ethnie. In: End / Herold / Robel (eds): *Antiziganistische Zustände*, pp. 41–66, here p. 47.

32 Ibid., p. 53.

of Pieter Brueghel, Jacob van Felsen, Caravaggio, Hieronymus Bosch, Simon Vouet and many others) and in textbooks.[33] Imagined as such, fortune telling is often represented as an interaction between the self and the Other. The contrast is often based on the distinction between nature and culture, but the real emphasis is on gender difference. These images show fortune telling as a feminine craft. The women who practice it are in turn associated with superstition and folk magic; their services are used by women whose gender-specific lack of reason makes them prone to irrational thoughts. Fortune telling imagery thus exemplifies a gendered discourse of alterity with complex layers of social, cultural, and ethnic differences.

Romanticism served to popularize the figure of the "beautiful Gypsy-woman" that was already firmly established as a counter-image to bourgeois femininity. Examples include Alexander Pushkin's *Zemfira* (1827), Victor Hugo's

33 Peter Bell / Dirk Suckow: Lebenslinien – Das Handlesemotiv und die Repräsentation von ‚Zigeunern' in der Kunst des Spätmittelalters und der frühen Neuzeit. In: Uerlings / Patrut (eds): *‚Zigeuner' und Nation*, pp. 493–549.

Esmeralda (1831) and Prosper Mérimée's *Carmen* (1845). At the intersection of exoticism and orientalist discourses, the "beautiful Gypsy woman" with her "wild nature" that cannot be tamed, her "natural ways" and her "promiscuity" become the object of projection for masculine sexual longing. Often, as in *Carmen*, she appears as a *femme fatale* who brings misfortune. Only through her death can the bourgeois order of gender be re-established. Further, this capricious, erotic "Gypsy woman", dancing for all to see, is often portrayed in opposition to the bourgeois ideals of stability and uniformity. This dancing image is present in many forms – like on European postage stamps and in countless films, from early cinema to recent productions and even on current reality TV.[34] (Fig. 1–3)

Born Musicians

The alleged connection frequently made between Roma and music remains unquestioned by many authors who write about Roma, regardless of their area of concentration, expertise and the historical specificity of their scholarship. The unchanging nature of the alleged knowledge of the centuries-long historical and cultural evidence pertaining to Roma as born musicians serves as a reminder of the forceful prejudice against Roma. They are thrust into a culturally constructed relationship with music, thus further freezing the overall discursive formation: Roma musicians. As there are many accomplished and talented Roma musicians in the world, the prevailing discourse largely continues to epitomize them as intrinsically substandard musicians. The same discourse pigeonholes Roma as street, restaurant, and wedding entertainers, to whom access beyond this milieu is largely denied.

It was Michel Foucault who emphasized the radically historicized nature of discourse; as there are slight variations in discursive practices of representation through time and space, the uniformity of Roma musicians stereotyping across historical periods is unsettling and parallels Foucault's description of a regime of truth. This 'knowledge' as a form of power, once applied to the material world, effectively becomes true. A Barthesian semiotic analysis of signifiers shows that they are not just present but unchanging across cultural production, from the fifth-century poem of *Schah Nameh* to contemporary literary and cinematic works. The signifiers in this case would be Roma people (rarely alone, often in a group of three or more) playing an instrument (most often a violin), by a camper, on fairgrounds, by a campfire, on the street in an urban area, as an escort to a rural wedding setting or at a restaurant by the patrons' table. The signified ones

34 See Annabel Tremlett: *My Big Fat Gypsy Wedding*: Demotic or Demonic? Race, Class and Gender in 'Gypsy' Reality TV. In: *The Sociological Review* 62,2 (2014), pp. 316–334.

are concepts, such as music, musicians and "Gypsies". Following Barthes, this is linked to an ideology: substandard musicians, disfranchised people, and the general dichotomy of 'us' versus 'them'. We thus end up stereotyping Roma as born musicians, whose occupation as such is directly linked to their wretched lives and essence, 'othered' to the point of no possibility of coexistence. De facto music stereotyping has neatly created processes by which Roma can be made into "Gypsies", Europe's Other, in perpetuity.

Borrowing again from Richard Dyer, the stereotype of a "Gypsy musician" rests on a few simple and easily grasped characteristics: shoddy dress and travelling in a group with an instrument in hand. Next, the reduction of everything to those traits about the person materializes and is as perceptible as much in turn-of-the-century literature as in contemporary media. In his 1912 book *Blicke in das Leben der Zigeuner*, German author Engelbert Wittich writes that music is that which is innate to every "Gypsy".[35] They play without knowing a single note. Roma music somehow translates into the essence of what it means to be Roma, and by extension Wittich emphasizes the wildness and violence intrinsic to the "Gypsy character". To exemplify his assertions, Wittich speaks of astonishing Roma children, each endowed with an artistic/musical skill, which they possess solely because they are Roma. His better known contemporary, Gerhard Stein, after extensively describing the physiognomy of Roma, turns to the psychological characteristics and declares that the way they play music is in their blood.[36] Authors writing about Roma often invoke such myths of innateness, which leads to both exaggeration and simplification of traits and therein fosters stereotypes. Jumping to a present-day example, the award winning American film *Brasslands* depicts two brass orchestras competing for a prestigious award; while the non-Roma orchestra is introduced by narrating of its origins and history, the Roma orchestra (clearly marked as such) needs no introduction: just a few images and no words can reduce, simplify, and exaggerate them to the point of complete identification. Finally, these characteristics are fixed without change, as if timeless. *Schah Nameh*, the epic poem written eleven centuries ago about Persia's ancient history, is thus continually evoked as an authoritative text (especially among those writing and reading about Roma) despite being widely unknown in the West.[37]

35 Engelbert Wittich: *Blicke in das Leben der Zigeuner*. Striegau: Kuß 1911, p. 7.

36 Gerhard Stein: *Zur Psychologie und Anthropologie der Zigeuner in Deutschland*. Gräfenhainichen: Schulze 1938, p. 79.

37 In the fifth-century Persian poem, *Schah Nameh*, written by the poet Firdousi, the only musicians referred to by name are the so-called Luri musicians; the poem makes mention that 10,000 such musicians were hired by the king of Persia for an Indian celebration. Some historians

After the rules of the game have been spelled out and fixed, stereotyping continues with the 'us versus them' dichotomy, or what Dyer calls "splitting"[38]; it is applied to Roma as to no other minority in Europe, and it could be summed up as summoning the quintessential antitheses of the normal and abnormal, the acceptable and unacceptable. The delineation of boundaries and the strict rules of belonging send Others into what Stuart Hall calls a "symbolic exile"[39]. Stein poignantly illustrates this practice of exclusion by drawing a chart that qualitatively assesses differences between "Europeans" and "Gypsies", specifically referencing music. The European rubric reads: "Concerts, gregariousness, dance, great masters", while the "Gypsy rubric" includes: "ecstasy, woods, love, sadness, earning money".[40] The incompatibility of the races is glaring. Similar rhetoric carried into National Socialism with its most prominent "Gypsy researcher" Eva Justin, whose work is based on her observations of forcefully orphaned children and their developmental progress (or rather lack thereof) in school. Justin observes that the only area in which Roma children perform well is song.[41] As the other non-Roma children systematically progress, the Roma children cannot grasp complex, abstract concepts required of their peers at the higher levels; their blood determines their fidgety and restless nature, and they possess no capacity to perform more than fairly in school, but in their dance, song, and music one witnesses the depth and reach of the "Gypsy heart" – the untamed and animalistic enjoyment of vigorous health and physical drives.[42] However, even in those musical occupations in which they supposedly thrive, they are still not equal to other Germans. In other words, the music they play and the way they play are too "Gypsy-like".

The most important facet of stereotyping is the gross inequality of power. The "violent hierarchy"[43], as Richard Dyer calls it, refuses any illusion of peaceful

acknowledge the possibility of a connection between the Luri and the Roma people who came from India to Iran, assimilating with the Luri, but warn that any tangible evidence is still to be revealed. There is no direct reference to Roma in this poem. See Michael Witzel: Autochthonous Aryans? The Evidence from the Old Indian and Iranian Texts. In: *Electronic Journal of Vedic Studies* 7,3 (2001), pp. 1–115.

38 Richard Dyer: *The Matter of Images: Essays on Representations.* London / New York: Routledge 1993.

39 Stuart Hall: The Spectacle of the 'Other'. In: Id. (ed.): *Representation: Cultural Representations and Signifying Practices.* London: Sage 1997, pp. 223–290, here p. 257.

40 Stein: *Psychologie*, p. 86: "Konzerte, Geselligkeit, Tanz, große Meister" vs. "Extase, Wald, Liebe, Traurigkeit, Geldverdienen", our translation from the original German.

41 Eva Justin: *Lebensschicksale artfremd erzogener Zigeunerkinder und ihrer Nachkommen.* Dissertation Friedrich-Wilhelms-Universität, Berlin 1943, p. 49.

42 Ibid., p. 52.

43 Dyer: *The Matter of Images.*

coexistence. The established hegemony assures that the Other remains excluded, and the powerful fashion their world according to their value systems; importantly, the ruling groups need the Other, as their own hegemony rests on this defining exclusion.

Gabrielle Tyrnauer's article recounting Roma orchestras in concentration camps, one of which was Auschwitz, stands as one of the most literal and concise archetypes of this hegemony. In particular, she cites stories by camp survivors and their accounts of the SS staff's "music appreciation." One of the stories is about the "Auschwitz Gypsy Orchestra", which was organized by the SS Officer Board. On May 25, 1943, the Gypsy Orchestra held a concert for the SS, which was interrupted when the musician-prisoners were sent back to the barracks and gassed on special orders.[44]

As the capacity to other can come from within power structures, it is also found among the ranks of the othered. An "authentic" voice, although something of a rarity, is frequently used to bemuse the non-Roma interests that often lie in hearing the reiteration of their preconceived fantasies of Roma; that which would not support their beliefs but would be classified as inauthentic or deceitful. The position of a native informant often comes down to supporting established strategies and ideologies. On a theoretical level, this type of othering is well-captured by Slavoj Žižek (mostly stemming from his discussion of antisemitism), who talks about the belief held by power structures that there is always more behind what is being presented; the search for the "it" that the Other demonstrates or *allows* us to see. Žižek describes the attainment of the real kernel as both overdetermined (always something more than the object itself) and unattainable. Lastly, the search for the "it" allows the powerful researcher to rummage continuously through the history and culture of the less powerful people, revisiting written literature and creating new tomes that stabilize the culturally constructed dichotomy of the omnipotent versus the powerless. Roma music, the Romani woman and by extension the Roma, are perceived as something more than meets the eye; envisioned as such, both are infinitely measured and changed, allowing for the continuous scientific (and less scientific) identification of the constructs "Gypsies", "Gypsy woman" and "Gypsy music." Lastly, the search for the "it" is unremitting as it furthers the dichotomy of power relations. (Fig. 4–6)

44 Gabrielle Tyrnauer: Mastering the Past: Germans and Gypsies. In: Diane Tong (ed.): *Gypsies: An Interdisciplinary Reader*. New York: Garland 1998, pp. 97–114, here p. 109.

The Continuity of Antiziganism

Even in present-day media, Roma people are marked both visually and narratively as "Gypsies". The stigmatizing image of eccentric, convivial "Gypsy life" has endured as lexicons and dictionaries make only half-hearted attempts at revisions. The 1989 Oxford English Dictionary's first definition for "Gypsy" is still racially marked, describing "Gypsies" as "a wandering race of Hindu origin".[45] The majority of current print and television reporting relies on conventional antiziganist stereotypes in its choice of images and narration by reinforcing the spectators' cultural frame of interpretation. Historical knowledge has also been combined with current images of 'poverty' and 'deviant behavior'. The Roma people and the cultural construct of "Gypsy" quickly and easily commingle in the media by means of introductory remarks such as "they are Roma who call themselves Tzigan, Gypsies".[46] Covert references, e.g. colorful skirts, ethnic minority, travelers, clans, or extended families function as codes

45 See Ian Hancock: Gypsy Mafia, Romani Saints. The Racial Profiling of Romani Americans. www.radoc.net/radoc.php?doc=art_f_bias_profiling&lang=en&articles=true (accessed 15.08.2016).

46 "It is the Roma who have appropriated Gypsy for themselves" / "Es sind Roma, die sich selbst Tzigan, Zigeuner nennen" (Einwanderer-Elend: Die neuen ‚Gastarbeiter'. In: *Spiegel TV*, 05.06.2011).

Fig. 4–6
Left: Thadeusz Rybkowski: *A Gypsy family at a campfire*. Oil painting, 1894.
Above: Trading card, early 20th century.
Right: Record cover and tour poster by Fanfare Ciorcarlia: *Baro Biao. World Wide Wedding*, 1999.

for the same; such euphemisms as "those belonging to national minorities" are nothing more than airs put on for ostensible political correctness.[47] As a result, in many TV news reports, an entire collective system of symbols unfolds quickly. The characteristics attributed to Roma can be summed up very briefly: begging, larceny, fraudulence, taking unfair advantage through quick wit or criminality, abusing social services (a trait usually paired with the image of the parasite), having a nomadic existence, bearing an overabundance of children, squalor,

47 See the *Frankfurter Allgemeine Zeitung* on the Occupy movement in the downtown district: "Weeks ago, the camp had acquired a bad reputation, because more and more homeless people, drug users, inebriated persons, and members of national minorities had moved in." (Katharina Iskandar: Polizei räumt Occupy-Camp in Frankfurt. In: *Frankfurter Allgemeine Zeitung*, 06.08.2012.) For further examples see Markus End: *Antiziganismus in der deutschen Öffentlichkeit. Strategien und Mechanismen medialer Kommunikation*. Heidelberg: Dokumentations- und Kulturzentrum Deutscher Sinti und Roma 2014; Wulf D. Hund: ‚Schwarzes Volk', ‚Herrenloses Gesindel' und ‚Kinder der Freiheit'. In: Id. (ed.): *Fremd, faul und frei. Dimensionen des Zigeunerstereotyps*. Münster: Unrast 2014, pp. 5–20.

violence, and a lack of discipline with regard to bodily functions, such as public urination.[48]

Especially powerful is the *interlacing* of discursive fields with the Roma-discourse. For example, an overlapping with the discourse on flight and asylum become obvious. In this case, accusations about the abuse of political asylum and benefit fraud are highlighted. These elements of discourse have been tied to the media coverage of immigration since the 1980s and are now picked up again when reporting about Roma. The link to the discourse centered on Islamophobia is also notable; here, the symbols and patterns – like unbridgeable cultural differences and the oppression of women – that stigmatized Muslims are now also affixed to the Roma. Regarding the structure of the majority of news coverage, we are still dealing with the dichotomy of early modern times. Even today, these figures of "Gypsies" are shown in complete opposition to dominant society.

The discourses about Roma – the spoken words, images, conventionalized modes of representation and narration – are real deeds that produce knowledge and determine how something is to be understood and interpreted; however, they can be understood as symbolic violence. Their power stems from their respective history, the one entrenched and personified in the potential for conflict.[49] It is not the individual intentions of one speaker, but rather the cultural and historical practices of the language usage that are essential for the conflict's power. Discourses can lead to structural violence as they generate actions and produce meaning resulting in othering and exclusion; they are also responsible for new institutions and laws. Alongside symbolic and structural violence inherent to the historically informed discourses about Roma runs parallel physical violence, which is legitimized by conflict-ridden speech. Referencing once again the Human Rights First report, there is evidence that most acts of violence occur in areas where local political leaders openly resort to anti-Roma rhetoric, whereby

48 We are referring to a huge body of news reports: "Immigrant Misery. The new 'Gastarbeiter'" / "Einwanderer Elend. Die neuen Gastarbeiter" (*Spiegel TV*, 05.06. 2011); "From Bucharest to the German welfare state: Rumania-town in the Harzerstrasse" / "Von Bukarest in den deutschen Sozialstaat: Klein Rumänien in der Harzerstraße" (*Spiegel TV*, 11.09.2011); "From a neighborhood to a ghetto: doom and gloom in Duisburg Hochfeld" / "Vom Wohngebiet zum Ghetto: Untergangsstimmung in Duisburg Hochfeld" (*Spiegel TV*, 05.11. 2012); "The Horror-house in Berlin. Life amidst trash and urine" / "Das Horrorhaus von Berlin. Leben zwischen Dreck und Urin" (*Spiegel TV*, 20.6.2015), and talk shows: "Squalor there, fear here. Are the destitute from Eastern Europe arriving now?" / "Elend dort, Angst hier. Kommen jetzt die Armen aus Osteuropa?" (*Maybritt Illner*, 28.02.2012); "Begging, free loading, collecting donations – is our compassion being abused?" / "Betteln, Schnorren, Spenden sammeln – wird unser Mitleid ausgenutzt?" (*Anne Will*, 05.12.2012); "The poverty-immigrants. Is Germany overstretching itself?" / "Die Armutseinwanderer. Ist Deutschland überfordert?" (*Menschen bei Maischberger*, 26.02.2013).

49 Judith Butler: *Excitable Speech: A Politics of the Performative*. New York: Routledge 1997.

even police become implicit in antiziganistic language and deeds of brutality. Between the language of public discourse that speaks of Roma's otherness and need for expulsion, deportation, and incarceration, along with the popular language that continues to describe Roma as little else but "thieving kidnappers" and "asocial low-lives", there forms a clear pathway wrought with bigotry often resulting in virulent conflict.

Current discourses capture a remarkable discrepancy in the representation of Roma vis-à-vis that of other minorities in Europe. Despite the taboo on biological racism in European media, the representation of and policies toward Roma people are a blind spot in the European public sphere. There has been no fundamental rupture post-1945 in antiziganist ideology. The stigma within these stereotypes leads to delineating social conditions along ethnic lines, that is, to a transformation of contingent social conditions into immutable ethnic problems.

In the context of the long history of antiziganism, the figure of the "Gypsy" can be understood as an instrument and an outlet for the development of the nation-state. Even in the twenty-first century, Roma people are imagined and stigmatized as the "Other" in order to channel and direct national and European developments. In many cases, political ruptures are followed by an intensified stigmatizing discourse about Roma, which in turn have direct consequences. In Germany, for example, the recent semantics of describing Roma as a threat to the nation reached its peak with the new definition of the German nation after the fall of the Berlin Wall and the unification of both German states (as the 1992 pogrom in Rostock-Lichtenhagen suggests). Since 2000, entry into the EU of East European countries has formed additional discursive intensification. Parallel to an escalation of antiziganist media coverage over terms such as "poverty-driven migration", there have been many political, police-related, and social incidents resulting in the deportation of Roma people from France and Italy, and even the murder of Roma people in the Czech Republic and Hungary.

This dissociative quality of stereotypes becomes especially salient in the current distinction between 'good' and 'unwanted' refugees. Parallel to the current media coverage of the "Culture of Welcome" in Germany, Roma continue to be largely excluded and discriminated against by means of an increasingly harsh legal situation. In 2015, the establishment of the so-called 'safe third states' in Montenegro, Albania, and Kosovo in southeastern Europe is clearly aimed at the exclusion of Roma people. Lastly, the concentration of refugees from southeastern Europe in so-called "Balkan Centers" in Bavaria with the objective of quick deportation shows an attitude that is certain to have ever-greater repercussions for Roma – and Europe.

Reviews

Olga Alekseeva / Hans-Georg Heinrich:
Ethnic Minorities of Central and Eastern Europe in the Internet Space.
Frankfurt am Main: Lang 2013.
Jeff Shires

The internet is an odd mixture of sources – commercial and non-profit, official and unofficial and public and personal. All of these elements reflect and define the identities of those who use them. Olga Alekseeva and Hans-Georg Heinrich's book *Ethnic Minorities of Central and Eastern Europe in the Internet Space* examines how minority and immigrant cultures display ethnic identity via public forums on the internet. The authors' intent is to study "why and how ethnic groups present themselves on the internet." (13) The text is part of the larger research project entitled "Interplay of European, National and Regional Identities: Nations between States along the New Eastern Borders of the European Union. A Cross-National Study of Trans-Boundary Social and Ethnic Groups in Europe (ENRI-East)." (5) Alekseeva and Heinrich focus on twelve minority groups which are the result of the collapsed "European empires, including the Communist regime" (5): Russians in Latvia and Lithuania, Hungarians in Slovakia and Ukraine, Belarusians in Lithuania and Poland, Ukrainians in Poland and Hungary, Slovaks in Hungary and Poles in Ukraine, Lithuania and Belarus.

The authors make an overarching presumption, which they do not defend, concerning the internet: "Communication through blogs and forums is a case of channeled political activity. In its political dimension, the internet has replaced and complemented classical print and audiovisual media as well as traditional forms of political articulation such as demonstrations or meetings." (14–15) There are two parts to this assertion that need to be examined.

First, the internet has "replaced and complemented" other media. The claim that the internet has "complemented" traditional media is uncontroversial. Traditional media companies have expanded onto "second screens" in an attempt to broaden their reach. The claim that the internet has "replaced" traditional media, however, is suspect. If we take news as our example, broadcast and print sources still reach a much larger audience overall than any specialized portal or news site. An increasing proportion of people are getting news via social media but that news is likely to have been shared from traditional media outlets. Blogging sites do have an influence on traditional news media, especially concerning political discourse. The question of who sets the agenda for political discourse for a nation, group or ethnicity, the media or the professional bloggers, is very much up for debate. Indeed the definition of whom or what a journalist is has been thrown into question by the presence of 'citizen journalists.' However, media companies own many of the blogging sites that are used to drive the news. This calls into question the independent nature of blogging and 'citizen journalists.' (While the authors are claiming the internet has "complemented and replaced" traditional media, they make significant use of traditional media websites. Online versions of traditional media sites make up almost one-third of the internet sites considered by Alekseev and Heinrich.)

Second, the internet has "replaced and complemented" forms of political activity. There are several internet technologies that have made organizing and mobilizing large groups of people quickly. The use of Facebook and Twitter helped to coordinate movement and get thousands of people into the streets during the 'Arab Spring'. The question is whether online communities can simply mobilize or actually supplant physical communities. Does discussion in online forums and social media transfer over to political action or do they narcotize the individual into believing he or she has already made a difference? It would have been interesting to test the participation in individual in forums with the participation of those individuals in the actual political process.

Methodologically, the survey samples "text fragments" from ethnic internet sources and, through content analysis, locates major themes in the fragment samples for each group. The study is limited by several factors which Alekseeva and Heinrich acknowledge (limited access to internet in rural areas, not considering those who prefer print thus eliminating older members of the group). The authors sample from online periodicals, news and broadcast portals and organizations for each of the twelve groups. They search each site for selected keywords using the site's search function or text clouds on the site. From those results, a random sample of text fragments is obtained and subjected to content analysis through simstat/wordstat and a number of categories and keywords are developed. These are used to determine issues of importance to each minority ethnic community. The categories are developed well and defined thoroughly. The authors, however, attempt to generalize the results of the analysis of a few sites to the community at large. For example, the authors state that the "[d]read of assimilation and the loss of the Hungarian mother tongue is the dominant feature of the Ukrainian Hungarians." (127) It is perhaps more accurate to say that this is the concern of a particular subset of Ukrainian Hungarians. The extrapolation of the data to the community at large is made difficult by the limitations the authors already acknowledged. While Ukrainian Hungarians may fear the loss of the Hungarian language, the data cannot support the making the claim on a wide scale.

Alekseeva and Heinrich present an interesting methodology to study ethnic groups embedded in host countries. Their approach shows that there is much to be gained by this analysis. There is much discussion in the short (around 150 pages) book on definition, methodology and results. More time could be spent on the conclusions drawn from each group. The analysis of the results is done well with each group laid out logically and the important issues to that group of sites detailed. The conclusions concerning each group, as mentioned above, are overgeneralized to the population as a whole. There is great merit to expanding this study to examine ethnic groups through social media although realizing, however, that certain countries limit the access of internal groups to this medium.

John Nauright / Alan G. Cobley / David K. Wiggins (eds):
Beyond C. L. R. James: Shifting Boundaries of Race and Ethnicity in Sport.
Fayetteville: University of Arkansas Press 2014.
Tim Keogh

This past year, prolific sport historian Tony Collins decried the irrelevance of his sub-discipline, claiming "sport is the great undiscovered country of the historical world." For Collins, the study of sport provides insight into the most important fields of scholarship, namely global and gender studies.[1] Judging by the scholarship in *Beyond C. L. R. James: Shifting Boundaries of Race and Ethnicity in Sport*, sport is indeed a useful lens to explore such topics in the global context. Editors John Nauright, Alan G. Cobley, and David K. Wiggins use C. L. R. James' *Beyond a Boundary*, the famous critical analysis of cricket and colonialism, as the foundation for a wide-ranging collection of articles analyzing globalization and its relationship to gender, race, and ethnicity. Nearly all authors go beyond their particular sports to engage these broader issues and contribute to the scholarly debate as a result.

Beyond C. L. R. James is a compilation of presentations given at a 2013 50th anniversary conference for *Beyond a Boundary*, looking to take C. L. R. James framework into the 21st century and in new directions of academic inquiry. Following Sir Hilary McD. Beckles' introductory assessment of West Indian cricket since C. L. R. James' publication, the book dives into historical analyses about how minority ethnicities and racial groups are constructed through sport. The chapters range widely, including how cricket cultivated a sense of white racial superiority in colonial Australia, or alternatively, how Australian Aborigines recent participation in sport, while a victory for minority opportunity in the country, has been nonetheless attributed to racist biological anomalies or non-human 'other' almost magical traits. Other chapters look at the importance of Zulu stick fighting to Zulu masculinity and colonial resistance, how Italian-Americans used sport and their physicality to gain respect within the racial hierarchies of 20th century America, or how media interest in the racial and gender backgrounds of black female athletes historically neglected their athletic abilities and accomplishments. Douglas Booth and John Nauright provide the most interesting article on the topic, about how race was performed through the body in South Africa, from black middle class cricketers who demonstrated 'appropriate' behaviors on-field to their colonizers, to the deep discussions of body parts and physical performance of non-white players during the Apartheid era.

The book's third section takes up similar themes in the context of global migration, how sport can shape the ethnic and gender identities of migrants, promote integration, or perpetuate a sense of separation. For example, while Muslim Turkish male immigrants

1 Tony Collins: The History of Sport beyond Sports History. In: *North American Society for Sport History*, 05.05.2016. http://www.nassh.org/NASSH/content/president%E2%80%99s-forum-taking-charge-future-sport-history-academic-institutions-iii (accessed 05.05.2016).

embrace soccer as a means to acculturate in Denmark and Germany, gender norms regarding female physical activity restrict Turkish women from using sport to integrate. Gender ideas are not easily broken, particularly regarding the body. Sport is just as likely to serve as a means to perpetuate gender roles in immigrant communities, as Thomas Michael Walle illustrates in his study of Pakistani Muslim cricket players in Oslo, Norway. These men perform their gender identity among one another separate from their ethnic position in Norwegian society. Anand Rampersad likewise shows how cricket provides a means for Indo-Caribbean peoples to at once solidify their ethnicity while also integrating within Caribbean national identity. Charles Freuhling Springwood's article is the highlight for this section, discussing basketball and Oaxacan ethnicity, arguing that Oaxacans embraced sport to distinguish themselves from broader Mexican population who denigrate them as "indios" and not as a way to emulate American culture. Basketball became an ethnic marker, carried with them to the United States, as basketball games keep the Oaxacan community intact across national borders. *Beyond C. L. R. James* is a good place to start.

The last section, "Crossing Boundaries/Maintaining Boundaries" is similar to the sections above, though focuses on the racial divisions evident through sport and is the weakest section overall. Two strong chapters discuss racial hostilities expressed through sport. Religious and increasingly racial boundaries are violently apparent in Association Football in Northern Ireland, as the longer history of sectarian strife has been complicated since Eastern European immigration and the globalization of players, and largely Protestant fans express their racism publicly during games. British Asians have likewise faced hostility from British citizens for rooting against the English cricket team, leading to doubts about their 'Britishness' and the possibility of integration, which disregards their 'hybrid' cultures. The two weaker chapters include a discussion of 'adventure' sports as an "unproblematic" racial zone for white middle class participants to build social capital, enjoy racial privileges, and transcend the anxieties of "whiteness", which claims these sports are almost exclusively "white" without statistics. The last chapter interprets Usain Bolt's 2008 100-meter race (less than 10 seconds long), and his pre- and post-race celebrations as anti-colonial cultural resistance, an unconvincing claim.

Aside from the few weaker chapters, *Beyond CLR James* demonstrates exactly what Tony Collins claims sport history can do – provide insight into how race, gender, and ethnic divisions and identities are formed, restructured, transgressed, or deconstructed throughout history and across the world. All chapters utilize cultural theories to ground their work; Lipsitz, Foucault, Said, Lefebvre, various theorists of whiteness, subaltern, and nationalism studies are referenced. The scholars in this collection, including sociologists, historians, and anthropologists, are engaging literatures and contributing to scholarship well beyond the sports they study. Perhaps it is time others go beyond their fields and consider sport in their research on race, ethnicity, and/or gender, particularly in the transnational and global context.

Hermann Wellenreuther:
Heinrich Melchior Mühlenberg und die deutschen Lutheraner in Nordamerika, 1742–1787. Wissenstransfer und Wandel eines atlantischen zu einem amerikanischen Netzwerk.
Berlin: Lit 2013.
Frank Kleinehagenbrock

In his comprehensive book, Hermann Wellenreuther examines the life of Heinrich Melchior Mühlenberg. The volume is a collection of research on the fascinating Mühlenberg, the rise of social structures in North America, and the opportunities that German Protestantism created during the 18th century. In general, it focuses on lesser-known parts of early modern American history.

Heinrich Melchior Mühlenberg hailed from a small German town and grew up in a craftsman's family. Despite his humble roots, he attended the University of Göttingen to become a theologist, standing between traditional Lutheran positions and pietism as it had developed in Halle. Although it is doubtful that he would have been a convincing preacher, Mühlenberg faced a career as a minister in his early life. However, he was chosen to go to America – as a Hanoverian subject, he was sent to Pennsylvania to organize church structures for German Lutherans.

The new society in which Mühlenberg found himself was characterized by loose feudal bindings, distinct civic participation and a greater variety of confessions – although different from his life in Germany, he was able to adapt to America easily. German tradition stated that he had to search for order in a world that offered freedom; in America, signs of that freedom were social and political structures without clear definitions. However, Mühlenberg found that he had become part of a world that cried for pragmatism and forced him to make decisions on his own.

Wellenreuther explains how Mühlenberg changed in the years after his arrival in Philadelphia – how his way of thinking became more independent from the bindings of the old world and how his new circumstances sharpened his intellect. His biggest challenge was to obtain a permanent position among the Lutheran community in Pennsylvania, where unreputable preachers and ministers sent by other German princes were simultaneously active. In addition, Lutheran parishes had an important function in integrating the rising numbers of German immigrants into American society. Mühlenberg found out that Lutherans from Southern Germany, especially from Württemberg, were skeptical of his Hallensian background. It was thus important that his Hallensian network helped him import religious pamphlets and books from Germany, which were of continuing importance for the Lutherans in Pennsylvania.

Mühlenberg's networks are at the center of Wellenreuther's research, which are identifiable by his correspondence. Mühlenberg left many letters that demonstrate his intellectual development. The Philadelphia minister wrote over 1,600 letters, over 1,000 of which have been preserved. These letters not only point to his social contacts in America, London and Germany, but to the process of emancipation that first arose at the end of the French and Indian War (Seven Years' War) and with the Pennsylvanian Church

Order of 1762, a document clarifying the positions of ministers and members of the congregation, which arose from conflicts in preceding decades. Mühlenberg's conduct during the American Revolution shows that he and the German Lutherans of Pennsylvania remained a special group of citizens that tried to keep out of the conflict with the British.

Wellenreuther also points out that Mühlenberg combined European and American practices in his life, and so did his parishioners. They brought European knowledge to their new world, but they were increasingly educated by their new Western surroundings. Mühlenberg's letters also suggest that the long distance spanning the Atlantic was an important factor in the 18th century – Europeans were unable to have much influence on decisions made in Philadelphia because they could neither react quickly to nor imagine circumstances overseas. Wellenreuther convincingly interprets this process as a kind of '*Konfessionalisierung*' that lacks elements of state building.

Wellenreuther's book demonstrates that it is possible to analyze networks not only as empirically measured social figures, but as social entities that shape people's experiences. He also suggests that German historiography should further examine American history. His dense reconstruction of a small "*Lebenswelt*" transfers elements of German '*Landesgeschichte*' to American history, and he makes a point that America, on its way to becoming an independent country, was shaped by a variety of social groups that were not included in the well-known narratives concerning British-American development.

Frederick White:
Emerging from out of the Margins. Essays on Haida Language, Culture and History.
Frankfurt am Main: Lang 2014.
Anna Hamling

"With this book I have one main goal: to inspire an appreciation of Haida language, culture and history [...] Certainly my treatment and topics about the Haida are not exhaustive, yet I am pleased to have this rare opportunity as indigenous person to offer such a book about my own culture" (13), explains Frederick White in the opening lines of his valuable book.

With this timely critical study, White fills the gap in an area that required more in depth research. The author was aware of his limitations in writing a story about Haida language and culture but decided to take upon himself the difficult task of sharing his research and knowledge that he acquired in the Haida community. White himself is Haida and was born in Prince Rupert, not in Haida Gwaii and has been marginalized in some ways by the Haida's Gwaii community.

The Haida of the Queen Charlotte Islands (Haida Gwaii) have fascinated all who have visited them, from the first explorers and travelers of the late 18th century to the anthropologists of the present. White explores the Haida's mythology and Haida humor from personal experience which is a new approach in comparison to previously written studies. The author explains that between 1860 and 1890 the total population of about 10,000 was devastated by a small pox epidemic that reduced the population to merely 800 people.

The text is based on White's research of archival sources covering documents, personal correspondence, Juan Perez's diary (that challenges the notion that Spain was the first European country to venture into Haida territory) and other published materials. It also includes many interviews with Haida Gwaii people. The book is divided in two thematic parts, Part One on "Haida Culture and History" and Part Two on "Haida Language, History, Struggles, and Future".

The second part of the book is of particular interest to linguists; it is an innovative and previously not explored area. It begins with a short introduction to the Haida language and some of its phonological, morphological and grammatical intricacies and then compares the different aspects of the current state of Haida language amongst the Haida communities in Alaska and Canada's northwest.

White's narrative enriches our knowledge of Haida Gwaii language and culture. *Emerging from out of the Margins* consists of 169 pages and is presented as a hardcover book. Detracting from the good presentation of information, however, there is a proliferation of typographical and stylistic errors as well as the repetition of information on numerous occasions. The bibliography is extensive and includes both recent and older critical works on the topic; however, the cited works in Spanish require careful and extensive typographical correction. This book would greatly benefit from further editing.

Overall in terms of content this book, written in an informative way, is a welcome addition to an authoritative work by Robert Bringhurst *A Story as Sharp as a Knife: The Classical Haida Myth Tellers and Their World* (1999). White's book serves as a good introduction for a non-specialist of Haida language and culture and might be an engaging read written in an accessible style for the specialists on Haida topics, students and public alike.

Table of Figures

Global Humanities
Studies in Histories, Cultures, and Societies

Edited by Frank Jacob

Published
01/2015 – On the Correlation of Center and Periphery
02/2015 – Religion and Poverty
03/2016 – Migration and State Power
04/2016 – Stereotypes and Violence

Further information:
www.neofelis-verlag.de/zeitschriften-reihen/global-humanities/